CONTORTION AND PRACTICES OF BODY FLEXIBILITY IN EAST ASIA:

Mongolia, China, Japan

I0092953

Mariam Ala-Rashi

Modern Vaudeville Press

Modern Vaudeville Press
113 E Mayland St
Philadelphia, PA 19144
United States of America
www.ModernVaudevillePress.com

Book Layout ©2023 Modern Vaudeville Press

ISBN: 978-1-958604-04-5

Library of Congress: 2023910599

Ordering Information:
Quantity sales. Special discounts are available on quantity purchases by corporations,
associations, and others. For details, contact the "Special Sales Department" at the
address above.

CONTENTS

The Kakubei Jishi

FOREWORD

When I was a teenager, I discovered the thrill of watching professional dancers who seemed to move and fly effortlessly over the stage while spinning amazing tales by their actions. I remember always leaving a dance performance with a light heart as if some of that grace and beauty had been bestowed upon me. In London in the 1960s, tickets to watch the Royal Ballet at Covent Garden were inexpensive and I was encouraged to attend by a friend who had worked with Dame Ninette de Valois, the founder of the Royal Ballet. There was such richness in that dancing!

Later, as a professional viola player, I worked in many pit orchestras and was able to see the extreme hard work that dancers put into their rehearsals. Situated in the pit, deep under the stage, was aware from the thumps and bangs of the massive amounts of energy the dancers expended in order to make their performances seem light and vivid.

I wandered from the artistic into the academic world of teaching and researching into cognitive psychology. We saw the discovery of what came to be known as "mirror neurons" in the brain around 2010. These are parts of the human brain that are said to activate both when an individual executes a specific motor act - and when the individual observes the same or similar act performed by someone else. I realized that this went a long way to explaining my reaction (and the reactions of many!) to watching dance: simply by watching, the mirror neurons in our brains are exercised in lightness, grace, and beauty. As Mariam writes about the Mongolian Dara-ekhe performance, the expertly controlled languid movements of the dancers convey a spiritual message that echoes in the hearts and minds of the audience.

We are very lucky to have writers like Mariam. She has been able to combine her observations from a discipline of deep participant-observation in Mongolian, Chinese, and the Japanese Lion Dance preparation and training –she after all is an accomplished dancer in her own right– with a wide-ranging scholarly outlook. Her scholarship not only encompasses the historical aspects of contortion dancing, but also investigates the religious and cultural associations within a philosophical perspective.

One theme in her book that is worth noting and following is the balance between technique and cultural value. For me, as a musician, this is a very important theme.

The adoption of contortionist dancing by circuses –and the use of it as a vehicle to display a political message in China as taught rigorously by the Beijing International Art School– emphasizes the technical end of the spectrum. The spectacle value of contortionist dancing has been enriched, as she illustrates, by influences from other disciplines in the entertainment industry. In China, in keeping with the implications of mirror neuron theory, dancers must exhibit extreme perfectionism in their performances to convey the messages of the strength of Socialist culture, of a Chinese national identity, and of the need for control and discipline in the everyday lives of audiences. The image of the circle that is ultimately depicted in the bending of the body symbolizes perfection and is rooted deeply in Chinese philosophy. A Chinese audience will return from such performances imbued with the ideal of the citizen subject in their minds and hearts.

...But there is a "cultural value" end of the spectrum as well, as she illustrates with her description of the Lion Dance in Japan. In Japan, the children are not encouraged to practice eight or more hours a day, as in China, to perfect their techniques. Modern Japanese instructors view with disquiet the supposed practices of trainers of child contortionist dancers in the numerous Kakubei Jishi troupes of the Edo period, with their rigid training regimes and disregard for the well-being of the children. Although some children do attain physically remarkable performances, the approach in Japan is child-centered, and dancers do only what they feel able to do. As a result of demographic changes in Japan, the existence of the Lion Dance tradition is in jeopardy, and Mariam writes of her deep concern with this trend.

Mongolian contortionist dancing perhaps illustrates a midpoint between these two extremes. The Mongolians are a nomadic people, and nomadic people inherently retain as few objects as possible to maintain their lifestyle; and they live in dwellings called Ger in which there is little enough space to throw bodies around. So, contortionists move in spatially restricted dance spaces, allowing audiences to share extraordinary movements in their minds with the dancers. But as Mariam points out, Mongolian contortionist dancers also convey messages in their postures as well as their dress, artifacts, and choices of color: messages that come from deep within Mongolian culture and religion. To the Mongolian mind, these elements speak a language in which non verbal discourses are framed. Symbols and messages do not exist only on pages, they can be read from the displays of the dancers - if the viewer knows the language of these symbols.

I have always been captivated by the image of the great warrior Chinggis Khan who enjoyed watching and sharing Mongolian contortionist dancing with his guests. A man who reached for extremes, who demanded extremes from his skilled horsemen, he would have felt his mind and heart gladdened and encouraged by the displays of dancers who exhibited messages in their dancing of extreme bodily movements and cherished cultural symbols.

Mariam perspicaciously observes that training in Mongolian contortionist dance in the West has concentrated on technique; the rich language of Mongolian culture which speaks immediately to the Mongolian soul is not passed on with any great emphasis. In the West, such adornments are in danger of becoming mere symbols of "orientalism."

The nomadic life of the Mongolian people means a lack of written and geographic records, so we have no material evidence going back thousands of years–as Mariam shows from the Ancient Egyptian and Greek depictions. Yet, as she points out, for a discipline to flourish, as modern Mongolian contortionist dance has done, there must be deep cultural roots. It was a great pity that Mongolian contortionist dance failed to get into the UNESCO list of Intangible Cultural Heritage in 2011. Perhaps Mariam's monograph, and scholarly research inspired by it will revive an interest in elevating this tradition to the list.

Mariam's ability to observe and analyze the practice of training and preparation, and to embed this into a scholarly context is outstanding - she certainly straddles metaphorically in an over-split between these two worlds! Her sympathy with the people of Mongolia shows clearly in these pages, and her fond personal depictions of the contortionist dancers and teachers she has encountered in her journeys show vividly that her heart and mind follow her dancer's body. Contortionism (or "contortionist dance" as I have preferred to refer to it) as she points out is not simply about bodily flexibility, it is a discipline that should be lived. I draw from her account that it should nourish cultural understanding of where we as a species have come from, and to enable us all to see what we are capable of. Our minds and hearts must always join with the graceful but extreme movements of the dancers who have dedicated their lives to convey these messages to us.

Jurek Kirakowski
Senior Lecturer, University College Cork
Cork, Ireland, May 2023

Mongolian Contortion
an ethnographic inquiry
Mariam Ala-Rashi

Mongolian Contortion

AN ETHNOGRAPHIC INQUIRY

ACKNOWLEDGEMENTS

I take this opportunity to thank the Regional Officers of Asia and the Pacific of the UNESCO Living Heritage Sector for supporting this research, as well as to Yargai Galtat for the translation from Mongolian and Chinese into English and for creating the magnificent illustrations for this article. My sincere gratitude also goes to my Family, to Dr. Jurek Kirakowski for sharing his invaluable knowledge, to Thom Wall for helping develop the piece, to Jean-Luc Bedryk, Nomin Tseveendorj, Urnaa Uranbileg, Jackie Ward Kehrwald, Ayumi Moco Osanai, Agiimaa Jargalsaikhan, Oyuna Erdene Senge and Otgo Waller for their encouragement, support and attention. I also place on record, my sense of gratefulness to everyone, who directly or indirectly, has helped me in this venture.

INTRODUCTION

This paper proposes to examine body contortion in Mongolia, looking specifically at its history, genesis, theory and functions and presents points of discussion regarding its cultural values in Mongolia by considering social and historical aspects. It aims to analyze traditional training and performance methods, as well as the development of contortion styles through an anthropological lens. This ethnographic research considers traditions, symbolism, rituals and shared meanings within the Mongolian society and makes use of primary research methods such as the participant observation triangulated with interviews and informal conversations with local contortion practitioners in Mongolia. This research is further contextualized with Mongolian literature; encyclopedias of Mongolian circus history and folk arts; images, photographs, press releases; as well as public documentation provided by UNESCO regarding the safeguarding and inclusion of *Traditional Mongolian Contortion* into the UNESCO List of Intangible Cultural Heritage.

The rationale for this paper is the increasing popularity of contortionism, with a growing number of contortion practitioners worldwide. When compared to other performing arts – including other disciplines within the circus – very little has been written about the Art of Contortion. Despite the lack of a contortionism bibliography within the academic field, the author is uniquely qualified to discuss the subject. The author undertook substantial field research in Mongolia between 2013 and 2016, training as a full-time student of contortion, as well as working with contortion coach Nomin Tseveendorj as a participant-observer in a variety of settings. This treatise also builds upon the author's research in China, Mongolia and Europe and her prior works *The Art of Contortionism. An Introduction to and Analysis of Chinese Contortionism in a Historical, Political and Social Context*[1] and *Mapping Contortion in Japan-Part One, Two and Three*[2].

During her time in China, the author arranged a series of formal and informal interviews with the students of the *Beijing International Art School* and professional acrobats of the associated *China National Acrobatic Troupe*. These interviews served as the foundation for aforementioned papers and continue to offer insights when examined through different lenses.

In summation, this paper aims to answer the following questions: What is Mongolian contortion? What is its history, genesis, development and function in Mongolia? Which aspects make *Traditional Mongolian Contortion* unique and how are they tied to Mongolian culture, society and traditions? Although many cultures around the world show evidence of hyper-flexibility being cultivated in rites or performances, few show the same intricate development as can be found in Mongolia. To comprehend the development of Mongolian contortion, three main figures whose contributions to this art-form were of utmost importance need to be introduced: Madame Tsend-Ayush Togoonchuluun, contortionist and coach, Honored Artist of Mongolia (1958), State Prize Winner (1971) and People's Artist of Mongolia (1978), first contortionist of the Mongolian State Circus and founder of the first contortion school in Mongolia. Majigsuren Dashpuntsag, contortion coach and second contortionist of

1   Ala-Rashi, Mariam. *The Art of Contortionism. An Introduction to and Analysis of Chinese Contortionism in a Historical, Political and Social Context.* USA: Amazon KDP Press, 2019. 5.
2   Ala-Rashi, Mariam. "Mapping Contortion in Japan-Part One, A History." CircusTalk. March 10, 2020. Accessed April 18, 2020. https://circustalk.com/news/mapping-contortion-in-japan-part-one-a-history

the Mongolian State Circus, State Prize Winner (1971) and Honored Artist of Mongolia (1981); and finally, Norovsambuu Budbazar, contortionist and coach, honored with the State Prize (1971), the People's Artist Award (1980), and awarded Honored Artist of Mongolia (1966). How their contributions shaped the development of Mongolian contortion will be explored throughout this paper.

Contortion or contortionism, broadly defined, is a movement pattern and performance art form in which the performer is bending and twisting his or her body into seemingly impossible positions, with the effect of letting the body appear "boneless". An extreme level of physical flexibility is necessary and gained over years of daily practice. Nowadays contortionism is usually part of a circus program and is performed to music in front of a live audience. A contortion performance appears superhuman since the extreme body flexibility of the performer exceeds that of the general public.[3]

Between 2013 and 2015 the author spent eight months over the course of two years in Ulaanbaatar, the capital of Mongolia, to conduct short-term field research and to study Mongolian contortion while at the same time being a full-time student at the *Beijing International Art School* in China. After completion of her studies in China in 2015, she became a full-time student of Nomin Tseveendorj, director of the contortion department at the *Mongolian National Circus and Ulaanbaatar Ensemble* at the *Ulaanbaatar Chuulga Theatre* from 2015 to 2016. While in Mongolia, she gained insights into the Mongolian society, the nomadic lifestyle of the Mongolian people and their culture, traditions and customs which seemingly pervade every facet of contortionism. She had the opportunity

---

3   Ala-Rashi, Mariam. *The Art of Contortionism. An Introduction to and Analysis of Chinese Contortionism in a Historical, Political and Social Context.* USA: Amazon KDP Press, 2019. 5.

to visit numerous events that showcased the diversity of Mongolian contortion in different contexts and facets, and was able to visit and train at contortion schools to observe the training curricula and the synergy between teacher and students.

Ulaanbaatar, the capital of Mongolia, is characterized by the nomadic lifestyle of the Mongolian people as well as the political impact of the Soviet Union on large parts of the city's apartment complexes, built in the unmistakable Soviet "Plattenbau" style. The city reflects the numerous transformations this country went through and displays the division between economic growth and nomadic lifestyle, with a modern skyline that surrounds the *Sukhbaatar Square* in the center of Ulaanbaatar and the city of tents with herds of cattle that extends around the outskirts of the capital. These transformations are not only visible in the city's appearance. They leaked into the microcosms of the Mongolian society and its customs, traditions and even performing arts such as Mongolian contortion and influenced training development, aesthetics and contortion styles. In the context of globalization, Ulaanbaatar and its economy--including the entertainment industry--are expanding rapidly on the world market. While innovation is necessary to meet the demands of the international entertainment market, with companies such as Cirque du Soleil broadening the market for contemporary contortion acts, it ultimately threatens traditional aspects of the performing arts that are repressed in this fast-growing industry. In an effort to safeguard Mongolian contortion, members of the state circus who advocate for the preservation of the traditional form of Mongolian contortion appealed to the United Nations in 2011 to have *Traditional Mongolian Contortion* included into the UNESCO List of Intangible Cultural Heritage. Unfortunately, the plea was unsuccessful and has been withdrawn before it could be evaluated by the UNESCO committee[4]. As a result, this research project is partly motivated by the unfortunate development of the plea and aims to elucidate the cultural values of *Traditional Mongolian Contortion* by presenting ethnographic data and positioning this art form in scholarly literature. It therefore, presents the following research data collected following best ethnological practice, ethical standards and highest respect to the Mongolian culture and its people.

To provide a clear overview of Mongolian contortion and its development, this paper has been divided into five segments: The genesis of Mongolian contortion, the development of contortion techniques and styles, training methods in Mongolia, the development of aesthetics and, finally, a proposal for the safeguarding of *Traditional Mongolian Contortion.*

---

4   In an email exchange with UNESCO, it was revealed that the petition was withdrawn due to an „unfavourable recommendation provided by the subsidiary body at that time." A number of artistic disciplines were also being petitioned that year, and it seems that contortionism was one of numerous elements from Mongolia that were under consideration for the list of intangible cultural heritage.

THE GENESIS AND DEVELOPMENT OF CONTORTIONISM IN MONGOLIA

Very little has been recorded about the history and the development of contortion practices in Mongolia, and the following overview is based on what literature and qualitative studies are available. Given the nature of these sources, the information contained therein needs to be interpreted with caution. Both ancient texts and modern surveys require an understanding of possible response biases.

An understanding of the artistic development of Mongolian contortion will be explored in different contexts such as international artistic exchange during the Silk Road era and examines the influence of the Soviet Union that ultimately led to the establishment of the Mongolian circus.

This paper further examines the history of Mongolian contortion in relation to three possible theories regarding its genesis and development and analyzes the function of Mongolian Contortion within the context of each theory. Throughout this paper when referring to Chinggis Khan (Чингис Хаан, born likely 1162), the spelling that is most commonly used in Mongolia was utilized. Notwithstanding, one ought to recognize that there are other spellings, such as *Genghis Khan, Genghis, Chingis, Jinghis* or *Jenghiz*. The word for "Mongolian Contortion" is *uran nugaralt* (уран нугаралт). *Nugaralt* is the literal translation of bending/folding. When the modifier *uran* is added in front of a word related to a profession, it means that this person is a professional/or the best at this particular profession. In Mongolia, *uran nugaralt* is translated to "Professional/ Beautiful/Ultimate Bender".[5]

During the research process and in interviews with members of the Mongolian circus community numerous narratives on how the Art of Contortion has developed in Mongolia were discovered. Throughout this segment, these narratives are acknowledged and in addition further findings of this research will be examined to refine a feasible theory. This section therefore concludes with three theories about the genesis of Mongolian contortion; the first is a traditionally given one which refers to ancient Mongolian history, the second arises from a consideration of Mongolian contortion as a folk art expression of the Mongolian people perhaps connected to religious performance, and the third arises from evidence about the influence of the Mongolian State Circus on Mongolian contortion with an entertainment centered function. The difference between these three theories is, in the end, one of preferred perspective and orientation; although they may seem to conflict, each theory offers a unique look at the same performing art.

Theory One – Court Performances in the 13th Century

The first theory about the genesis of Mongolian contortion is one that was often introduced during interviews with local contortion practitioners in Ulaanbaatar and it pointed towards the compendium of chronicles *Jami' al-Tawarikh*, a history book that was written at the beginning of the 14th century in the Mongol *Ilkhanate* (a political entity ruled by a *khan*, a political entity in the southwestern sector of the Mongol empire, ruled

5   Oyun-Erdene, Senge, personal communication, December 23, 2020.

by a military leader or ruler, or *khan*). It was written by Rashid-al-Din Hamadani, born in 1247 in Iran: a statesman, historian and physician who served as court historian and vizier to the *Ilkhan* court and who expanded the university at Rab'-e Rashidi, which later published the majority of his works. The *Jami' al-Tawarikh*, also known as *World History*, datable to 1314, was produced in the city of Tabriz, the modern-day Iran. It encompasses major events in world history and explores different cultures and countries such as the Mongol and Turkish tribes, the history of the Mongols, starting with Chinggis Khan, but also that of the Indians, Chinese and Franks.[6]. Some parts of the *Jami' al-Tawarikh* have been published in Mongolian history books, stating that Chinggis Khan had a proclivity for watching Mongolian contortion during court performances.

This narrative is popular among Mongolian locals and frequently comes up in conversations about Mongolian contortion and is as well used on cultural websites that introduce Mongolian culture. Mongolian author and blogger Sodnom Ulzee, for example, shares the story of contortionists, performing in court for Chinggis Khan: "The art of contortionism in Mongolia goes back at least to the 13th century. It was a favorite form of entertainment for the mighty Genghis Khan." [7] This theory is so omnipresent that it can be found as well in general media with news agency *Reuters* stating that Mongolian contortion was developed in the palace of 13th century warlord and national hero Genghis Khan.[8] Similar versions

6   Only a few parts of the original manuscript have survived. These are currently displayed at the Edinburgh University Library, the Khalili Collections and the Topkapi Palace Istanbul.
7   Pigg, Sodnom U., "Mongolmom: Mongolian Contortionist" Blogspot. April 23, 2018. Accessed April 09, 2020.
https://mongolmom.blogspot.com/2018/04/mongolian-contortionist.html
8   Thomas, Nathalie, "Mongolian child contortionists stretch for international success." Reuters, July 7, 2016. Accessed November 26, 2020. https://www.reuters.com/article/us-mongolia-contortionists-idUSKCN0ZN0DK

of this narrative speak of Mongolian folk dances with emphasis on body flexibility as being one of the emperor's favorite forms of entertainment. This theory, which finds itself repeated by both practitioners and the public media, is tempting. However, numerous governments have a reputation for manipulating their own history books for the benefit of their agenda, which why this theory should be treated with some caution.

With this first theory, one could argue that Mongolian contortion has a far-reaching history that goes back to the 13th century with its function, as depicted in the narratives presented here, being mainly for entertainment purposes as court performances. It is, therefore, either rooted in folk dance that incorporates elements of body flexibility, or it has already developed into an independent art form by that time, with performances mainly presenting body flexibility. However, other perspectives exist.

Theory Two – Tradition, Nature, Dance and Ritual

The second theory discusses the development of Mongolian contortion in a more recent time frame. In her book "Монголын уран нугаралт - Mongolian Contortion", Norovsambuu Budbazar, honored with the State Prize (1971), the People's Artist Award (1980), awarded Honored Artist of Mongolia (1966) and one of Mongolia's most influential contortion trainers, gives insight into the history and development of Mongolian contortion and enumerates the most prominent contortionists and contortion coaches of her country. Three of the most influential and innovative figures in the history and development of Mongolian contortion since the establishment of the Mongolian State Circus (Монголын Үндэсний Цирк), are Madame Tsend-Ayush Togoonchuluun, Majigsuren Dashpuntsag and Norovsambuu Budbazar (particularly in that order), whose contributions to the art form will be introduced and examined appropriately throughout this paper. Already in the introduction, she emphasizes the importance of dance, music and the preservation of tradition and cultural heritage to the Mongolian people: "Freedom loving, happy people of the land of the blue sky have [a] very ancient and rich historical and cultural heritage. Anyone who watches the traditional dances preserving special features of different national minorities, festivals, melodic songs's [sic] festival he [sic] thinks that Mongolia is the country of song and music."[9]

Perhaps most tellingly, the book cover depicts three female contortionists, a Buddhist *Tara* (Mongolian: *Dara-ekhe*), the skylight of a Mongolian yurt (Mongolian: *Ger*), Mongolian traditional ornaments and a starry sky. The reference to tradition, preservation and music together with the imagery and symbolism, hints how contortion performances in Mongolia are created, how their distinguishing features from region to region are preserved through the present day, and how they are valued and perceived both by the Mongolian society as well as its performing artists, which will be analyzed in passing throughout this article.

In her chapter *Mongolian Contortion,* Norovsambuu creates a timeline where she divides the development of Mongolian contortion into three periods: Period One describes the history and genesis of Mongolian contortion prior to 1940, listing numerous male and female artists who displayed their body flexibility by dividing them into front and back benders. The 1940s represent Period Two where the concept of circus, including training structures, was first introduced to Mongolia by the Soviet Union, followed by the establishment of the Mongolian State

---

9   Budbazar, Norovsambuu. Монголын уран нугаралт - *Mongolian Contortion* (Ulaanbaatar: Selengepress Co., Ltd, 2011), 20.

Circus in 1941. Period Three encompasses the development between 1960 to 1980 and catalogs influential and innovative female contortion coaches and their contributions. Comprising the genesis of contortion in Mongolia prior to 1940, she describes the elements of body flexibility in folk arts when contortion in Mongolia has not yet developed into its current form. She asserts that Mongolian contortion is rooted in various traditional Mongolian dances that are performed in different regions of Mongolia with elements of body flexibility and deep back-bends, where dancers kneel and bend back and forth.[10] In addition, Norovsambuu lists numerous front and back benders who practiced and performed body flexibility prior to the 1940s and implies that the ability to perform body flexibility has been a widespread skill among the Mongolian population.

If we turn to the failed 2011 appeal, we see details about how the art-form has been preserved and continued. In 2011 the Arts Council Mongolia, together with Norovsambuu as head of a steering committee, appealed to the United Nations to have Mongolian contortion included in the UNESCO List of Intangible Cultural Heritage. The Arts Council Mongolia established the cultural heritage program that focuses on promoting cultural heritage to the general public, improving the preservation of heritage sites, building the capacity of cultural heritage organizations, and transmitting intangible cultural heritage (ICH) to younger generations, assisting Mongolian museums & schools with heritage education curriculum development.[11] Together they submitted an introductory video along with photographs of Mongolian contortionists to support the bid. In addition to archival footage of Mongolian contortionists, Norovsambuu introduces in detail the history of contortion in Mongolia:

10   Norovsambuu, Монголын уран нугаралт - *Mongolian Contortion, 20.*
11   Arts Council of Mongolia. "Heritage Program" January 01, 2012. Accessed December 08, 2020. http://artscouncil.mn/heritage-program-introduction/

Contortion admires and recognizes Mongolian women's beauty and gracefulness. The art form known as Mongolian contortion has developed over a long history of Mongolia. It is considered as one of the traditional performing arts. The early development of Mongolian contortion started back in the 16th and 17th century when the first Mongolian theatre Saran Khukhuu was founded by the great nobleman Dazanravjaa. At this theatre the contortion act was influenced by the rituals and religious rituals as well. ... The traditional Mongolian contortion is influenced by traditional Mongolian dance, ornaments, animals, including frog and frown [sic], and rituals such as the fire rituals and so on. [12]

The footage used in the video displays different groups and solo artists performing contortion poses with a resemblance to animals, Mongolian ornaments and Buddhist images executing for example folded hands and bowing heads. The costume colors, displaying religious themes, are gold and red and the headpieces are similar to those as seen on statues of Buddhist deities.[13] Another scene displays the young Norovsambuu as a student of Madame Tsend-Ayush Togoonchuluun, contortionist and coach, Honored Artist of Mongolia (1958), State Prize Winner (1971) and People's Artist of Mongolia (1978). In the training scene, it appears that Madame Tsend-Ayush is studying traditional Mongolian ornaments and later shares her knowledge with the 9-year old Norovsambuu by using

12   UNESCO, "Representative List-2011, Mongolian traditional Contortion (Mongolia)" UNESCO. June 23, 2011. Accessed January 10, 2020. https://ich.unesco.org/en/13-representative-list-00411?include=film.inc.php&id=05328&width=500&call=film
13   Questions remain, however, about the relationship between contortionism's Buddhist roots and the emerging Soviet circus machine. It is feasible that spiritual practices, rituals and their reference in performing arts were altered by the Soviet circus sector.

these elements of the ornaments as templates or pattern for the contortion poses. Additionally, footage of folk dancers is shown, who kneel on the floor, performing deep back-bends with their heads touching the floor and who execute complicated arm movements with overextended joints that make their arms, wrists and fingers appear boneless (Figure 1).

Figure 1: *Performance of the Mongolian National Song and Dance Academic Ensemble showcasing deep backbends during a dance performance at the Mongolian National Theatre* (2015/2016). Mongolia. Photograph courtesy of Yargai Galtat

In 2013, filmmaker Pearly Jacobs interviewed Norovsambuu and Nomintuya Baasankhuu, former contortionist and historian for the non-government organization Arts Council Mongolia, regarding the appeal to UNESCO. Here Norovsambuu again specifies the connection of Mongolian contortion to dance and links it to a folk dance called *Biyelgee* which requires the previously mentioned kneeling on the floor while performing deep back-bends.[14]

---

14   Jacobs, Pearly. „Mongolia: Contortionists aim for UNESCO Recognition."

The theory that Mongolian contortion is rooted in religious performances has been supported as well by Madame Tsend-Ayush Togoonchuluun, contortionist and coach, Honored Artist of Mongolia (1958), State Prize Winner (1971) and People's Artist of Mongolia (1978). Andréane Leclerc, contortionist and graduate from the *National Circus School of Montreal*, cites Madame Tsend-Ayush with the following:" Contortion came from Mongolia and was used in *tsam* dances, practiced by Buddhist monks and [performed] in shamanistic practices. It is said that it would be the will to surpass oneself in acrobatic dance which would have given rise to the contortion of today."[15] (Translated from French to English by the author.) Even today, Mongolian contortion performances often incorporate elements of folk dance, spiritual themes and Mongolian folklore. So much so, that an entire section is designated to folk dance in the *Encyclopedia of Mongol Circus-70 years of Mongolian Circus*. Musicians playing traditional instruments such as the *Morin Khuur* (horsehead fiddle) usually accompany a traditional contortion performance. In these settings, the contortionist usually wears a traditional costume in colors such as white, sky blue, red or gold together with a headpiece made of the precious materials, arranged in a style unique to the costuming of Mongolian contortionists (Figure 2).

In short, the second theory emphasizes contortionism's deep connection with Mongolian tradition, nature, dance and ritual. It reflects on the country's nomadic lifestyle, to cherish women's bodies and strength, and to preserve the cultural heritage of the Mongolian people. In the following

Eurasianet. August 23, 2013. Accessed June 24, 2017. https://eurasianet.org/mongolia-contortionists-aim-for-unesco-recognition
15   Leclerc, Andréane. *ENTRE CONTORSION ET ÉCRITURE SCÉNIQUE: LA PROUESSE COMME TECHNIQUE ÉVOCATRICE DE SENS* (Montreal: National Circus School of Montreal, 2013), 26.

Figure 2: *Mongolian Contortionist Urnaa Uranbilleg performing to traditional Mongolian Music.* Mongolia. Photograph courtesy of Urnaa Uranbileg

section on the aesthetics and creation process of contortion performances, these elements will be examined more comprehensively. Before this, the third theory remains to be presented.

Theory Three – The Establishment of the Mongolian State Circus

Theory one and two are largely based on oral history, qualitative interview data and the statements from our three main figures Majigsuren, Tsend-Ayush and Norovsambuu from their life during the pre-circus era (although Norovsambuu became Tsend-Ayush's student at the age of nine and inherited her knowledge). Theory three is based on tangible evidence such as archival data, interviews, photographs and video material that provide insight into the development of contortionism starting with the establishment of the Mongolian State Circus. Theory three does not necessarily abrogate the second theory that has been previously discussed.

It should be mentioned that none of these theories have been explored in depth by modern scholars. With the establishment of the Mongolian State Circus however, we have more archival data at hand in form of news articles, photographs and video material that demonstrate the development of contortionism in Mongolia from 1941 onwards, which is a dividing line in material evidence between the first two theories and theory three. Numerous Mongolian contortion practitioners and trainers believe, that Mongolian contortion developed into its current form from the 1940s on, with the installment of the first state circus in Mongolia.

Nomintuya Baasankhuu, historian of the Arts Council Mongolia explains in an interview with Pearly Jacobs that contortion really emerged as a performance act with the establishment of the Mongolian State Circus in 1941, which introduced its first official contortionist, Tsend-ayush (who like most Mongolians at the time used only a single name): "She is the one who really started the first contortion school in Mongolia. Later there was Majigsuren, the second contortionist of Mongolia. With her contortion became enriched, not only with flexibility but also with being strong and being able to balance the body." In 1958, Norovsambuu joined the circus as a nine-year-old after being spotted by Majigsuren as a potential talent. "All the different techniques we have, different positions and choreographs[sic], really come from these three people."[16]

---

16   Jacobs, Pearly. „Mongolia: Contortionists aim for UNESCO Recognition." Eurasianet. August 23, 2013. Accessed June 24, 2017. https://eurasianet.org/mongolia-contortionists-aim-for-unesco-recognition

The installment of the state circus was a crucial moment in the history of Mongolian contortion. Enkhbold Chuluunbaatar, assistant professor in the Department of Business Administration and strategic consultant who focuses on management issues of state-own enterprises in Mongolia, including cultural and creative industries, examines in his article *Mongolian Circus Industry in the Post-transitional Economy* the establishment and the development of the Mongolian State circus:

> The former Soviet Union set a turning-point in circus development with the renaissance movement in 1919, setting a standard of circus acts based on the techniques of ballet and gymnastics. Soon after the Soviet government established the world's first State College of Circus and Variety Arts in 1927 (the school was also known as the Moscow Circus School), the Russian circus emerged as the benchmark of circuses worldwide ("Chronology of Circus," 2008), resulting in the supremacy of Russian circus in the world's stage ... Not long after Russian circus rose to the world's acclaim, the spillover effect was strongly felt by Mongolia—the neighboring socialist country —leading to the birth of Mongolian circus. Mongolia was a satellite state that was closely aligned with the Soviet Union since 1921 (Rossabi, 2005). Mongolia was soon introduced to circus in the 1930s. The principal of the Moscow Circus School, Aleksander Voloshin, made multiple visits from 1931 to 1939 to scout Mongolian young talents to be trained in Moscow. In the first batch, 50 talents were selected to receive one-year circus training in 1940. These pioneers returned to Mongolia and established a circus group under the name of Mongolian Circus, with its

opening performance in July 9, 1941. Following the inaugural show, a circus training center was founded the next year.[17]

With this, the circus format and a consistent training concept were introduced by the Soviet Union which lead to the establishment of the Mongolian State Circus in the following years. It also led to a „standardization" of contortion routines presented on these stages. The third theory therefore, presents clear evidence and a timeline of the development of Mongolian contortion with the installment of a training curriculum from 1940s on and having an entertainment centered function. The introduction of these training concepts heavily influenced how contortionists would train and ultimately perform in the future. With Madame Tsend-Ayush, the first official contortionist and founder of the first contortion school, future contortionists would be instructed through a unified curriculum and training concept.

Having explored the three most prevalent theories regarding the genesis of Mongolian contortion it is crucial to include supplementary historical information to adequately address all possible developments. In past works, the author suggested that the genesis of Chinese contortionism dates back to around 771BCE, the spring and autumn period and the warring state period.[18] Although there is some debate amongst today's scholars, China's acrobatic history is considered to have originated between 2,000[19] and 3,000 years ago[20]. Furthermore, China established

17   Chuluunbaatar, Enkhbold. "Mongolian Circus Industry in the Post-transitional Economy." *International Journal of Cultural and Creative Industries.* Volume 1, 2 (2014): 68-74

18   Ala-Rashi, Mariam. *The Art of Contortionism. An Introduction to and Analysis of Chinese Contortionism in a Historical, Political and Social Context.* USA: Amazon KDP Press, 2019. 21.

19   Circopedia. (2018). Beijing Acrobatic Troupe. [online] Accessed December 15, 2020. Available at: http://www.circopedia.org/Beijing_Acrobatic_Troupe

20   The Soraya. (2012). The National Circus of The People's Republic of

foreign trading through the initiation of ancient networks such as the famous Silk Road from 114 BCE to 1450 CE, which automatically led to cultural and remarkable artistic exchange.[21] By 1279 the Mongolian empire had conquered large parts of China and Chinggis Khan had gained control over the Silk Road. Considering the closely intertwined history between China and Mongolia it is feasible that there has been an artistic exchange as well. It would not be the first time China had introduced acrobatic practices to another country. Recordings within one of China's largest cultural encyclopedias, *WapBaiKe*, assert that China introduced *Sanle*, later translated to *Sangaku*, to Japan in the 8th century. This was a precursor to what we call "circus" today, an artistic endeavor which included displays of juggling, pantomime, dance and acrobatics.[22]

Theories in Comparison

When taking all these possibilities into account it would bring us back to theory one of the *Jami' al-Tawarikh*. Considering all eventualities based on historical facts is crucial to create a complete image. However, scholarly literature on the development of contortion is sparse and in this lie the limitations of this paper.

Coming back to the second and third proposal it is obvious that there is distinct evidence to the third theory and less evidence to the second, but one should not go as far as to abandon the second theory. In his video *Body in Motion: Exploring the Art of Contortion* filmmaker Sarnai Tessitore argues: "If the art of contortionism once existed in Mongolia it should be

China presents Cirque Chinois. [online] Accessed December 15, 2020. Available at: https://www.thesoraya.org/assets/Uploads/education/archive/pdf/CirqueChinois-CueSheetrev.pdf

21   Ala-Rashi, Mariam. *The Art of Contortionism. An Introduction to and Analysis of Chinese Contortionism in a Historical, Political and Social Context. 23.*

22   WapBaike. (2019). Sanle. [online] Accessed 23.12.2019. Available at: https://baike.baidu.com/item/%E6%95%A3%E4%B9%90

evident in historical paintings, drawings or literature. No such proof seems to exist."[23] Nonetheless, written evidence is not the only means to preserve intangible cultural heritage. Tradition does not develop overnight and the fact that Mongolian contortion would have become one of the signature performance art-forms of its country and the international brand that it is today while incorporating cultural aspects of the Mongolian society, solely through the establishment of the state circus and a training curriculum, is questionable. It places too much weight on the influence of imposed Soviet culture: there must surely have at least been an existing predisposition or loose social practice. The development of Russian circus in the USSR and how it influenced the establishment of the circus industry in Mongolia is outlined by Enkhbold Chuluunbaatar and illustrates how it became an instrument in cultural policymaking:

> The former Soviet Union set a turning-point in circus development with the renaissance movement in 1919, setting a standard of circus acts based on the techniques of ballet and gymnastics. Soon after the Soviet government established the world's first State College of Circus and Variety Arts in 1927 (the school was also known as the Moscow Circus School), the Russian circus emerged as the benchmark of circuses worldwide ("Chronology of Circus," 2008), resulting in the supremacy of Russian circus in the world's stage. Circus became an even more prominent piece of culture and a point of pride; it played an important role in the development of cultural policy in the Soviet Union. Not long after Russian circus rose to the world's acclaim, the spillover effect was strongly felt by Mongolia—the

---

23   Sarnai Tessitore, "Body in Motion: Exploring the Art of Contortion." Sarnaifilm. February 16, 2015. Accessed April 02, 2020. https://www.youtube.com/watch?v=vfVJ37icGjg&t=317s

neighboring socialist country —leading to the birth of Mongolian circus.[24]

In contrast, American anthropologist Adrienne L. Kaeppler defines in her article *Dance Ethnology and the Anthropology of Dance* the development of movement in human societies and their preservation through systems of knowledge:

> Structured movement systems occur in all known human societies. They are systems of knowledge - the products of action and interaction as well as processes through which action and interaction take place- and are usually part of a larger activity or activity system. These systems of knowledge are socially and culturally constructed by a group of people and primarily preserved in memory. Although transient, movement systems have structured content; they can be visual manifestations of social relations, the subjects of elaborate aesthetic systems, and may assist in understanding cultural values.[25]

The passing on of intangible culture through knowledge, folklore, traditions and oral history and social practice is a crucial process to keep cultures alive. In his video, Sarnai Tessitore interviews Majigsuren who clarifies the circumstances of missing evidence in paintings and literature:

> Mongolian flexible dance movements were passed throughout many generations, long before the contortionists [as an] individual circus act were established. So, I believe there were

24   Chuluunbaatar, Enkhbold. "Mongolian Circus Industry in the Post-transitional Economy." *International Journal of Cultural and Creative Industries.* Volume 1, 2 (2014): 68-74

25   Kaeppler, Adrienne L. "Dance Ethnology and the Anthropology of Dance." Dance Research Journal 32, no. 1 (2000): 116-25. Accessed December 17, 2020.

contortionists in Mongolia many years ago, just that they were not called contortionists. For instance: A Western Mongolian ethnic dance requires the knees on the ground as the back bends [sic]. Such examples prove that flexible individuals existed in the past."[26]

Intangible cultural heritage, as it is passed on from one generation to the next, does not always live on in paintings and literature, it lives on as well in practice and the customs of the people. Although there has not been any evidence in paintings or literature, one has to take into consideration that the Mongolian people lived and, in part, are still living a nomadic lifestyle up until today. Other modern „circus" disciplines have left evidence all across the globe as they emerged from ancient times. Millennia-old evidence of jugglers exists in the tombs of Egypt as well as on disparate islands in the south Pacific, for example. These cultures had physical homes that they developed, allowing the preservation of images of jugglers – and sometimes their tools.[27] Ancient Mongolia, however, left no such monuments to their people and daily practices. The traveling life entails a lot of limitations and enforces a reduction to a minimum of necessary items. I therefore, disagree with the statement that only literature and paintings give proof to a society's development and argue that there is an *embodied evidence* that can be seen in the *practices* of the Mongolian people. A lack of material evidence is not a lack of history. Its function would therefore, serve both as a means to preserve culture and tradition, as well as for entertainment purposes. By exploring the lifestyle of ancient Mongolian nomads, environmental activist and communication strategist Khulan Batkhuyag shares her knowledge on how Mongolian nomads

---

26   Tessitore, "Body in Motion: Exploring the Art of Contortion." Sarnaifilm. YouTube.

27   Wall, Thom. *Juggling - From Antiquity to the Middle Ages: the forgotten history of throwing and catching.* USA: Modern Vaudeville Press, 2019.

have preserved their intangible heritage while traveling with a minimum of essential items:

> I was surprised by how little they owned. At first, I thought it was because they moved about four times a year. [...] You only carry what you need. But then I learned there's a deeper philosophy behind it. Historically, nomads believed that we are only passing through this life, that people come and leave naked, so they believe that there's no point in building anything that destroys nature or in being greedy for materialistic things when your life expectancy is only less than 100 years. Instead, they invest in tradition, heritage, history and pass it from generation to generation.[28]

Thus, not only a practical understanding of the nomadic lifestyle is depicted but also a philosophical signification of how traditions and intangible cultural heritage were preserved.

Another important notion that should not be overlooked is the encounter of body flexibility among tribe members in remote regions of Mongolia, who discover their body flexibility independently, as stated in the introductory video for UNESCO:

> The biggest contortion center in the North-West area [of Mongolia] is in the city of Erdenet. Many talented, young contortionists continued [sic] to be found in remote regional areas. Despite living nomadic lifestyles largely influenced by

---

28   Khulan Batkhuyag, "The Ancient, Earth-Friendly Wisdom of Mongolian Nomads." TED. September 01, 2020. Accessed October 19, 2020. https://www.ted.com/talks/khulan_batkhuyag_the_ancient_earth_friendly_wisdom_of_mongolian_nomads#t-480297

urban trends and with limited exposure to the performing and circus arts, these young contortionists have discovered their own natural flexibility and grace. This rare, innate ability is quite remarkable and not often seen anywhere else in the world.[29]

The accuracy of this statement cannot currently be validated as there are no scholarly papers that analyze Mongolian contortion and its relationship to genetic predisposition. Since the introductory video aims to convince the UNESCO committee to include Mongolian contortion in the UNESCO list of intangible cultural heritage, one could argue that it draws on an idealized image of the unique development of contortion in Mongolia and, therefore, further research would be needed to defend this statement on a scholarly level. The statement, however, if proven to be accurate, could reveal important details regarding the history of contortion, its genesis and development in ancient Mongolia. It also informs us about the far-reaching ability of body flexibility throughout the Mongolian population and further research could illuminate as to why Mongolia has been a melting-pot for body flexibility over the past decades.

All in all, the aforementioned data that has been examined in correlation to the proposed theories offers different outcomes regarding the genesis of Mongolian contortion: Each theory not only has the potential to stand alone, there is also the possibility that these theories are intertwined or partially build on one another. Understanding the limits of material evidence when studying nomadic cultures, one can argue that the final form of Mongolian contortion as we know it today was based on earlier forms and practices of body flexibility that were rooted in folk dance,

29   UNESCO, "Representative List-2011, Mongolian traditional Contortion (Mongolia)" UNESCO. June 23, 2011. Accessed January 10, 2020. https://ich.unesco.org/en/13-representative-list-00411?include=film.inc. php&id=05328&width=500&call=film

religion and the depiction of nature. Having been a practitioner of Mongolian contortion herself since 2013 the author had the opportunity to experience the traditional contortion training as well as attending traditional contortion performances firsthand. The connection of the Mongolian people to nature, tradition and religion is undeniable and their day to day life is deeply rooted in traditions that continue to this day to be highly valued and cherished. It seems possible, therefore, that the second and third theory are actually linked and that Mongolia has a history of body flexibility prior to the establishment of the state circus and the introduction of structured training concepts. As there is no anthropological evidence to support the claim at present, the author leaves this question for future researchers to explore. It appears evident that Mongolian contortion is deeply rooted in nature, traditional art forms including music, dance, fine arts (ornaments), spiritual practices (Buddhism and Shamanism) as well as the practice to preserve the legacy of their ancestors in narratives.

It is feasible that traces of body flexibility existed in the past with flexible performers being located all over Mongolia, and that with the establishment of the circus concept a structure was introduced that unified the Mongolian contortionists. Thus, a training and performance concept was installed that gave the Mongolian artists an additional outlet to honor their roots and the stories of their ancestors and to cherish nature in the form of Mongolian contortion.

On the grounds of these observations and participant observations during my training sessions I contend that it is likely that Mongolian contortion developed *from* Mongolian folk dances and practices of body flexibility *into* the modern, autonomous circus discipline we see today.

In conclusion, this section aimed to illuminate the genesis and function of Mongolian contortion and proposed three different theories advanced by Mongolian contortionists and historical experts. These theories consider Mongolian contortion to have arisen from one of three places. The first gives credit to court performances for the great Chingghis Khan in the 13th century. The second theory asserts that Mongolian contortionism was rooted in folk dance with elements of body flexibility, religious practices and depictions of nature, and the third theory proposes that Mongolian contortion came into existence with the installment of the circus concept in Mongolia during the 1940s. With this, three of the most influential contortionists in Mongolian history Madame Tsend-Ayush, Majigsuren and Norovsambuu have been introduced in this section and their expertise regarding the genesis and development of Mongolian contortion has been taken into account. Additionally, the appeal of the Arts Council Mongolia together with Norovsambuu as head of a steering committee to have Mongolian contortion included in the UNESCO list of intangible cultural heritage has been examined. Finally, a fourth option was proposed, wherein theories two and three, were combined as a feasible origin of Mongolian contortion in one breath with acknowledging the limitations of this research study due to sparse scholarly literature regarding this art form.

Having explored the historical aspects of Mongolian contortion, the next section will examine the development of training concepts, contortion styles and techniques following the establishment of the circus concept in 1941. In order to fully grasp the evolution of Mongolian contortion, it is imperative to illuminate the contributions of the three main figures of Mongolian contortion in the following section: Tsend-Ayush, Majigsuren and Norovsambuu.

DEVELOPMENT OF CONTORTION TECHNIQUES AND STYLES

The Mongolian State Circus was established in 1941, setting the stage for developments within the Art of Contortion. Having already introduced the three main figures of the art form, Madame Tsend-Ayush, Majigsuren and Norovsambuu, their contributions will be examined by looking at the training concepts, contortion styles and techniques. Archival video material will be drawn upon, supplemented by the author's training experience in Mongolia when pertinent.

With the import of the circus in the 1940s new training curricula and techniques were introduced to the Mongolian artists. Numerous contortion movements that had already been established and performed internationally by contortionists from for example China, Europe, the U.S. as well as other countries, were introduced to the Mongolian artists through a structured training curriculum designed in the Soviet Union. In her book Монголын уран нугаралт - *Mongolian Contortion*, Norovsambuu introduces a detailed timeline which will be analyzed throughout this section, that allows the reader to observe the gradual development of contortion techniques and styles and informs about important events in the evolution of Mongolian contortion. In the pages that follow, a variety of seemingly disparate factors will be explored. The country's traditions, nomadic lifestyle, and geographic isolation each played an important role in the development of contortionism, as well as political influence through the Soviet Union with the establishment of the Mongolian state circus in 1941, and the first contortion school founded by Tsend-Ayush in 1959.

Figure 3: *Mongolian Contortionist Agiimaa Jargalsaikhan, one of Majigsuren's last contortion students, practicing the Marinelli Bend, called zubnik (зубник) in Mongolia* (2014). Mongolia. Photograph courtesy of Agiimaa Jargalsaikhan.

In her publication, Norovsambuu lists in a timeline different milestones in the development on Mongolian contortionism, where contortion techniques and styles have been performed by local contortionists for the first time in Mongolia, such as the Marinelli bend, called zubnik (зубник) in Mongolia (Figure 3)[30], hand balancing, and the balancing of breakable props, such as cups or plates to name a few examples. It also informs us about a significant development in the presentation of this art-form, evolving from the display of figurative gestures of ethnic dances, rituals

---

30   A world-renowned and exclusive contortion trick, is the Marinelli bend, named after H.B. Marinelli (1864-1924), who was a male contortionist of Italian descent that grew up in Germany. He performed internationally in vaudeville shows under his stage name "The Boneless Wonder". The Marinelli bend is considered one of the most extreme and difficult contortion tricks

and folk art to an entertainment centered focus/commodity/premise/ specialty.

Current knowledge, however, does not entirely encompass the developments of contortionism in the Soviet Union in the 1930s and 1940s, which makes it difficult to say with certainty which styles of body flexibility or gymnastics, and which techniques and poses have been imported to Mongolia by the Soviet Union, and which were discovered through practice independently during this particular era by Mongolian contortionists. Today, the terms used for contortion poses in Mongolia are a blend of Russian and Mongolian wordage, with some Russian terms supplanting the Mongolian words for even the most basic poses. Poses in Russian language include *Chpagat* (split), *Stoik* (handstand), *Most* (Bridge). Poses with Mongolian names include *Gants Gar* (one-arm handstand), *Buurunhii* (triple fold), *Jim* (push-up/press-up). Shapes that are created with the legs, as well as duo contortion tricks, don't have specific names and are usually called after the basic contortion position that is performed in the trick.[31]

In her book, Norovsambuu introduces Tsend-Ayush, Majigsuren and herself as some of the three most influential contortionists in Mongolia, who have invented and established different techniques and styles that are categorized nowadays as classical and *Traditional Mongolian Contortion*. It is not clear however as to what extent contortion techniques and movements have been invented by these three contortionists, and which have been imported from the Soviet Union.

---

31   Oyun-Erdene, Senge, personal communication, December 23, 2020.

To name one example: Norovsambuu asserts that Majigsuren was the first contortionist to *introduce* handstand into the Art of Contortion around 1948...

> ... [Majigsuren] was the second contortionist to perform her contortion acts in [the] Mongolian circus arena and her second performance was on the 1ˢᵗ of May 1948. She's the contortionist to perform the Marinelle [sic] bend contortion on the flower stand ... and then introduced the posture of handstand into the art of contortion.[32]

...however, given the limited sources available, we can neither confirm nor deny the statement. At the very least, this passage confirms that a fully-inverted handstand was an exciting innovation within Mongolian contortionism in the late 1940s.

As an artist, innovation and creativity are a prerequisite. When experimenting with one's own flexibility new poses and figures emerge. Norovsambuu continues to describe the creative process and how Tsend-Ayush reformed contortionism with the establishment of the first contortion school:

> Together with her student Norovsambuu she developed the acts of classical contortion contributing to the reformation in the development of Mongolian contortion. Her first performance titled "Flower on Flower" in [the] central circus arena was on 31ˢᵗ of December, 1959. On the 40ᵗʰ anniversary of [the] People's Revolution, both teacher and the student introduced the brand-new style of contortion and it was the result of their

32   Budbazar, Norovsambuu. Монголын уран нугаралт - *Mongolian Contortion* (Ulaanbaatar: Selengepress Co., Ltd, 2011), 21.

hard work. As the outcome of their artistic search and creativity, they created the equilibrium (balanced) contortion.[33]

From this, one could interpret that balancing techniques were invented by these artists. However, hand-balancing was a well-established circus discipline around the world at this point. It is likely that others around the world were performing inversions that required great flexibility, but it appears that in the late 1950s, Mongolian contortion masters were combining those two elements independently. What is known is, that Norovsambuu was famous for her contortion pose of balancing a vase with flowers on her head while being in a one-hand contortion handstand where she bends her back and places her feet next to her head.[34] Yet, distinct clarity whether or not handstand developed independently in the training process or was introduced by the Soviet circus industry as part of the circus curriculum, is not evident. Furthermore, another important fact is revealed in Norovsambuu's statement. It indicates that Tsend-Ayush together with her student Norovsambuu had developed a new category within Mongolian contortion, titled *classic contortion*, which presumably has been the first descendant of the *Traditional Mongolian Contortion* style. It further illustrates the velocity with which these artists shaped, produced and transformed Mongolian contortion styles during that era, by transforming a folk art into a complex hybrid of Russian-style hand-balancing techniques and body flexibility that stemmed from Mongolian folk art within less than a decade.

The independent development of contortion techniques and styles has as well been subject in an interview with aforementioned filmmaker

---

33   Norovsambuu, Монголын уран нугаралт - *Mongolian Contortion, 21.*
34   This famous pose is still performed today, having been passed down from student to student. Most notably, Enkhtsetseg and Otgontsetseg who both performed one-hand contortion handstands while balancing objects on their heads.

Sarnai Tessitore, where Mongolian contortion coach and performer Erdenechimeg recalls the influence of the Soviet Union and the evolution of Mongolian contortion techniques and styles:

> We were closed off from everything back then. We thought contortion existed only in Mongolia until we began exploring different parts of the world and discovered how this particular skill has a history of its own. [The] mouth balancing act actually is a famous trick, called the Marinelli technique, that came out in 1926. We were only allowed to travel to fourteen socialist and communist countries. Every move was watched and controlled.[35]

In addition, Mongolian contortion coach, student of Norovsambuu and author of *Twisted Tales-My Life as Mongolian Contortionist* Otgontsegtseg "Otgo" Waller concludes: "When I was little, I heard that America was such a horrible country, like...that's our enemy and they're so mean. You were basically almost brainwashed."[36] With this Erdenechimeg and Otgo give insight into the confined development of contortion in Mongolia during this particular era encompassing geographical seclusion and political propaganda that separated them from the rest of the world.[37] It illustrates the circumstances the artists found themselves in and gives insight into the creative process that was notably an isolated pursuit – both in terms of the individual artist who stretches alone in a room, and

---

35   Sarnai Tessitore, "Body in Motion: Exploring the Art of Contortion." Sarnaifilm. February 16, 2015. Accessed April 02, 2020. https://www.youtube.com/watch?v=vfVJ37icGjg&t=317s
36   Sarnai Tessitore, "Body in Motion: Exploring the Art of Contortion." Sarnaifilm. February 16, 2015.
37   More on the intersection of political propaganda and the circus can be found in the author's work *The Art of Contortionism*, Chapter 4: The Disciplined Body as Political Instrument.

as a nation of artists, living in an isolated country together. Questions, however, remain: to what extent is Mongolian contortion the result of importing another land's culture? What poses were created by Mongolia's first contortionists? It is certain that acrobatics, ballet and gymnastics had been well established already in the Soviet Union in the late 1940s. To name two prominent examples: The Bolshoi Ballet in Russia was founded between 1821-1825 and the Moscow Circuses were nationalized already in 1919. It is therefore plausible that disciplines such as handstand training and the balancing of objects became part of the circus curriculum in Mongolia, with the contortionists incorporating the new movements into their daily training practice and creative process.

However, alongside the large-scale impact of the Soviet Union, the contributions of these three influential artists Madame Tsend-Ayush, Majigsuren and Norovsambuu, who shaped the image of the Mongolian contortionist should be acknowledged in detail. As the founder of the first contortion school in 1959, Madame Tsend-Ayush was at the forefront of creating numerous groundbreaking acts and established the form of Mongolian contortion as we know it today. Her creations together with Norovsambuu and Majigsuren can be recognized as a chain reaction that initiated the professional development of contortionism in Mongolia. The development of contortion—and the styles unique to Mongolia—were thoroughly documented by Norovsambuu. Her records span from 1960 to 1980, and show a linear progression in the development of contortion styles:

> The contortion in Mongolia developed as an independent act of circus performance during [the] 1960s-1980s. During this time, the classic acts of contortion were emerging and could become the national acts of [the] Mongolian circus. Since [the]

late 1960s, Mongolian contortion divided into several forms of solo contortion, duo contortion, themed contortion and air contortion, duo and contortion by [a] group of contortionists. And therefore, backbend and frontbend contortion developed in their classic forms.[38]

Indeed, the creative progress between the 1960s and 1980s had a high impact on the art form, with new techniques, props and apparatuses being introduced to Mongolian contortion in cooperative work between Russian and Mongolian artists. In 1973, audiences witnessed for the first time two contortionists forming a pyramid, stacked as base and flyer, with the supporting contortionist being the *base,* and the artist performing on top of the base's body being called the *flyer.* Further developments in 1973 were the introduction of aerial apparatuses such as the rope, which allowed the Mongolian contortionists for the first time to perform in the air. By 1980 many performances of duo contortion acts had been developed, where one contortionist balances and executes tricks on top of another contortionist, and a variety of different props had been introduced to increase the entertainment factor and production value: The balancing of [breakable] cups and plates, balancing on multiple stacked benches, balancing on the short pole, balancing on the chair as well as performances with living animals such as pigeons.[39] These developments display the vast expansion of contortion techniques, styles and training developments and reflect that contortionists and new performance concepts were in high demand. It also shows that Mongolian contortion underwent multiple transformations within a short time, going from traditional contortion that may well indeed have been rooted in folk arts, ritual and nature, to

---

38   Norovsambuu, Монголын уран нугаралт - *Mongolian Contortion, 21.*
39   Norovsambuu, Монголын уран нугаралт - *Mongolian Contortion*, 22.

an entertainment-oriented art form that had to meet the demands of the fast-growing circus industry.

Furthermore, the evolution of Mongolian contortion did not stop there. It has since become an independent art form that is as well performed outside of the circus context. Following the example of the Mongolian state circus and the opening of the first contortion school in 1959, many independent contortion studios have since been founded to preserve the Art of Contortion, to promote Mongolian contortion abroad and to meet the market's demands for new performers. Mongolian contortion has become an international brand and new techniques are still being developed. Since the establishment of the Mongolian State Circus, a number of companies and performance groups have emerged, further shaping the market. The famous Cirque du Soleil, traditional circuses in North America and Europe, Varieté shows, as well as theme parks, cruise ships and more – all hire contortionists. Perhaps the best example of the continuing development of techniques is in the city of Darhan, in the North of Mongolia. This school, which was explored in detail in the UNESCO appeal, uses a scientifically-based curriculum to train contortionists. It includes a new form of Mongolian contortion that incorporates traditional and modern elements.[40]

To satisfy the international market, training techniques are constantly expanded and brought to high standard. Since Mongolian contortionists are internationally in high demand, Western talent scouts are visiting Mongolian contortion schools all year round to discover and recruit new talents. International circus institutions, such as the aforementioned

40   UNESCO, "Representative List-2011, Mongolian traditional Contortion (Mongolia)" UNESCO. June 23, 2011. Accessed January 10, 2020. https://ich.unesco.org/en/13-representative-list-00411?include=film.inc. php&id=05328&width=500&call=film

Cirque du Soleil as part of the contemporary circus genre, have a strong impact on the Mongolian circus sector and the Western influence of the *cirque nouveau* is reflected in contemporary contortion practice. As defined by the Chamäleon Theater in Berlin: "Contemporary circus, or Cirque Nouveau, is a young genre of performing arts developed in the 1970s in France. The genre is an exciting, independent art form defined by its willingness to blur genre boundaries that redefine traditional circus."[41] As a result of the influence of the new generation circus of the late 20th century, also known as *cirque nouveau* or cirque *contemporain*, and the influence of TV and social media platforms, traditional institutions with a long history in contortion practices have to co-develop in this fast-paced industry.

We have seen how contortion as an artistic discipline has responded to market forces. As new markets with identifying aesthetic styles emerge, we have seen contortionists balance their bodies in new ways, incorporate props, perform duets, and work with trained birds. Contortion has changed substantially over the past half century, in terms of its identifiable poses and its transformation will continue responding to the ever-changing entertainment industry- and market demands.

In conclusion, the previously examined contortion styles are summarized and a structure and timeline is proposed that categorizes the development of contortion styles by taking characteristics, function, techniques and aesthetics into account. Although the transitions between categories are somewhat fluid, one has to bear in mind that Mongolian contortion is ever-evolving and that a later style cannot be said to completely replace the previous style. *Traditional Mongolian Contortion*, for example, is

---

41   Chamäleon Theater Berlin. "Contemporary Circus/Cirque Nouveau." Chamäleon Theater Berlin. January 01, 2020. Accessed December 15, 2020. https://chamaeleonberlin.com/en/theatre/contemporary-circus

arguably one of the most performed styles of contortion in Mongolia. *Traditional Mongolian Contortion* is often showcased outside of the circus environment at events such as the *Naadam Festival*, as part of a theatre program, at cultural events and TV. The Tumen Ekh ensemble, for instance presents a rare selection of ancient Mongolian performing arts and culture to local and international audiences including the play of traditional instruments such as the *morin khuur* (horse head fiddle), Mongolian long song, epic and eulogy songs, a ritualistic shaman dance, an ancient palace dance, a Tsam mask dance and Traditional Mongolian Contortion.[42] Knowledge about the category of *Classic Contortion,* however, is extremely limited, relying almost exclusively on a single document. Should new sources emerge in the future, our understanding of classic contortion in Mongolia may shift considerably.

One may assume fairly confidently that, initiated in 1959 by Tsend-Ayush and Norovsambuu, the "classic" contortion style incorporates elements of classical ballet to create a fusion between the two disciplines contortion and ballet. Based on the political associations between both countries one may hypothesize that the classic style is influenced by techniques that were imported to Mongolia from the Soviet Union with an aesthetic focus on ballet or the aesthetic lines and silhouettes that are desired in ballet performances. Norovsambuu has choreographed numerous acts, as, for example the suggestively entitled, *Swan Legend*, that incorporate ballet technique. However, in order to be able to assert confidently that classic Mongolian contortion is influenced by ballet, it would be imperative to conduct further research. The following categorizations, therefore, serve as a suggestion and are based on current knowledge. They are not definite and merely serve as a starting point for further research.

---

42   Tumen Ekh. "About Tumen Ekh Mongolian National Song and Dance Ensemble." Thumen Ekh. January 01, 2020. Accessed December 15, 2020. https:// tumenekh.wordpress.com/about/

Changes in Contortion across Time: A Taxonomy of Stages in Mongolian Contortionism

The following is an annotated timeline, charting the changes to Mongolian contortion as it takes stages around the world. Note how the aesthetic results and functions are altered as world events and market forces also develop. While these are developments within Mongolian contortionism as an increasingly commercial product, it should be noted that traditional contortionists are still practicing their traditional performances in Mongolia throughout this time as well.

Prior to 1940, Folk Dance and Folk Acrobatics:

Characteristics: The presentation of body flexibility in folk acrobatics through independent performances *or* folk dances *incorporating* elements of body flexibility. Performances of folk acrobatics that showcase body flexibility often focus either on front bending *or* back bending with the performing artist being called front-bender or back-bender. Additionally, ritual practices and folk dances such as the *Biyelgee dance* are found that incorporate elements of body flexibility with deep back-bends and overextended arms, wrists and fingers.

Function: To reflect on the every-day life of the Mongolian people and their rituals and religious beliefs.

Aesthetics: The front bend (Mongolian: *Klishnik*) depicts images of animals such as the frog, the lying antelope or snake (to name a few), whereas the back-bend (Mongolian: *Kauchik*) depicts patterns of Mongolian traditional ornaments. The depiction is of traditional ornaments, animals and daily tasks of the nomadic lifestyle. Folk dances showcase unique movements and costuming with distinct patterns to represent various ethnic groups.

1940s, Traditional Mongolian Contortion:

Characteristics: Complex contortion techniques that depict traditional Mongolian ornaments and animal poses, as well as elements of folk dance such as arm movements and back-bends from the *Biyelgee dance*. It is rooted in nature, ritual and dance and depicts cultural traditions. Movements are elegant and controlled with an emphasis on strength.

Function: To preserve intangible cultural heritage, cherish the strength and elegance of the Mongolian woman and to narrate stories of Mongolian ancestors.

Aesthetics: Religious themes or traditional folk-art themes are presented. Traditional ornaments, animals such as the frog or lying antelope are presented. Costume headpieces represent the crowns of Mongolian queens and to acknowledge and cherish the strong Mongolian woman. Headpieces similar to those of Buddhist statues reflect on religious beliefs. Performances are usually accompanied by throat singers and traditional musical instruments such as the horse-head fiddle. Costumes in the early 1940s were two-piece costumes, similar to a bikini to showcase the muscle work. Later on, full-body suits were introduced. Simple props were used, such as a vase with flowers, that was balanced on the head.

1959, Classic Mongolian Contortion:

Characteristics: Merging of two disciplines namely ballet and contortion. The combining of fundamental movements of Mongolian contortion, utilizing its elegance and strength and incorporating ballet movements with contortion poses, while using the traditional aesthetic of modern ballet: tutus, leotards, tights, and pointe shoes.

Aesthetics: Contortion incorporating ballet movements, ballet aesthetics and costuming. Presented in ballet attire such as pink tights, white leotards, tutu-like skirts and pointe shoes or ballet slippers. Imagery and movements are often derived from popular ballets such as Tchaikovsky's *Swan Lake*.

Function: Entertainment.

Figure 4: Galtat, Y. (2020). *Mongolian Contortionist balancing Pigeons on her Head.* Artist: Yargai Galtat.

1960-1980, Modern Mongolian Contortion:

Characteristics: Aimed to surpass traditional practices and styles of the past and experiment with new ideas and techniques by incorporating props and apparatuses such as the balancing of objects, as well as the performances with living animals (e.g. pigeons) (Figure 4). From the 1980s, duo contortion acts were introduced.

Aesthetics: Versatile. Various themes, costuming, props and apparatuses are used to cater to the entertainment industry. To name a few, themes such as jungle and wild animals, cultural themes such as Egypt or China with matching costumes and music, as well as colorful fantasy themes were performed.

Function: Entertainment.

1990/2000 and onwards, Contemporary Contortion:

Characteristics: Influenced by Western concepts such as *cirque nouveau/ cirque-theatre*, combining theatrical techniques with contortion skills. Training curricula in Western circus facilities such as the *Cirque du Soleil* headquarters in Montreal are often scientific based and individualized by medical experts. *Performances*: Acts oftentimes do not stand alone and are choreographed as part of a complex project with seamless transitions between tricks and poses. Often aimed to follow a storyline and a theme, instead of focusing solely on extreme postures and tricks that are presented one after another, as it is custom in traditional circus. Other purposes: Commissioned performances of a particular theme and those that are produced to fit certain concepts such as TV shows and talent shows where the contortion act intertwines elements of other disciplines.

Aesthetics: Theatrical, versatile.

Function: Entertainment.

As previously suggested, a later style does not necessarily replace the previous style as they rather coexist to cater to various show concepts. Following the correspondence with the interviewees of this qualitative research, one of the trainers that was interviewed mentioned that within Mongolian borders the fundamental characteristics of *Traditional Mongolian Contortion* that emphasize strength and elegance, which are at the heart of this art form, remain within every consecutive contortion style mentioned here, but with the *aesthetic results* and *functions* to be altered. However, considering the previously examined influence of the Western circus industry, the introduction of new scientific training curricula and the demands of the international entertainment market, a continuous transformation of Mongolian contortion in the future is therefore likely.

With the influence of TV and social media, contortion has gained international popularity notably through televised competitions, such as *America's Got Talent* and multiple social media platforms such as Instagram and YouTube. Interviews with accomplished contortionists, for example Lilia Stepanova, Pixie Le Knot or Nina Burri, to name a few, have increased and give an insight into their background. Lilia Stepanova for example reached fame through her appearance on America's Got Talent, Pixie Le Knot was hired to display her body flexibility by playing an exotic prostitute with contortion skills in *Game of Thrones*. Nina Burri was internationally recognized after becoming one of the finalists on the Swiss' television show *Die grössten Schweizer Talente*. Following the promotion of contortion on television the content on social media platforms about body flexibility with, for example, online tutorials on how to increase flexibility, has increased exponentially.

Numerous contortion studios were established all over the world in recent years with many of them being led by Mongolian contortionists who have retired from performing and who offer authentic Mongolian contortion training intertwined with new, innovative techniques. Innovation and a healthy training approach are invaluable, especially for adult students who start contortion to complement other disciplines they perform that include enhanced body flexibility, such as dance. However, it is of importance to remember that in Mongolia *Traditional Mongolian Contortion* among other art forms such as folk dance and folk music serves to pass on intangible cultural heritage from one generation to the next. Norovsambuu and other long-established teachers, therefore, fear that the original form soon will be lost, with new generations of contortionists and teachers who follow innovative training techniques and who leave behind the historical value of this art form.

The efforts of the Arts Council Mongolia, therefore, aim to preserve and protect the original form beyond Mongolian borders, and have *Traditional Mongolian Contortion* included in the UNESCO list of intangible cultural heritage. It is proof that despite the decrease of *Traditional Mongolian Contortion* the cultural aspects of this art form are still highly valued among the Mongolian people.

The Periods of Mongolian Contortionism

Period One Antiquity - 1941	**Folk Dance** and **Folk Acrobatics**. Mongolian contortion prior to 1940, numerous **male and female artists** who displayed their body flexibility; divided into front (*klishnik*) and back benders (*kauchik*). Numerous Folk dances such as the **Biyelgee dance** require kneeling on the floor while performing deep backbends.
Period Two 1941 - 1960	The concept of **circus**, including training structures, was first introduced to Mongolia by the **Soviet Union**. This was followed by the establishment of the **Mongolian State Circus** in 1941. Mongolian contortion becomes a circus discipline.
Period Three 1960 - 1980	The development and stylization of contortion continues between 1960 to 1980. This features the acknowledgement of **influential and innovative female contortion coaches** and their contributions. Various contortion styles/categories are established **in response to changing market forces, changing aesthetics and requirements of the entertainment industry**.

CONTORTION TRAINING

Having explored the historical development of contortion techniques and styles, contortion training in Mongolian circus institutions is now presented. The following section gives insight into the selection process, the training methods of the contortion school, the daily training duration, the training environment and the synergy between teacher and students. In Mongolia, the performance art form contortionism is taught in governmental circus institutions as well as independent contortion schools. The research focus of this paper is mainly on contortion schools in Ulaanbaatar, visited by the author between 2013 and 2016. The author's experiences as a full-time student of Contortionism at the National Mongolian Circus at the Ulaanbaatar Chuulga Theatre are also considered.

Among archery, horse riding and wrestling, contortion is a discipline that is considered an art-form and one of the main athletic practices of Mongolia. Inferring from the author's observation during her time in Mongolia, where contortion is regularly performed in theatres as part of a theatre program that involves an orchestra, actors, singers and dancers, one could conclude that contortion is highly valued in Mongolia. While working, living and studying contortion in Mongolia between 2013 and 2016 the author became acquainted with many Mongolian families, most of had at least one female family member that practiced or performed contortion. It appeared, that contortionism is an art-form practiced mainly by female artists and that it had almost a similar popularity in Mongolia among little girls as, for example, ballet in England, France and Russia. In her book *Twisted Tales-My Life as Mongolian Contortionist,* Otgo Waller states that during the rule of the Soviet Union in Mongolia, being selected as a contortion student was one of the highest cultural honors a child could be bestowed upon at the time, and it appears that the discipline is still very popular among children today.[43] Most circus institutions offer contortion classes to prepare students from an early age for the profession as a contortionist (Figure 5). To guarantee an efficient and successful contortion education, students begin their training at the age of around four or five when bones, muscles and connective tissues (such as ligaments and tendons) can quickly adapt to the training methods. The focus of the training is on strength, elegance, flexibility and distinct control over the body so that most difficult tricks can be performed in a slow, controlled and graceful manner. The decision of whether or not a practitioner executes

Figure 5: *Contortion Training at the Mongolian State Circus.* Mongolia. Photograph courtesy of Urnaa Uranbileg.

---

43   Waller, Otgo. *Twisted Tales-My life as a Mongolian Contortionist.* Bloomington: Balboa Press, 2017. Kindle.

contortion solely as a hobby, or to further their training towards a career as professional contortionist remains with their families. However, for many young practitioners becoming a professional contortionist represents the opportunity to travel and to follow an international career path.

Between 2013 and 2016 the author had the opportunity to visit and train at numerous contortion schools in Ulaanbaatar. The overall concept and environment of those schools were uniform. Training rooms are typically equipped with layers of thick carpets, rugs, yoga mats, yoga blocks and wooden blocks for handstand training, benches to perform stretching exercises on, as well as numerous balancing props to perform hand-balancing on. Within the training space, each student has her own designated training spot with the teacher walking around and providing corrections and individual support to each student. The opening hours and timetables of schools vary, but most of them are open between 9 am and 5 pm. Some schools divide students by age with children arriving in the morning hours and teens and adults practicing in the afternoon and other schools divide students by level. The average training duration for each student, however, lies between three to five hours of daily practice Monday through Friday, with additional hours of choreographic training for upcoming performances.

During her full-time contortion training at the contortion department of the *Ulaanbaatar Chuulga Theatre*, the author studied usually between 1 pm and 6 pm together with teenage and adult students. The morning hours were reserved for the students between the age of four to twelve. After finishing the training session with the teacher, contortion students of all ages were advised to stretch at home on their own for at least two more hours throughout the day, whenever possible.

The training facilities in Mongolia vary from school to school. Some schools rent space in former factory buildings, some classes are held in the living room of the teacher's home, and some teachers rent training rooms at local fitness studios. The *Ulaaanbaatar Circus Ensemble* as part of the *Mongolian National Circus* operated from the *Ulaanbaatar Chuulga Theatre*. During the winter months, the contortion training was held in a tiny space, a former dressing room, with a minimum of at least ten students crammed in. The theatre had plenty of training space to offer but the small room had the luxury of a heater, and with a harsh Mongolian winter from September to May, with temperatures well below -45° Celsius, it was the best option to stay warm during the contortion training (Figure 6). In fact, the more people would stay in the tiny training space, the more comfortable the temperatures.

Figure 6: *Contortionist Urnaa Uranbileg executing a handstand during Winter on a frozen Lake in Mongolia.* Mongolia. Photograph courtesy of Urnaa Uranbileg.

During the morning hours, most children were accompanied by their mothers who would wait in the training room for the duration of their daughters' practice. Some of the mothers had been contortionists themselves at some point and had since retired from training. Although the overall training atmosphere was very strict and goal-oriented as deadlines for upcoming shows had to be adhered to, it was as well a social gathering, with mothers and teachers conversing about their daily life while watching their children stretch and bend. The same applies to the relationship between the teacher and adult students, as conversations were not only restricted to exchanging training related topics. However, as training was taken seriously, a professional mannerism during training hours was always expected.

To be accepted to the contortion class, the teacher would ask the applicant to join a trial class for one day. The teacher would then observe the applicant and give her simple tasks to test her body flexibility. The selection process for children who wish to become professional contortionists however, is based on their overall training performance, training attitude and willingness to commit to a rigorous contortion program. The decision to move a student from the classroom to the stage is ultimately made by the teacher. The average duration of the full-time training for a young student, however, is six to eight years of daily, intensive practice. Yet, even after completion of their contortion training, many students remain in contact with their teacher. Professional contortionists oftentimes leave Mongolia to perform abroad for a few months or a few years and return to their teacher after completion of their contract to work on new choreographies and to stay fit until the next contract.

The relationship and the power dynamic of master teacher and student are therefore of utmost importance for a successful training outcome. The stretching of the spine for example, is at the heart of a contortionists training and contortionism is one of the most complex ways to enhance the flexibility of this delicate part of the body, and therefore requires professional knowledge. The contortion coach represents a vital role during the training sessions as the synergy between coach and student is dependent on mutual trust and respect. The assisted backstretch for instance is where the teacher bends the back of the student who is laying on her chest with her legs resting on the shoulders of her coach and her chin placed on a wooden block to increase the stretch of the upper spine (Figure 7).

Figure 7: *Contortion Coach Nomin Tseveendorj executing an assisted back stretch with student Mariam Ala-Rashi* (2015). Mongolia. Copyrights: Mariam Ala-Rashi.

This stretch makes it difficult to breathe and requires some mastery over the body and its fear responses. In order to achieve a deep backstretch that succeeds the natural movement of the spine and attached muscles, the practitioner must breathe calmly, and relax entirely, while trusting that the coach is aware of how far the back can be stretched without causing any injuries. Only then is the success of a professional contortion training ensured.[44] The relationship between teacher and student often lasts many years until the contortionist retires from performing and they often stay friends beyond their professional affiliations.

---

44   Ala-Rashi, Mariam. *The Art of Contortionism. An Introduction to and Analysis of Chinese Contortionism in a Historical, Political and Social Context.* 54-55.

Teacher and director of the contortion department at the *Mongolian National Circus and Ulaanbaatar Ensemble* Nomin Tseveendorj is the granddaughter of Madame Tsend-Ayush who trained her in contortionism from the age of eight. Later she would be trained by Norovsambuu before signing a contract as contortionist and character with Cirque du Soleil for the show *Alegria*. After numerous successful years working with Cirque du Soleil, she returned to Mongolia to teach contortion, hand balancing and aerial arts. Today she runs her own contortion school *Khun Sarnai* named after a documentary about Mongolian contortion that was initiated by her grandmother. Throughout the author's training with her, she prepared numerous contortionists for their international long-term contracts with high-profile circus companies in Asia, Europe and America, initiated auditions for Cirque du Soleil, and choreographed for unique events such as the launch of *Mongolia's Got Talent* in 2015. The curriculum's focus was not only on flexibility but also to build stamina, strength and resilience in order to provide energetic, athletic and at the same time graceful choreographies.

Apart from the flexibility training students were instructed to execute a high amount of conditioning workouts that would prepare them for the rigors of the discipline and which would cater to the unique aesthetic requirements of Mongolian contortion. In her interview with Pearly Jacobs for the video creator marketplace *Storyhunter* Norovsambuu gives insight into the unique aspects of Mongolian contortion training:

> Another significant trait is that we Mongolians have developed our own training techniques. Mongolian contortion performances are highly complex and of a high level of difficulty. Our performances don't only depend on the flexibility of the

back and limbs, but also incorporate a lot of strength and fine balance elements.[45]

These aesthetic aspects that are desired in performances and that make Mongolian contortion unique are at the center of Nomin Tseveendorj's training curriculum.

Having explored the training curricula of numerous contortion institutions in Europe and Asia it appears that in most countries the training sequences and exercise arrangements are largely universal, proven and time-tested as a contortionist usually starts to stretch her legs and hips first and then proceeds to stretch the upper body, while simultaneously keeping her legs and hips warm and flexible. This is to build and maintain flexibility throughout the whole body. The contortion training, therefore, starts with practicing over-splits for both box/middle and front splits by using a bench to place the front foot on. Compared to Chinese contortion training where the student would bounce while executing over-splits to enhance the stretch, the Mongolian training requires the student to hold the stretch without bouncing and increase the stretch through the weight of the upper body. After five repetitions of "sitting" in the over-split for about one to two minutes each, the teacher will assist the stretch and push the back leg down, so that the upper thigh may touch the floor (Figure 8). The assisted stretch forces the body to move beyond the natural capacity and combined with daily repetition aims to increase the flexibility towards extreme results. Numerous variations of passive and active leg stretching follow before moving on to the stretching of the upper body.

---

45   Storyhunter. „Mongolian Contortionists Vie to Become Cultural Icon." YouTube. September 23, 2013. Accessed January 10, 2020. https://www.youtube.com/watch?v=3G3OkrV3R-s

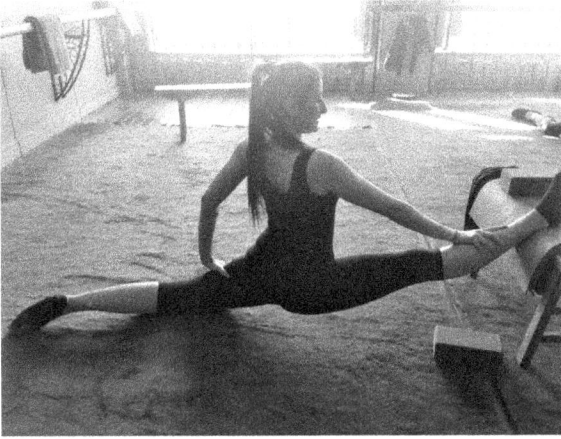

Figure 8: *Mariam Ala-Rashi executing an overspilt on a bench* (2013). Beijing, China.Copyrights: Mariam Ala-Rashi.

The bending of the spine always *follows* the leg stretches as it is crucial to warm-up the leg muscles and hips first, in order to achieve maximum flexibility in the muscles of the upper and lower back. Therefore, a contortionist's training sequential starts from toe to head. The stretching of the back is at the heart of a contortionist's training and contortion training is one of the most complex ways to enhance the flexibility of this delicate part of the body, and therefore requires professional knowledge and practice. [46] Once the body is fully warmed-up and the muscles and tendons are soft and flexible the choreographic work and performance preparation begins. The work of a professional contortionist is a full-time job with training and choreographic work Monday through Friday and with performances on the weekends.

Having explored the training aspects of Mongolian contortion, the next section will explore the creative process by considering aesthetics, elements of spiritual practices, hidden meanings and symbolism that are incorporated in the choreographic work, performance concepts and costuming.

---

46   Ala-Rashi, Mariam. *The Art of Contortionism. An Introduction to and Analysis of Chinese Contortionism in a Historical, Political and Social Context*. 53-54.

DEVELOPMENT OF AESTHETICS

Contortion is a performing art form that consists of purposefully selected sequences of extreme body flexibility. By scrutinizing its aesthetics and by identifying its traditional and cultural values, characteristics that make Mongolian contortion unique are examined. As previously discussed, *Traditional Mongolian Contortion* may well have evolved from folk dances, such as the *Biyelgee* dance, and folk acrobatics that showcased individual performances of the front bending and back bending. It also incorporates elements from religious practices and rituals of Buddhism and Shamanism and cherishes the beauty, grace and strength of the Mongolian woman. This section explores the linkage between folk dance and folk acrobatics, traditions and spiritual practices to illuminate the aesthetic development of *Traditional Mongolian Contortion* by emphasizing the similarities between folk arts and the circus discipline.

Folk Arts, Symbolism, Color Codes

The back bending in contortionism is linked to folk dances with elements of body flexibility, specifically the *Biyelgee* dance which embodies the nomadic life of the Mongolian people. It was established that contortionism, in its modern, codified sense, was developed in the 1940s. However, the traditional folk dance *Biyelgee* is identified not only by its rhythm and dance poses, but also its reliance on deep bending motions, drawing on the dancer's body flexibility. It first evolved in the West of Mongolia around the 13th century among nomadic tribes and was mainly performed within the limited space of the Mongolian *Ger*. Nowadays numerous variations of the dance are practiced and represent distinct characteristics of different ethnic groups of Mongolia. The impact that this traditional folk dance had on the circus industry and *Traditional Mongolian Contortion* respectively is so significant, that an entire section was designated to this versatile art form in the *Encyclopedia of Mongol Circus-70 years of Mongolian Circus*:

> Biyelgee dances are typically confined to the small space inside the Ger (nomadic dwelling) and are performed while half sitting or cross-legged. Hand, shoulder and leg movements express aspects of Mongolian lifestyle including household labor, customs and traditions, as well as spiritual characteristics tied to different ethnic groups. Biyelgee dancers wear clothing and accessories featuring color combinations, artistic patterns, embroidery, knitting, quilting and leather techniques, and gold and silver jewelry specific to their ethnic group and community. The dances play a significant role in family and community events such as feasts, celebrations, weddings and labor-related practices, simultaneously expressing distinct ethnic identities and promoting family unity and mutual understanding among different Mongolian ethnic groups (Translated from Mongolian to English).[47]

Biyelgee dance presents a versatile spectrum and reflects on different aspects of the Mongolian people.

Every ethnic group has its own style of performing the *Biyelgee* dance. The *Bayid* and *Dörvöd* tribes dance while balancing cups filled with *airag*

---

47   Batbold, Yo. Монгол циркийн нэвтэрхий толь | Mongol tsirkiin nevterkhii toli: *Encyclopedia of Mongol Circus-70 years of Mongolian Circus*. Ulaanbaatar: National Library of Mongolia, 2011. 339. (Translated from Mongolian to English.)

(a fermented dairy product) on their heads while their knees are bent outwards. The *Buryat* dance in a circle and the *Zakhchin* lean forward with their upper bodies and squat during the dance. Each ethnic group incorporates different elements into the dance as they reflect on their every-day life, their environment and traditions. Since the space in the *Ger* (Figure 9) is limited, the majority of movements is executed with the upper body, the arms and through facial expressions. Here one can clearly recognize dance movements that mimic daily tasks and labor such as sewing, horse-riding, cooking, herding cattle and so on. In a video about the dance, prepared by the UNESCO for Intangible Cultural Heritage, the dance is described with the following characteristics:

Figure 9: *Mongolian Ger* (2015). Mongolia. Copyrights: Mariam Ala-Rashi

While sitting cross-legged, in squatting position or while kneeling on the floor the upper body performs movements such as swinging, shaking, waving, stretching movements of the upper parts of the body, fist, hands, shoulder, chest and head [together] with [a] beautiful flexible swift in slow frequencies. This Biyelgee dancing ritual symbolizes happiness, [a] healthy and wealthy life of families, children, and the whole community…Every ethnic group has its own Biyelgee dances that features their uniqueness and distinctive guises."[48]

The front and back bending of the upper body together with specific gestures are the focal points of the dance and combined with the expressions of the dancer the narrative and meaning of the dance are communicated to the audience. When observing these specific features of the upper body movements such as the back and front bending, the overextension of joints, as well as the balancing of objects on the head, a connection to the development of *Traditional Mongolian Contortion* is easily comprehensible. It ties in as well on the previously analyzed theories that were proposed in the first section of this article, exploring the genesis of Mongolian contortion. Furthermore, the unique and distinctive guises of the *Biyelgee* dance inform us about the development of costume styles of *Traditional Mongolian Contortion* that complement the performance by promoting a specific narrative.

Seeing how codified and nuanced the dance's choreography is, it comes as no surprise that Biyelgee dancers approach their costumes with a similar attention to detail. Performance costumes in Mongolia, whether for dancers, singers or contortionists are elaborate and created with great care for detail. Correspondingly, the development of contortion costumes underwent numerous transformations, conforming to the aesthetic requirements of each era. Pictures from the early days of *Traditional Mongolian Contortion* depict the contortionists in bikini-like costumes to showcase every muscle used during the performance (Figure 10). Later,

---

48   UNESCO. "Mongol Biyelgee: Mongolian Traditional Folk Dance." UNE-SCO-YouTube. September 27, 2009. Accessed January 10, 2020. https://www.youtube.com/watch?v=yAfUZ81E42I&t=7s

full-body suits and leotards became the main choice for costuming. Color codes, as recognizable in dance costuming such as the *Biyelgee* dance, have as well been an important part in the Mongolian society. The color blue, for example, symbolizes the sky, and the color gold symbolizes imperial authority or spiritual aspects. Sharon Hudgins, author and former university professor who specializes in U.S.-Soviet strategic relations, describes in her article *Tsatsal: The Symbolism and Significance of Mongolian Ceremonial Milk Spoons* the importance of dairy products and the symbolic significance of the color white in Mongolian culture:

> Mongolians consider dairy products to be "white foods" (tsagaan idee), a special category of food. The colour white has long had a sacred role in Mongolian culture. Traditionally whiteness has been associated with women, and white is considered to be the "mother" of all colours, which descend from it. White also has a number of positive attributes: light (as opposed to darkness), innocence, purity, nobility, kindness, honesty, happiness, prosperity, respect, high social status-and all naturally white coloured things, from milk to clouds, are considered to possess these properties. In addition, the word milk (süü) itself connotes warm and pleasant feelings to Mongolians.[49]

Furthermore, a traditional Mongolian wardrobe is characterized by its variety of magnificent headdresses. Each ethnic group has its own particular headdress which also informs about the wearer's hierarchical status. Mongolian queens, for instance, would wear specific headpieces in combination with elaborate jewelry to express their status (Figure 11 & 12). In *Traditional Mongolian Contortion*, headdresses represent an

---

49   Hudgins, Sharon. "Tsatsal: The Symbolism and Significance of Mongolian Ceremonial Milk Spoons." Mongolian Studies 36 (2014): 41-77. Accessed December 11, 2020

Figure 10: Galtat, Y. (2020). *Contortionists in Bikini-like Costumes to showcase every Muscle that is being used during the Performance.* Image courtesy of Yargai Galtat.

Figure 11: *Backstage at the Mongolian National Theatre Ensemble in Ulaanbaatar. With friendly Permission of the Head Designer, Mariam Ala-Rashi is trying on the costume of Queen Mandukhai Khatun backstage at the costume design department* (2015). Mongolia. Copyrights: Mariam Ala-Rashi.

Figure 12: *Mongolian Contortionist Urnaa Uranbileg wearing a traditional Mongolian costume.* Mongolia. Photograph courtesy of Urnaa Uranbileg.

Figure 13: *Mongolian Contortionist Urnaa Uranbileg wearing a blue Contortion Costume adorned with Traditional Mongolian Ornaments, Jewelry and a Headpiece.* Mongolia. Photograph courtesy of Urnaa Uranbileg.

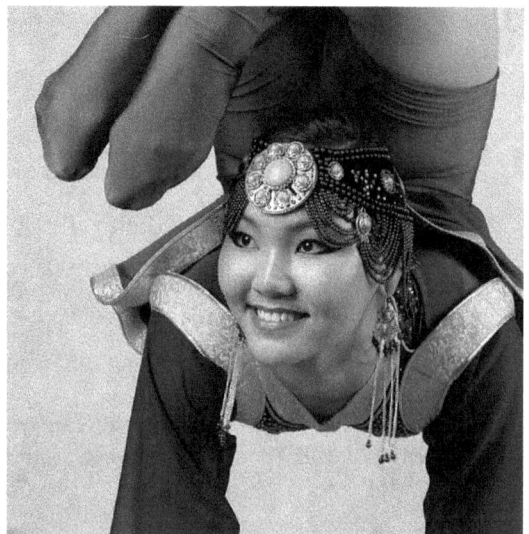

essential part of the costume and are worn to honor the ancient queens of Mongolia (Figure 13). Traditional ornaments, symbols, color codes and natural iconography and animals, in particular, play an important part in the aesthetics and creative development of contortion and have derived from the characteristics of folk dance, as pointed out as well by the Arts Council Mongolia for UNESCO: "Mongolian contortion is distinguished by a truly elegant form of movement, based in Mongolian traditional performing arts."[50] In an interview in 2016 with Yargai Galtat, costume designer at the *Mongolian National Theatre* and Dorjpurev Ganbold, director of the *Mongolian National Song and Dance Academic Ensemble*, about the symbolism that is found in Mongolian folk arts, the delicate and detailed work that goes into costume designing was analyzed.

It is important to go beyond the purely performance aspects of Mongolian contortion. Although the art form is clearly spectacular, as evidenced by its international renown, the spectacle can obscure the deep symbolic themes associated with Mongolian contortion. In order to clarify an example of traditional aspects of the symbolic meaning of ornaments, costume colors and specific patterns found in traditional Mongolian folk dance is examined in the following section. Traditional ornaments are a distinctive element of this type of dance, and merit a small discussion on their own. Within the dance we find gestures and movements that relate to spiritual themes and practices which likewise merit attention. All these may well vary from region to region in Mongolia, and we find current teachers and practitioners are very aware of the need to preserve tradition.

---

50   UNESCO, "Representative List-2011, Mongolian traditional Contortion (Mongolia)" UNESCO. June 23, 2011. Accessed January 10, 2020. https://ich.unesco.org/en/13-representative-list-00411?include=film.inc.php&id=05328&width=500&call=film

With regard to symbolic meaning between everyday life and spiritual practices, let us take for an example the *Biye Chini Boliyo* dance, as discussed by Yargai Galtat and Dorjpurev Ganbold. The motive of the *Biye Chini Boliyo* dance, performed by a pair of male and female dancers, is to represent a good life and communicate blessings for the young couple. By intertwining this premise, the choreography and the costume design, the overall structure of the dance gains profundity. In this case, colors and symbols for good luck can be found in the costume design.

As dairy products are a substantial part in the nutrition of the Mongolian people, the basic color of the costume is white and represents a pure heart that is white like milk. The color red is used to cover walls, pillars and the furniture of a *Ger*, and therefore, the chest piece of the costume is red and shaped like the wooden main pillars and ornaments of the *Ger*.[51] The pattern of the hat (Figure 14) symbolizes the pointy ceiling window of the *Ger*, called *toono* (skylight) and the skirt of the female dancer depicts the pattern that is typically found on the walls of the *Ger*. The hat of the male dancer is gold, and the female dancer is wearing a silver hat which draws a connection to religious paintings in Mongolia that often display a silver moon and a golden sun that circle around each other for eternity.[52] In the context of the dance performance these colors represent the eternal love of the young couple. The sun and the moon are also the highest points in the sky that can be seen through the skylight of the *Ger*, and therefore represent blessings for a long life that is strong like that of a king and a

---

51   Altankhuyag. "Mongolian Ger Structure." Altankhuyag-B-Blogspot. 2020. Accessed March 22, 2020. https://altankhuyag-b.blogspot.com/2015/02/mongol-geriin-butets.html

52   As established earlier, the color gold is associated with imperial power and one could argue that the male dancer is resembling the sun, wearing the gold hat to represent the power of the sun, a king and probably ultimately Chingghis Khan. Whereas the moon can appear white and silver at times, which is associated with femininity, milk and purity, and which why the female dancer is wearing a silver hat.

queen[53]. Traditional Mongolian ornaments include symbols for each member of the couple. The man wears the *Khaan Buguivch*, or „King's Bracelet," which represents honesty, peace, and love. The woman wears its opposite, the *Khatan Suikh*, the "Queen's Bracelet" which represents

Figure 14: *Golden Hat of the Male Dancer.* (2015). Mongolia. Photograph courtesy of Yargai Galtat.

Figure 16: *Costume Belt in the Design Process.* (2015). Mongolia. Photograph courtesy of Yargai Galtat.

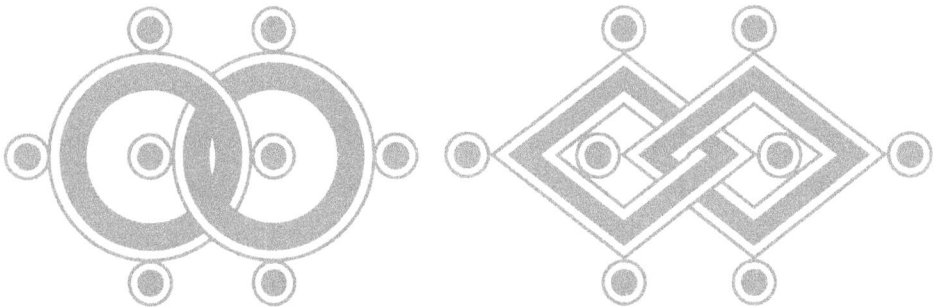

Figure 15: *Costume Belt Pattern for Khaan Buguivch (left) and Khatan Suikh (right).* (2020). Image courtesy of Yargai Galtat.

---

53   Suld Suldee. „бие чинь болъё." YouTube, October 6, 2018. Accessed October 20, 2020. https://www.youtube.com/watch?v=mdMAm1jQkjU&ab_chan-nel=SuldSuldee

love, invincibility and honesty. These symbols are attached to the belts of the male and the female dancer (Figures 15 & 16).

This is just one example that shows how the environment and lifestyle of the nomadic people of Mongolia are incorporated into folk arts. To fully unpack the symbolic importance behind costuming in traditional displays of Mongolian contortionism would take volumes. Beyond these symbols, elements such as ornaments and colors are also right with meaning—in contexts within contortionism and other seemingly unrelated Mongolian folk arts. When looking at *Traditional Mongolian Contortion*, one can find similar patterns.

Traditional Ornaments

To turn now to traditional ornaments which are omnipresent in Mongolian culture and belong to the decorative arts. As established earlier in this paper, the nomadic lifestyle dictates a minimalistic way of living which why even the smallest utensils in a nomadic household are abundantly adorned with ornaments. Traditional ornaments are therefore depicted on furniture (Figure 17), kitchen utensils, saddle accessories, in traditional clothing and stage costuming (Figure 18), on pillars of the *Ger*, in jewelry, buildings and doorways and even on traditional instruments. In Mongolian contortion, ornaments are embodied through specific movements: The front-bend, called *Klishnik*, depicts images of animals such as the frog, the lying antelope or snake (to name a few). The back-bend, called *Kauchik*, depicts patterns of Mongolian traditional ornaments. A classification of traditional Mongolian ornaments was presented by design expert Tsogzolmaa Byambajav for the Mongolia

Figure 17: *Traditional Ornaments on furniture inside a Mongolian Ger of the Terelj National Park.* (2015). Mongolia. Copyrights: Mariam Ala-Rashi.

Figure 18: *Ornaments on stage props, costumes and musical instruments. Performance of the Mongolian National Song and Dance Academic Ensemble.* (2016). Mongolia. Photograph courtesy of Yargai Galtat.

colloquium at the Humboldt University Berlin in 2014, dividing them into four main categories:

1. Geometrical ornaments used for interior and furniture to grant a stable and secure life.
2. Animals.
3. Natural Phenomena such as mountains, fire, water, plants and the stars in the sky.
4. Religious/Spiritual Ornaments.[54]

To give one example on how traditional Mongolian ornaments are created consider a simple pattern which is that of the Mongolian bighorn sheep as explored in an introductory video of Magsarjalam Khovor-Erdene, teacher of the design technology department of the Shine Mongol Harumapuji School, who provides videos for children on how to handcraft traditional Mongolian ornaments. Here, the basic shape of the horns of the Mongolian bighorn sheep is outlined and then set side by side to create the pattern of a traditional ornament.[55] The function of this particular ornament is to wish prosperity to a nomadic tribe or family that owns sheep (Figure 19).

The subcategory of horn and antler ornaments эвэр угалз (Ever Hee) as presented by Tsogzolmaa Byambajav, belongs to one of the early ornamentations in Mongolian history and not only depicts sheep horns but also deer and reindeer horn and can be combined with a myriad of

54   Byambajav, Tsogzolmaa. „Traditionelle Mongolische Ornamentik und ihr Gebrauch im Wandel der Geschichte." Presentation. Humboldt-Universität zu Berlin. Berlin. December 10, 2014. Accessed December 11, 2020. http://munx-tenger. de/fileadmin/Redaktion/Dokumente/06_Kultur/066_Ornamentik/2015-01-17_ Traditionelle_Mongolische_Ornamentik_Praes_Seiten.pdf
55   Magsarjalam Khovor-Erdene. "[ЦАХИМ ХИЧЭЭЛ] Дүрслэх урлаг 2-р анги Эвэр угалз" Magsarjalam Khovor-Erdene. March 27, 2020. Accessed May 10, 2020. https://www.youtube.com/watch?v=arZuVF7kEJA

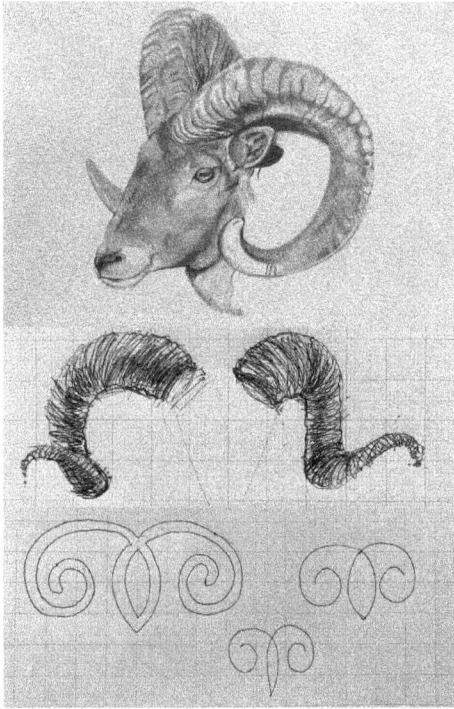

Figure 19: *Example of how the Sheep horn Ornament, called зэр угалз (Ever Hee), is created. (2020)*. Image courtesy of Yargai Galtat.

other ornaments. One of the most prominent examples of the representation of sheep horns in Mongolian costuming and ornamentations are the costume variations of Mongolian queens, the so-called *deel* robes. As part of the costume the women flatten their long hair and fixate it on each side of the head to resemble sheep horns (Figure 20). This particular *deel* costume even served as inspiration for queen Amidala's famous robe in the Star Wars movie *The Phantom Menace*.

There are large numbers of different ornaments within these five categories and each of them comprises a particular meaning that can then be embodied through the movements of folk arts and *Traditional Mongolian Contortion* (Figure 21). Some meanings of these ornaments are for instance strength, love, solidarity, protection, prosperity, longevity and good health. When used in a contortion performance, it can create and communicate a distinct narrative that may reflect on a people's everyday life, represent a specific ethnic group or transmit a spiritual meaning, depending on the context of the performance. Considering these aspects, *Traditional Mongolian Contortion*, when presented to a Mongolian audience, can communicate the rich culture of the Mongolian people and interact at a deep emotional level with the audience, but presented to an untrained eye it might appear as a mere display of extreme body flexibility.

Figure 20: *Representation of sheep horns in Mongolian costuming and ornamentations. The Deel Robes of Mongolian queens. Performance of the Mongolian National Song and Dance Academic Ensemble. The Ornaments Khaan Buguivch (left) and Khatan Suikh (right) of the King's and Queen' bracelet are represented in the background* (2015). Mongolia. Photograph courtesy of Yargai Galtat.

Figure 21: *Example of how Traditional Ornaments are incorporated into Contortion Movements. Ornament:* эвэр угалз *(Ever Hee).* (2020). Design and Copyrights: Yargai Galtat.

However, ornaments and folk arts are just two of the main elements in the complex framework of *Traditional Mongolian Contortion*, which brings us to the next element: Spiritual practice.

Spiritual Practice

Next, we consider the element of spiritual practice as it is often portrayed in traditional contortion performances. Contortion choreographies with a spiritual or religious context often incorporate specific gestures and movements such as sitting cross-legged, folding hands and the performing of *mudras* (hand gestures) with a resemblance to Buddhist statues. One of the Buddhist deities that are worshiped in Mongolia is the *Tara* (Mongolian: *Dara-ekhe*) which is often depicted in *Traditional Mongolian Contortion*. As seen in group performances, oftentimes one artist performs the contortion act on a contortion table, while the other contortionists are seated cross-legged in front of, or around the main performer while executing mudras.[56] The costume for *Dara-ekhe* performances is almost always gold-colored with a headpiece that resembles the deity's crown. The movements are mostly slow and elegant to create a spiritual atmosphere and to showcase the contortionist's outstanding body control.

During her research in Ulaanbaatar in 2015, the author had the opportunity to visit the *Mongolian National Theatre* regularly and gained unique insights into the extensive creative work that went on behind the scenes. The author was able to observe the costume designers and the training of the actors, dancers and musicians of the *State National Song and Dance Academic Ensemble of Mongolia*. A particular performance

56   UNESCO, "Representative List-2011, Mongolian traditional Contortion (Mongolia)" UNESCO. June 23, 2011. Accessed January 10, 2020. https://ich.unesco.org/en/13-representative-list-00411?include=film.inc.php&id=05328&width=500&call=film

the author was able to study through all stages of the creative process (from costume design to final performance) was that of the *Dara-ekhe*, performed by the outstanding contortionist Tsetseglen Odgerel (Figure 22). This performance tells the love story between a monk and a deity with the contortionist transforming into a golden statue at the end of the act.[57] The choreography emphasized the slow and controlled movements, showcasing the technique of the artist in a gleaming gold-metallic colored bodysuit that transformed the contortionist into a life-like *Tara* (Figure 23) These expertly-controlled, languid movements—although technically impressive—served a greater purpose: conveying the spiritual message of the love story.

Figure 22: *Contortionist Tsetseglen Odgerel performing as Dara-ekhe.* (2016). Mongolia. Photograph courtesy of Yargai Galtat

---

57   Tsetseglen Odgerel. „Tara /Dara-ekhe/ contortionist Tsetseglen Odgerel and Mongolian Talented Dancers." Tsetseglen Odgerel-YouTube. December 29, 2018. Accessed January 10, 2020. https://www.youtube.com/watch?v=M4uzsv9JbvA

Figure 23: *Contortionist Tsetseglen Odgerel's final transformation into a Dara-ekhe-A Buddhist Tara.* (2015). Mongolia. Photograph courtesy of Yargai Galtat

Juxtaposed with the other elements sometimes hidden meanings are incorporated into *Traditional Mongolian Contortion*, such as color codes, the symbolism of traditional ornaments and specific movements that reflect the every-day life of the Mongolian people. The function of the spiritual performances is easily noticeable and even the untrained eye can usually detect that there are spiritual elements within the movements communicated through the performance. Yet, it is the composition and balance of all the above-mentioned elements, that create an outstanding performance, and that make *Traditional Mongolian Contortion* unique.

Although we have now had a cursory look at the general development of Mongolian contortion, it is important to remember that each region of the country is home to its own particular aesthetic values and performance qualities.

As explored throughout this article, each ethnic group inherits its own portrayal of the *Biyelgee* dance. It has been noted by Mongolian contortion instructors that many members of remote, tribal populations discover an innate body flexibility. When asked about the independent development and characteristics of contortion practices in different parts of Mongolia, some of the interviewees confirmed that different ethnic groups and teachers in other cities of Mongolia incorporate their own characteristic aesthetics, techniques, movements and gestures into their contortion practices and performances. It is therefore feasible that, similar to the different styles of the *Biyelgee* dance, the main category of *Traditional Mongolian Contortion*, should include subcategories that represent the traditional contortion styles of each ethnic group in the North, South, East and West of Mongolia.

However, further research and extensive fieldwork in remote regions of Mongolia would be necessary to analyze and categorize these particular styles and aesthetics, and to determine how the people of a region and their collective form of Mongolian Contortion incorporate very specific attributes into *their* version of contortion.

Passing on a tradition is important, especially in times of great change and social transformation. Folk arts in most cultures are traditionally passed on to younger generations through apprenticeships or home-tutoring within the family, clan or neighborhood. Similar traditions apply to the inheritance of Mongolian contortion which is entrusted to next generations as a holistic discipline comprising physical practice and the knowledge about its cultural values. Both, Nomin Tseveendorj (Figure 24) and Tumurbaatar Bud, founder of the internationally well-known contortion studio *X-Roses*, are the grandchildren of Madame Tsend-Ayush, and both have established remarkable careers as contortion performers and instructors. Following the footsteps of their grandmother, they continue to educate new generations of contortionists to pass on this traditional art form, with each generation of contortionists contributing its own characteristics, techniques and aesthetics to it. However, advocates of *Traditional Mongolian Contortion*, like Norovsambuu and the Arts Council Mongolia, fear that, in favor for contemporary contortion styles and the job opportunities that come with them, the traditional art form soon will be lost.

Figure 24: *Contortion Coach Nomin Tseveendorj (center) with her Contortion Students.* Mongolia. Photograph courtesy of Nomin Tseveendorj

SAFEGUARDING OF TRADITIONAL MONGOLIAN CONTORTION

The safeguarding of *traditional-style Mongolian contortion*—the form based on folklore, cultural symbolism, and ritual—faces numerous challenges, which can be divided into three main categories: the export of Mongolian contortionists to the world's stage, the growing popularity of Mongolian contortion in the West, and the transformation of performing arts through political influence and cultural dominance. The first challenge is that, as influences from abroad are brought back to Mongolia, there is a tension and a danger that novel, non-traditional training methods and concepts supplant the traditional and that the deep meaning of Mongolian contortion is lost in a consideration of technique. We must also be aware that there are other cultures in which contortion is a traditional feature and there is a tendency to blend all these practices into a generic concept of 'contortionism', simply put, a display of impressive flexibility, which loses the specific regional differences between countries and traditions. The second main challenge is that the growing popularity of Mongolian contortion in the West threatens to transform this tradition within Mongolia into a commodity as the world's entertainment market continues to homogenize thanks to social media and televised talent shows, and with traditional contortion being shaped and subjected to the theatrical and entertainment needs of a changing world. Already we see young Mongolian girls dreaming of and training to present their skills on world stages and seeking international contracts as a way to establish a career overseas/in the West. And thirdly, as we have remarked on several occasions throughout this article, but essentially out of scope of what is intended to cover in terms of the distinct character of Mongolian contortionism, it must be pointed out that political influence, cultural domination and repression are also dangers that have already been seen to beset Mongolian contortion as a tradition which is peculiarly and specifically rooted in Mongolian culture, lifestyle, and religion.

First Challenge: Lost Meaning in a Consideration of Technique

Mongolian contortionists are recruited to perform overseas and are exposed to foreign performance and training styles, which has likely already led to innovations within contortion in the past and which is a phenomenon that could alter the artist's understanding of their art. Depending on the focus of the show and requirements of the artistic director or producer of a production, the contortionist will provide her contortion skills as a "canvas" so that new aesthetic aspects, suitable for the respective performance, can be applied. Of course, new artistic influences are part of the creative process and important for each performer. This does not automatically mean that the performer will start to neglect the traditional art form she once learned, but the change of the environment, different aesthetic standards, requirements and training curricula and the market's demand for new and innovative spectacles might dilute unique aspects of *Traditional Mongolian Contortion*. The threat to the traditional art form lies as well in the transmission from one generation to the next and the market's demands that disempower the artist, as pointed out by Enkhbold Chuluunbaatar:

The limited size of the local market, the non-conducive environment to grow (low pay, fierce competition, and less appreciation of talents), and the open market have pushed the best talents to find opportunities to perform abroad, causing the "talent drain" in Mongolian circus industry. Once settled, some will stay to become a trainer or open a training center abroad. There are approximately 300 [Mongolian] artists who work as performers and trainers in over 40 countries. Their skills and contributions are well-recognized, indicated by the significant positions that they hold in the world circus arena.[58]

Many Mongolian trainers who offer contortion classes abroad create new training concepts that combine traditional Mongolian training techniques with modern science by using the support of medical experts of circus arts to meet international training standards. This raises the question to what extent the traditional aspects of the art form are preserved and communicated to the next generation of contortionists. The decrease, however, does not only continue on foreign soil. Norovsambuu, together with the Arts Council Mongolia, also fear the traditional art form could be replaced by modern styles in Mongolia:

As the times pass the inheritor of this traditional form of contortion is getting rare and preserving the traditional style is getting more difficult. Although in today's globalized world Mongolian contortion is flourishing further in modern and classical styles. However, it is crucial to preserve the traditional Mongolian contortion. [59]

58   Chuluunbaatar, Enkhbold. "Mongolian Circus Industry in the Post-Transitional Economy." *International Journal of Cultural and Creative Industries.* Volume 1, 2 (2014). 73
59   UNESCO. *Representative List-2011, Mongolian traditional Contortion (Mongolia).* UNESCO: 2011. Accessed January 10, 2020. https://ich.unesco.org/

Many countries, such as China, Russia, India, Japan, practice *body flexibility* and *contortionism* in their cultures, with a myriad of functions and different values and appreciation within the respective societies of each country. There are few entries in Contortionism's bibliography, which makes it difficult to protect as an established performing art. This paper endeavors to help remedy that oversight. It would be wrong, for example, to acknowledge the discipline *contortion* solely as an art form of the Mongolian culture. The term *contortion* serves as an umbrella term to describe a discipline that includes different styles and different cultural values, depending on the country it is being practiced and performed in. It can be argued, that no one single country could demand agency over an entire discipline, but that the different styles, each unique to their country, each on its own, like *Traditional Mongolian Contortion,* including their values, functions, aesthetics and recognition within the society, can be accepted as intangible cultural heritage.

Second Challenge: Exploitation and Appropriation

The growing popularity of Contortionism as a circus discipline in the West also poses a threat to *Traditional Mongolian Contortion*. Mongolian Contortion has become an international brand in the circus industry. Its practitioners are promoted by leading entertainment companies as world class performance artists, transmitting that message across international news- and media outlets. Sandi Croft, artistic director for Cirque du Soleil's show *O* states in an interview with CNN: "When you want a top baseball player, sometimes you look in America. Where we need a contortionist,

en/13-representative-list-00411?include=film.inc.php&id=05328&width=500&-call=film

we look to Mongolia".[60] While Contortion is a traditional art-form in Mongolia and a number of surrounding countries, it has recently become a fast-growing trend and spectacle in Western countries due to the impact of televised talent shows and social media. More and more adults discover this performance art form either as a hobby or as a way to improve their professional performance skills in dance, acrobatics or gymnastics. As evident in many European contortion schools, contortion becomes labeled simply as a tool to improve body flexibility, rather than being acknowledged as an art form and ethnic practice in its own respect. This method is not new, as other art forms such as ballet, to name one example, have been reduced for a single, mechanical goal. Some of the greatest athletes such as Arnold Schwarzenegger, world champion in boxing Vasyl Lomachenko, NFL player Eddie George and many Olympic athletes took ballet classes to improve their strength, foot work, balance and flexibility. The authenticity, cultural heritage and history of Mongolian contortion, therefore, needs preservation and protection to avoid exploitation and cultural appropriation.

As explored in the previous research study *The Art of Contortionism*[61], many Western contortion instructors who travel to Asia to study contortion in Chinese or Mongolian training facilities, do not communicate any or very limited historical and cultural knowledge about the contortion style to their students in the West. This might be due to the limited time the Western student is spending at the facility, it may be caused by language barriers, or it is simply not of interest nor within the scope of

60   McKenzie, Sheena. „Head over heels for Mongolia's mind bending contortionists." CNN. 2013. Accessed December 11, 2020. http://edition.cnn.com/2013/09/06/world/asia/mongolians-bend-over-backwards-contortionists/index.html

61   Ala-Rashi, Mariam. (2019)*The Art of Contortionism. An Introduction to and Analysis of Chinese Contortionism in a Historical, Political and Social Context.*

the lesson. As with many performance disciplines, coaches often decide what information and techniques they communicate to their students. However, surely each teacher has the responsibility to acknowledge and protect the cultural aspects of the art form they are passing on to next generations of performing artists, whether that be contortion, dance or other performative art forms. The rich aspects of the Mongolian culture that is reflected in *Traditional Mongolian Contortion* as explored throughout this paper, is not acknowledged in many training facilities in the West – not an omission of malice, but one of naiveté. The history of contortion is simply not known by many of its practitioners today.

While one part of the contortion curriculum in Mongolia has the clear function of passing on tradition and cultural values, it is often a merely technical approach in the West and serves as a means to improve body flexibility. It would be desirable to provide contortion practitioners in the West with cultural knowledge about the art form they are executing for multiple hours every day, to develop a similar recognition among contortion students as it is the case with, for example, the knowledge many yoga practitioners have.

The origins and health benefits of Hatha (fitness) Yoga are well-known among practitioners and have been discussed in a multitude of health, fitness and fashion magazines and TV shows where it is acknowledged as a holistic practice that originated in India. In contrast, the author's qualitative research in Europe revealed that many contortion practitioners could not recall the countries this art form originated from, despite their teachers having trained extensively in Mongolia or China. The knowledge is oftentimes simply not passed on to the Western students during class. Now, this might have been partially caused by language barriers between local teachers in Mongolia and China and their foreign students, but is in great part caused as well by the lack of scholarly literature and knowledge simply not being made available in popular literature. Furthermore, once the artistic discipline is elevated by academic study, it seems possible that an appeal to UNESCO might be successful.

Third Challenge: Political Influence and Cultural Dominance

The third challenge which requires extensive independent research is the transformation of performing arts through political influence and cultural dominance. Before the concept of *circus* was introduced by the Soviet Union to Mongolia in the 1940s, body flexibility was simply a form of folk arts. The establishment of the Russian circus, and its decision to employ flexible Mongolian „contortionists", led to a new understanding of body flexibility in Mongolia. Now, this activity wasn't *just* a cultural practice—it had show-business implications (and the hope of economic freedoms) tied to it as well. The impact of the introduction of circus had a massive impact on Mongolia's economy.

Chinese, Mongolian and Japanese contortion and body flexibility are all mainly rooted in dance practice and folk arts. In China, acrobatics are rooted in folk dances of harvest celebrations and in Mongolia it is folk dances that represent the nomadic lifestyle and the diversity of ethnic groups in Mongolia. In Japan the Lion Dance *Kakubeijishi* is referred to by locals as dance and performers are considered dancers and actors who are depicting Japanese landscapes through body flexibility.[62] According to historical records, it has been argued earlier in this paper that in China

---

62   Ala-Rashi, Mariam. "Mapping Contortion in Japan. Part Three: Cultural Heritage and the Lion Dance." Circus Talk. 2020. Accessed April 10, 2020. https://circustalk.com/news/mapping-contortion-in-japan-part-three-cultural-heritage-the-lion-dance

and Mongolia the practice of body flexibility has been renamed *contortion* and re-categorized as a circus act at a later stage (in Mongolia in the 1940s and in China when it became the "Peoples Republic of China"). Prior to the concept of *circus*, body flexibility was either performed independently or belonged in the dance category as part of folk dances. As Majigsuren one of the founders of Mongolian contortion stated in her interview, Mongolian Contortion has only been named *Contortion* after the installment of the circus in Mongolia, which ultimately transformed this folk art, changing its function by transforming a spiritual practice and traditional folk art into a commodity with entertainment purpose. Mongolian contortionism is an ethnic practice and more intrinsic than simply an 'art form' among the Mongolian people. To label something as 'folk art' in a Western understanding of the term 'art' is to divorce the practice we are referring to from the culture from which it sprang. Once one has made that divorce by labeling it, then the object that was labeled as 'folk art' can become a commodity.[63]

It is a similar situation with Chinese contortion: When China became the "Peoples Republic of China", first premier Zhou EnLai officially renamed contortion from "Body Art beyond Limits" to "Rou Shu" and categorized contortion within the traditional acrobatic family.[64] It appears that prior to the re-categorization, *Body Arts beyond Limits* was an independent art form. However, the examination of the repercussions of the political impact on folk arts is beyond the scope of this paper. Further research could aim to illuminate the positive and negative aspects of political influence on folk acrobatics and circus arts.

---

63   Kirakowski, Jurek, personal correspondence, August 03, 2020.
64   Ala-Rashi, Mariam. *The Art of Contortionism. An Introduction to and Analysis of Chinese Contortionism in a Historical, Political and Social Context.* 24.

It is noteworthy that the aforementioned appeal to UNESCO to include *Traditional Mongolian Contortion* into the list of intangible cultural heritage was withdrawn before it could even be considered by UNESCO. In correspondence with UNESCO, the author was informed that Mongolia had withdrawn this nomination file in 2011 before its examination by the Intergovernmental Committee due to the unfavorable recommendation provided by the subsidiary body at that time. [65] Further details are not available at this point and the reasons for the withdrawal are unclear. Before attributing this failed application to an instance of cultural repression; the lack of scholarly literature about the Art of Contortion, in general, might be considered as one of the contributing aspects.

In direct comparison, the *Biyelgee* was inscribed on the list of intangible cultural heritage in need of urgent safeguarding already in 2009. This might be because dance as a genre is a well-researched and well-funded field, while the art of contortionism is underrepresented in scholarly literature leading to the misconception that contortionism is a purely entertainment element of circus acts.-

Although this paper has only scratched the surface of such a complex art-form, it outlines completely the value of contortionism yesterday and today. Further research is necessary to cover deeper aspects of this art form in different contexts. In what ways were specific attributes of Mongolian (traditional) contortionism exported to the West by the Soviet Circus establishment? What are the roles and values of the male and female contortionist in Mongolia? What is the status of a male

---

65   UNESCO. *Evaluation of Nominations for Inscription in 2011 on the Representative List of the Intangible Cultural Heritage of Humanity (item 13 on the agenda).* UNESCO: 2011. Accessed January 10, 2020. https://ich.unesco.org/en/13-representative-list-00411#13.33

contortionist when compared to the status of a female contortionist? Do male contortionists perform *Traditional Mongolian Contortion* as well or contemporary/modern contortion only? Which "subcategories" of *Traditional Mongolian Contortion* are executed in remote regions of Mongolia and how do they represent the characteristics of each ethnic group? Which ornaments are of particular value within a contortion performance and how are they combined to create a specific narrative? What is the historical connection between Chinese and Mongolian contortionism and the possible hybrid nature of contortionism in Inner Mongolia? What is the value of contortion in Mongolia today? Is it an art-form, intangible cultural heritage, a sport, or something in between?

It is imperative to position the art of contortionism in scholarly literature as an aspect of valuable Mongolian heritage, to open up this valuable field for future discussion and research, that contributes to a better understanding of this art form for current and future contortion practitioners and to the preservation of this unique element of Mongolian culture for Mongolian people. It is also the author's hope that such academic inquiry helps elevate the status of the Circus Arts on the whole, as a rich collection of diverse art-forms with unique histories and cultural values.

BIBLIOGRAPHY

Ala-Rashi, Mariam. *The Art of Contortionism. An Introduction to and Analysis of Chinese Contortionism in a Historical, Political and Social Context.* USA: KDP Press, 2019. 21.

Ala-Rashi, Mariam. "Mapping Contortion in Japan. Part One: A History." Circus Talk. 2020. Accessed April 10, 2020. https://circustalk. com/news/mapping-contortion-in-japan-part-one-a-history

Ala-Rashi, Mariam. "Mapping Contortion in Japan. Part Three: Cultural Heritage and the Lion Dance." Circus Talk. 2020. Accessed April 10, 2020https://circustalk.com/news/mapping-contortion-in-japan-part-three-cultural-heritage-the-lion-dance

Altankhuyag. "Mongolian Ger Structure." Altankhuyag-B-Blogspot. 2020. Accessed March 22, 2020. https://altankhuyag-b.blogspot. com/2015/02/mongol-geriin-butets.html

Arts Council of Mongolia. "Heritage Program" January 01, 2012. Accessed December 08, 2020. http://artscouncil.mn/ heritage-program-introduction/

Batkhuyag, Khulan. "The Ancient, Earth-Friendly Wisdom of Mongolian Nomads." TED. September 01, 2020. Accessed October 19, 2020. https://www.ted.com/talks/khulan_batkhuyag_the_ancient_ earth_friendly_wisdom_of_mongolian_nomads#t-480297

Bolor-Erdene Enkhbaatar. "MobiCom-Naadam Greeting." Bolor-Erdene Enkhbaatar-YouTube. July 10, 2014. Accessed January 10, 2020. https://www.youtube.com/watch?v=320Z5SEou1M

Budbazar, Norovsambuu. Монголын уран нугаралт - Mongolian Contortion. Ulaanbaatar: Selengepress Co., Ltd, 2011. 20.

Chamaeleon Theater Berlin. "Contemporary Circus/Cirque Nouveau." Chamaeleon Theater Berlin. January 01, 2020. Accessed December 15, 2020. https://chamaeleonberlin.com/en/theatre/contemporary-circus

Chuluunbaatar, Enkhbold. "Mongolian Circus Industry in the Post-Transitional Economy." *International Journal of Cultural and Creative Industries.* Volume 1, 2 (2014): 68-74

Circopedia. (2018). Beijing Acrobatic Toupe. [online] Accessed December 15, 2020. Available at: http://www.circopedia.org/Beijing_Acrobatic_Troupe

Hint Mag. *What's the Deel?* Hint Fashion Magazine. February 26, 2017. Accessed March 10, 2020. https://hintmag.com/2017/02/26/mongolian-deel-february-26-2017-0206-fashion/

Hudgins, Sharon. "Tsatsal: The Symbolism and Significance of Mongolian Ceremonial Milk Spoons." Mongolian Studies 36 (2014): 41-77. Accessed December 11, 2020

Jacobs, Pearly. *Mongolia: Contortionists aim for UNESCO Recognition.* Eurasianet. August 23, 2013. Accessed June 24, 2017. https://eurasianet. org/mongolia-contortionists-aim-for-unesco-recognition

Kaeppler, Adrienne L. "Dance Ethnology and the Anthropology of Dance." Dance Research Journal 32, no. 1 (2000): 116-25. Accessed December 17, 2020.

Khuyg Khuygaa. "Уран нугаралтын түүх." Khuyg Khuygaa-YouTube. November 21, 2016. Accessed March 20, 2020. https://www. youtube.com/watch?v=YGuuBd8t06E

Leclerc, Andréane, "ENTRE CONTORSION ET ÉCRITURE SCÉNIQUE: LA PROUESSE COMME TECHNIQUE ÉVOCATRICE DE SENS". Thesis. Montreal: National Circus School of Montreal, 2013. 26.

Magsarjalam Khovor-Erdene. "[ЦАХИМ ХИЧЭЭЛ] Дүрслэх урлаг 2-р анги Эвэр угалз" Magsarjalam Khovor-Erdene. March 27, 2020. Accessed May 10, 2020. https://www.youtube.com/ watch?v=arZuVF7kEJA

McKenzie, Sheena. „Head over heels for Mongolia's mind-bending contortionists." CNN. 2013. Accessed December 11, 2020. http://edition.cnn.com/2013/09/06/world/asia/mongo-lians-bend-over-backwards-contortionists/index.html

Neirick, Miriam. "When Pigs Could Fly and Bears Could Dance. A History of the Soviet Circus. Wisconsin: The University of Wisconsin Press. 2012.

Pigg, Sodnom U. *Mongolmom: Mongolian Contortionist*. Blogspot. April 23, 2018. Accessed April 09, 2020. https://mongolmom.blogspot.com/2018/04/mongolian-contortionist.html

Storyhunter. „Mongolian Contortionists Vie to Become Cultural Icon." Storyhunter-YouTube. September 23, 2013. Accessed January 10, 2020. https://www.youtube.com/watch?v=3G3OkrV3R-s

Suld Suldee. „бие чинь болъё." Suld Suldee-YouTube. October 6, 2018. Accessed January 10, 2020. https://www.youtube.com/watch?v=mdMAm1jQkjU

Tessitore, Sarnai. "Body in Motion: Exploring the Art of Contortion." Sarnaifilm-Youtube. February 16, 2015. Accessed April 02, 2020. https://www.youtube.com/watch?v=vfVJ37icGjg&t=317s

The New York Times Archive. *The Hidden Mongolia*. The New York Times: December 13, 1981. Accessed February 20, 2020. https://www.nytimes.com/1981/12/13/magazine/the-hidden-mongolia.html

The Soraya. (2012). The National Circus of The People's Republic of China presents Cirque Chinois. [online] Accessed December 15, 2020. Available at: https://www.thesoraya.org/assets/Uploads/education/archive/pdf/CirqueChinois-CueSheetrev.pdf

Thomas, Nathalie, "Mongolian child contortionists stretch for international success." Reuters, July 7, 2016. Accessed

November 26, 2020. https://www.reuters.com/article/ us-mongolia-contortionists-idUSKCN0ZN0DK

Tsetseglen Odgerel. „Tara /Dara-ekhe/ contortionist Tsetseglen Odgerel and Mongolian Talented Dancers." Tsetseglen Odgerel-YouTube. December 29, 2018. Accessed January 10, 2020. https://www. youtube.com/watch?v=M4uzsv9JbvA

Tsogzolmaa Byambajav. „Traditionelle Mongolische Ornamentik und ihr Gebrauch im Wandel der Geschichte." Presentation. Humboldt-Universität zu Berlin. Berlin. December 10, 2014. Accessed December 11, 2020. http:// munx-tenger.de/fileadmin/Redaktion/Dokumente/06_ Kultur/066_Ornamentik/2015-01-17_Traditionelle_ Mongolische_Ornamentik_Praes_Seiten.pdf

Tumen Ekh. "About Tumen Ekh Mongolian National Song and Dance Ensemble." Thumen Ekh. January 01, 2020. Accessed December 15, 2020. https://tumenekh.wordpress.com/about/

UNESCO. *Representative List-2011, Mongolian traditional Contortion (Mongolia).* UNESCO: 2011. Accessed January 10, 2020. https:// ich.unesco.org/en/13-representative-list-00411?include=film. inc.php&id=05328&width=500&call=film

UNESCO. *Evaluation of Nominations for Inscription in 2011 on the Representative List of the Intangible Cultural Heritage of Humanity (item 13 on the agenda).* UNESCO: 2011. Accessed January 10, 2020. https://ich.unesco.org/en/13-representative-list-00411#13.33

UNESCO. "Mongol Biyelgee: Mongolian Traditional Folk Dance." UNESCO-YouTube. September 27, 2009. Accessed January 10, 2020. https://www.youtube.com/watch?v=yAfUZ81E42I&t=7s

University of Edinburgh. *Rashid al-Din's History of the World, 714 A.H. (1314 A.D.).* Edinburgh Collections: 2020. Accessed February 20, 2020. https://collections.ed.ac.uk/iconics/record/51419

University of Edinburgh. *The World History of Rashid al-Din, 1314. A Masterpiece of Islamic Painting.* Libraryblogs Edinburgh: 2014. Accessed February 20, 2020. http://libraryblogs.is.ed.ac.uk/blog/2014/07/14/the-world-history-of-rashid-al-din-1314-a-masterpiece-of-islamic-painting/

Wall, Thom. (2019) *Juggling - From Antiquity to the Middle Ages: the forgotten history of throwing and catching.* USA: Modern Vaudeville Press, 2019.

Waller, Otgo. *Twisted Tales-My life as a Mongolian Contortionist.* Bloomington: Balboa Press, 2017. Kindle.

WapBaike. (2019). Sanle. [online] Accessed 23.12.2019. Available at: https://baike.baidu.com/item/%E6%95%A3%E4%B9%90

Yo, Batbold, Монгол циркийн нэвтэрхий толь | Mongol tsirkiin nevterkhii toli: *Encyclopedia of Mongol Circus-70 years of Mongolian Circus.* Ulaanbaatar: National Library of Mongolia, 2011. 339

LIST OF FIGURES

Figure 1: Performance of the Mongolian National Song and Dance Academic Ensemble showcasing deep backbends during a dance performance at the Mongolian National Theatre (2015/2016). Mongolia. Photograph courtesy of Yargai Galtat. (Note: Faces of ensemble anonymized.)

Figure 2: Mongolian Contortionist Urnaa Uranbileg performing to traditional Mongolian Music. Mongolia. Photograph courtesy of Urnaa Uranbileg.

Figure 3: Mongolian Contortionist Agiimaa Jargalsaikhan, one of Majigsuren's last contortion students, practicing the Marinelli Bend, called zubnik (зубник) in Mongolia (2014). Mongolia. Photograph courtesy of Agiimaa Jargalsaikhan. (Note: person in background anonymized.)

Figure 4: Galtat, Y. (2020). Mongolian Contortionist balancing Pigeons on her Head. Artist: Yargai Galtat.

Figure 5: Contortion Training at the Mongolian State Circus. Mongolia. Photograph courtesy of Urnaa Uranbileg. (Note: Students anonymized.)

Figure 6: Contortionist Urnaa Uranbilleg executing a handstand during Winter on a frozen Lake in Mongolia. Mongolia. Photograph courtesy of Urnaa Uranbileg.

Figure 7: Contortion Coach Nomin Tseveendorj executing an assisted back stretch with student Mariam Ala-Rashi (2015). Mongolia. Copyrights: Mariam Ala-Rashi.

Figure 8: Mariam Ala-Rashi executing an overspilt on a bench (2013). Beijing, China.Copyrights: Mariam Ala-Rashi.

Figure 9: Mongolian Ger (2015). Mongolia. Copyrights: Mariam Ala-Rashi

Figure 10: Galtat, Y. (2020). Contortionists in Bikini-like Costumes to showcase every Muscle that is being used during the Performance. Image courtesy of Yargai Galtat.

Figure 11: Backstage at the Mongolian National Theatre Ensemble in Ulaanbaatar. With friendly Permission of the Head Designer, Mariam Ala-Rashi is trying on the costume of Queen Mandukhai Khatun backstage at the costume design department (2015). Mongolia. Copyrights: Mariam Ala-Rashi.

Figure 12: Mongolian Contortionist Urnaa Uranbileg wearing a traditional Mongolian costume. Mongolia. Photograph courtesy of Urnaa Uranbileg.

Figure 13: Mongolian Contortionist Urnaa Uranbileg wearing a blue Contortion Costume adorned with Traditional Mongolian

Ornaments, Jewelry and a Headpiece. Mongolia. Photograph courtesy of Urnaa Uranbileg.

Figure 14: Golden Hat of the Male Dancer. (2015). Mongolia. Photograph courtesy of Yargai Galtat.

Figure 15: Costume Belt Pattern for Khaan Buguivch (left) and Khatan Suikh (right). (2020). Image courtesy of Yargai Galtat.

Figure 16: Costume Belt in the Design Process. (2015). Mongolia. Photograph courtesy of Yargai Galtat.

Figure 17: Traditional Ornaments on furniture inside a Mongolian Ger of the Terelj National Park. (2015). Mongolia. Copyrights: Mariam Ala-Rashi.

Figure 18: Ornaments on stage props, costumes and musical instruments. Performance of the Mongolian National Song and Dance Academic Ensemble. (2016). Mongolia. Photograph courtesy of Yargai Galtat. (Note: Faces of ensemble anonymized.)

Figure 19: Example of how the Sheep horn Ornament, called эвэр угалз (Ever Hee), is created. (2020). Image courtesy of Yargai Galtat.

Figure 20: Representation of sheep horns in Mongolian costuming and ornamentations. The Deel Robes of Mongolian queens. Performance of the Mongolian National Song and Dance Academic Ensemble. The Ornaments Khaan Buguivch (left) and Khatan Suikh (right) of the King's and Queen' bracelet are represented in the background (2015). Mongolia. Photograph courtesy of Yargai Galtat. (Note: Faces of ensemble members anonymized.)

Figure 21: Example of how Traditional Ornaments are incorporated into Contortion Movements. Ornament: эвэр угалз (Ever Hee). (2020). Design and Copyrights: Yargai Galtat.

Figure 22: Contortionist Tsetseglen Odgerel performing as Dara-ekhe. (2016). Mongolia. Photograph courtesy of Yargai Galtat. (Note: Faces of ensemble members anonymized.)

Figure 23: Contortionist Tsetseglen Odgerel's final transformation into a Dara-ekhe-A Buddhist Tara. (2015). Mongolia. Photograph courtesy of Yargai Galtat. (Note: Faces of ensemble members need to be anonymized.)

Figure 24: Contortion Coach Nomin Tseveendorj (center) with her Contortion Students. Mongolia. Photograph courtesy of Nomin Tseveendorj. (Note: Students anonymized.)

China's Bending Bodies:
Contortionists and Politics in China

Mariam Ala-Rashi

CHINA'S BENDING BODIES

CONTORTIONISTS AND POLITICS IN CHINA

TIMELINE OF CHINESE CONTORTION HISTORY

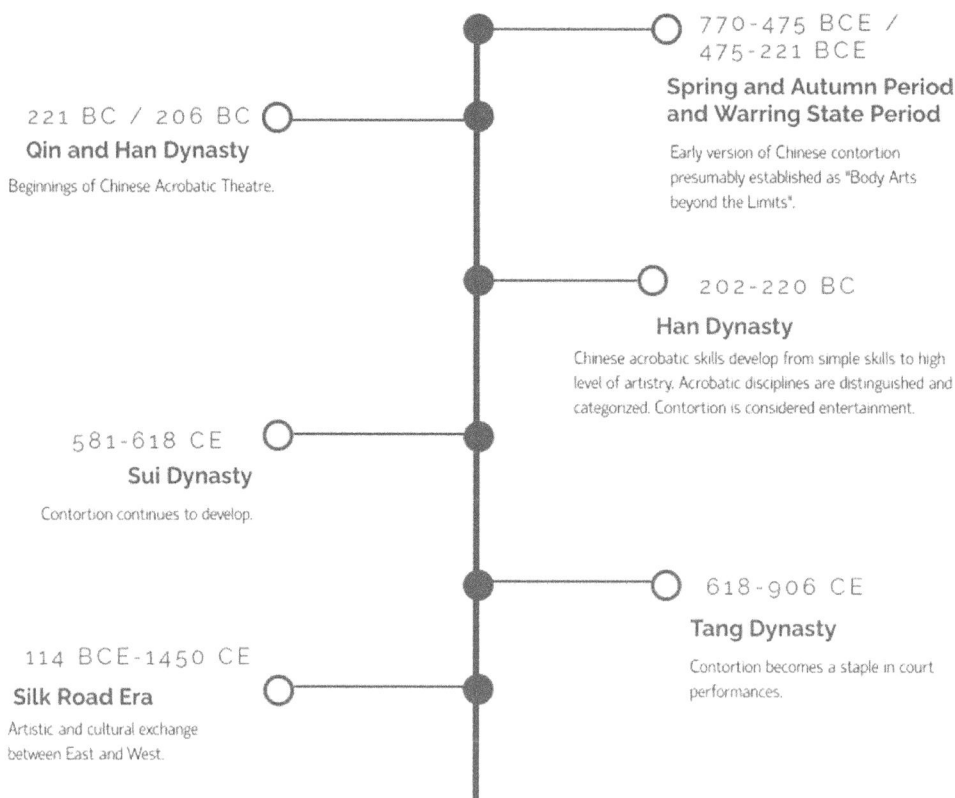

770-475 BCE / 475-221 BCE

Spring and Autumn Period and Warring State Period

Early version of Chinese contortion presumably established as "Body Arts beyond the Limits".

221 BC / 206 BC

Qin and Han Dynasty

Beginnings of Chinese Acrobatic Theatre.

202-220 BC

Han Dynasty

Chinese acrobatic skills develop from simple skills to high level of artistry. Acrobatic disciplines are distinguished and categorized. Contortion is considered entertainment.

581-618 CE

Sui Dynasty

Contortion continues to develop.

618-906 CE

Tang Dynasty

Contortion becomes a staple in court performances.

114 BCE-1450 CE

Silk Road Era

Artistic and cultural exchange between East and West.

1949

Founding of New China

Reformation of the acrobatics sector. Premier Zhou Enlai renames contortion from "Body Arts beyond the Limits" to "Rou Shu" (Rou=Soft/Flexible, Shu=Technique/Skills) and categorizes it within the acrobatic family.

1950

China National Acrobatic Troupe

Founding of the first state-run acrobatic troupe.

1966-1976

Cultural Revolution China

Utilization of acrobatics to demonstrate China's power, strength and prowess in international diplomacy.

1987
Cirque du Soleil starts hiring Chinese Acrobats

Late 20th century Chinese acrobatics focus more on incorporating other art-forms such as singing, dancing and acting.

2004-2009

Triple Marinelli Bend

Contortionist Wang Xiaoqiang performs record-breaking triple Marinelli Bend

A 19th century etching of the Temple of Heaven. *Temple of Heaven, Pekin.* 1887. Taylor, J.H. *China's Spiritual Need and Claims* (7th Ed.). P. 87.

A NOTE FROM THE AUTHOR

I first wrote this piece as part of my Master's thesis submitted in fulfilment of the requirements for the degree of MA Department of Dance University of Roehampton 2018. Since that time, I have discovered more information and material evidence to support this paper and to offer the interested reader, the scholar, the contortionist and contortion practitioner an even more substantial treatise about this art form. I have updated and expanded the 2018 piece by including more data from a wide range of literature, material evidence, oral history, current media reports, and correspondences with fellow scholars. All of the book's chapters have been revised in light of recent work in anthropology, archaeology, and political history.

This research study proposes an introduction to the performance art form *contortionism* by examining its theories and functions throughout the 20th and 21st century. It considers themes including the appropriation of contortionism during the golden age of Hollywood and discusses definition issues between contortionism and other disciplines that highlight body flexibility, such as gymnastics and yoga. By examining the genesis of contortionism in ancient China, it aims to explore parallels between the origins of Chinese contortionism and the establishment of Chinese acrobatics. It later dissects the political use of contortionism in socialist China and the development and institutionalization of acrobatic troupes since the founding of the People's Republic of China in 1949. Lastly, it draws upon a Foucauldian perspective by examining the parallels between the Western training of soldiers during the 17th and 18th century, and methods of traditional Chinese acrobatic training in the 21st century at the *Beijing International Art School*.

Throughout the writing of this monograph I have received a great deal of support and assistance. The work would not have been possible without the support of my supervisor Dr. Alexandra Kolb and all of the University of Roehampton Dance Department faculty members. I am grateful for their invaluable support and motivation, and for sharing their vast knowledge. I would also like to thank Thom Wall for helping develop this second edition, for his patient support and for providing me with the tools that I needed to choose the right direction to complete this monograph. I would like to thank my family and my partner Yargai Galtat for their wise counsel and sympathetic ear. You are always there for me. In addition, I would like to thank my friend Jean-Luc Bedryk who provided stimulating discussions as well as happy distractions to rest my mind outside of my research. I could not have completed this work without your support. Finally, I would like to place on record my sense of gratitude to Tian Feng, Professor Arthur Lewbel, Serchmaa Byamba, Wei Wei, Teng Li and everyone, who directly or indirectly, has helped me in this venture.

INTRODUCTION

This monograph examines the circus discipline and performance art-form *contortion* and the practice of *body flexibility* in China, looking specifically at its theories and functions as well as discussions across political, social, historical and performance studies. It analyses ancient traces and depictions of contortion practices, to advance the understanding of the practice of body flexibility, a flexibility far surpassing the average range of human limberness, in various cultures. It further analyzes its aesthetics and training methods in China through a Foucauldian[66] approach by considering Michel Foucault's book *Discipline and Punish-The Birth of the Prison*, where the social theorist describes how the human body was utilized by governments, as early as the 17th century. Striking similarities exist between the Chinese acrobatic schooling system and Western prison systems, as well as between their military and legal hierarchies. By drawing on multiple similarities between the Western system of prisons, military, and legal hierarchies, this study analyses how the education system in China "produces" disciplined, acrobatic bodies. It provides insight into the complex theories of contortionism, mainly throughout the late nineteenth and the twentieth century, exploring how the human body and its labor potential were utilized and leveraged by governments. This monograph further examines the etymology of the word *contortion* and its early emergence in print media.

---

66   Michel Foucault discusses in his book *Discipline and Punish-The Birth of the Prison* the Western system of prisons, the military, police and legal hierarchies in the discourse of power. It discusses social and theoretical mechanisms in Western governmental institutions to discipline the human body both in its mental/social spheres as well as the relationship between psychological and physical space.

The Oxford English Dictionary (OED) documents the first mention of the term *contortion* in 1611 by *R. Cotgrave Dict. French & Eng. Tongues,* defined as "the action of twisting or writhing; the fact of being twisted; distortion by twisting" (Oxford, 2018: A). In the context of performing arts, *contortion* or *contortionism,* is a movement pattern and performance art form in which the performer is bending and twisting their body into seemingly impossible positions, with the effect of letting the body appear "boneless." Contortionism requires an extreme level of physical flexibility, one gained over years of regular practice. The showcase of a contortion performance appears unnatural, as the performer's extreme body flexibility is so far outside of the "normal" range of motion of an untrained person. The term *contortionist* is defined by the OED as "A gymnast or performer who throws his body into contorted postures". Notably, in this early definition for *contortionist,* the OED uses the term "gymnast" to describe this performance art-form. The English-speaking world was initially introduced to contortionists in the British music hall, European variety theater, and traveling circus troupes. Back then, these activities were described in terms of gymnastics – as the modern art of contortionism developed in the West – and as audiences became more familiar with their practices – the language used to describe the acts also changed. One of the earliest evidences of the term *contortionist* in print can be seen in a circus advertisement in 1859 by K. Cornwallis in *Panorama New World I. 323 Cremorne Gardens:* "Wanted, male and female Equestrians, Tumblers [and] Acrobatic Performers, Contortionists" (Oxford, 2018: B). Though modern contortion is often seen in the context of a circus performance today, the practice of achieving extreme flexibility for public display has roots in many cultures.[67] A variety of the cultures that have been practicing body flexibility will be discussed in detail in the following chapters.

---

67   For more on these ancient roots in Mongolia see: Ala-Rashi, Mariam. *Mongolian Contortion-An Ethnographic Inquiry*. Philadelphia. Modern Vaudeville Press, 2021.

Fig. 1 (left) Performer: Mariam Ala-Rashi. *Ballet.* Germany (2011). Photographer: Hamid Sheikh.

Fig. 2 (above) Performer: Mariam Ala-Rashi. *American Tribal Fusion*, Germany (2010). Photographer: Rainer Westerwinter.

Fig. 3 (below) Performer: Mariam Ala-Rashi. *Belly Dance* (2012). Copyrights: Cicilia, Cat Dance Beijing.

Investigating the art-form contortionism stems from my artistic background as dance artist and contortion practitioner. As a professionally-trained dancer, I found myself naturally interested in the extreme abilities of contortionists and have memories of watching contortion routines on German television as a child. Being of both Western and Middle-Eastern descent, my professional dance education was shaped by a confluence of styles. I was first trained in Western stage dance such as ballet (Figure 1), modern dance, court dance, and Western fusion belly dance called American tribal fusion.[68] (Figure 2) In the Middle East and

68   Tribal Fusion: A Western form of belly dance and branch from American tribal style belly dance. It combines American cabaret belly dance, American tribal

in Europe, I studied raqs sharqy, widely known as belly dance. (Figure 3) The practice of body flexibility was part of my daily training curriculum at the ballet academy in Düsseldorf, Germany. The emphasis on body flexibility during my own dance routines that I performed as touring solo artist was expressed through floor-work (dance movements performed on the ground), which I used as highlights during my performances. (Figure 4, 5, 6) I often used backbends and split routines in my performances, and I found myself drawn to a more acrobatic style of dancing because of the possibilities and freedom of expression it offered, particularly in "fusion" dance styles where multiple genres are merged. In 2009, I decided to pursue a more specialized contortion training program. Studying the art of contortionism as an adult required professional training with contortion coaches who understood human flexibility outside of the dance world in order to maintain a healthy and successful training outcome. I started my own contortion training in 2010, and that year I was invited among other artists to perform for an event that was broadcast on national TV in Germany. Here I met the professional ballet dancer and contortionist Nina Burri, who performed her contortion act "Goldeneye." Nina Burri, from Switzerland, who was a former ballet dancer, decided to become a contortionist at the age of 30 and won multiple awards following her contortion education in China. She recommended to me the prestigious *Beijing International Art School*.

The *Beijing International Art School* (BJIAS) is one of the world's leading acrobatic institutions that offers training in a wide range of acrobatic disciplines (acrobatics= 杂技 zájì) with top-tier coaches. It is a governmental institution that fosters China's elite acrobats from as young

style belly dance and incorporates elements of body flexibility and other dance styles such as flamenco, Indian dance, Hip Hop, contemporary, modern dance and many more. Dance scholars currently discuss to re-name tribal fusion in an effort to avoid cultural appropriation.

Fig. 4 (left) Dance Performance Mariam Ala-Rashi at *Orientale* Germany (2010). Photographer: André Elbing.

Fig. 5 (above) Performer: Mariam Ala-Rashi. Beijing (2014). Photographer: Andreu Pardales.

Fig. 6 (below) Performer: Mariam Ala-Rashi. *Oriental Fusion*. Germany (2011). Copyrights: Arnd Wende.

as five years of age. Upon completion of their training program, these acrobats are frequently scouted and employed by leading producers in the entertainment industry. The school also operates the *International Department* aimed at foreign students who wish to be trained by those elite coaches. Here, visiting artists have the opportunity to train, develop their skills, and expand their repertoire amongst China's elite acrobats and under supervision of experts in their field. Disciplines taught at the school include equilibristics, contortionism, handstands, aerial hoop, straps, Chinese pole, and tumbling, among others. Notably, training duration, methodology, and aesthetic goals differ from one country to the next across the region. Mongolia and China, for example, are internationally known as the leading countries for contortion training and for "producing" the best contortionists in the world. In both countries, the art of contortionism is passed on from one generation to the next. However, their training approach and aesthetic goals differ significantly. In Mongolia, the average contortion student trains between three to five hours of each day (Monday through Friday), with additional hours of choreographic training for upcoming performances (Ala-Rashi, 2021: 43). The aesthetics of Mongolian contortion center around natural phenomena and spiritual elements. This is accomplished through slow, elegant movements that accentuate and uplift the strength of Mongolian women. Contortion training in China takes eight to ten hours (Monday through Friday) – twice that of their Mongolian counterparts -- with additional performance work in the evenings and on weekends. Chinese contortion coaches, in contrast, place the greatest value on technical prowess – dominating and surpassing the highest international benchmarks in training and stage performance. Chinese contortion focuses more on record-breaking effects such as the triple Marinelli bend, which will be explored in following chapters. The training at the *Beijing International Art School* (BJIAS) is high intensity and spans around 10 hours a day with the aim to exceed the highest levels of difficulty in an acrobatic discipline.

During my stay as a full-time student between 2011 and 2015, foreign students were allowed to share the training facilities with local students who practiced at the school daily. This served a particularly valuable (and motivating!) role for the foreign students, as they could see how immersive the contortionist lifestyle was for students at one of the world's top schools. In class, foreign students followed the same rigid rules and training techniques as their local counterparts, ensuring parallel access to the traditional Chinese training methods. My interest was to learn from world-leading teachers in China within the environment of the contortion culture, which was not available at that time in Europe. Only a handful of circus schools in Europe offered contortion training at the time, and most of them focused on training for children. This has changed in recent years with the growing popularity of contortion in the West.

The rationale for this monograph is the increasing popularity of contortionism, sparked by televised talent shows and social media and resulting in a growing number of contortion practitioners worldwide. Literature on this art form, its history, the value of body flexibility in different cultures, and training styles is sparse; as a result, current knowledge is inadequate. Oftentimes the practice of *body flexibility* in other cultures and the display of the performance art-form *contortion* are mistaken for one another. *Contortion* is oftentimes mistaken for *yoga* or *gymnastics* and vice versa, despite their functions and theories being entirely different. *Contortion* is a performance art-form. *Yoga*[69] is a holistic practice towards health and well-being. *Gymnastics* are a sport. Although these practices all display (and indeed, rely on!) physical flexibility, it is vital to understand their inherent differences and examine them in detail. By considering these differences, we can better understand ancient practices of body flexibility and examine their developments and uses throughout the ages.

Contortion is a folk art that stemmed from practices of body flexibility in different cultures as evident, for instance, in Mongolia and China. It was later stylized, adapted and commodified into a circus discipline. Exploring the historical development of Chinese acrobatic theatre, which contortionism was a part of; this research aims to discover a comprehensible link regarding the development of Chinese traditional contortionism that we see today. Due to lack of primary evidence regarding its genesis and development, contortionism has proved to be an under-researched field, with scarce scholarly literature. The insights shared throughout this

---

69   When referring to yoga, all forms are considered.

monograph are based on my personal research and fieldwork undertaken in China as student and participant observer at the *Beijing International Art School,* as well as during my visits of other local acrobatic schools. The knowledge of contortionism and physical flexibility within the circus was passed onto me through my contortion teachers, but only the practice allowed me to fully grasp its essence: A deep, physical understanding of the field which can only be attained through daily practice for years at the hands of expert coaches.

Records from ancient China however show evidence of contortion practices dating back about 2000 years. The murals of the ancient tomb of Liaoyang Bartaizi depict a girl performing a backbend on a black lacquered type of wooden platform, and a stone relief of "Hundred Entertainments" from the Eastern Han dynasty tomb in Dayi County in Chengdu, Sichuan displays a girl performing a contortion-like handstand with her feet bending forward in front of her face. In direct comparison to other countries with a deep-rooted contortion culture, such as Mongolia, China appears to be among the oldest. Distinguished from the *practice of body flexibility* that dates back centuries in other cultures such as India or Egypt, the performance art form *contortion* has been executed for entertainment purposes in China for thousands of years. Based on the material evidence currently present, it can be assumed that China was one of the originating countries of contortion performances.

The increasing popularity of contortion, as mentioned earlier, comes with the need for more knowledge about this discipline. This includes an analysis of its history and origins, theories and functions in various cultures and ages, as well as its development over the centuries. A clear definition allows us to distinguish practices of body flexibility (such as yoga) from performing arts (such as contortion) and sport disciplines (such as gymnastics.) It is a complex endeavor that aims to establish a foundation of knowledge that allows for expansion and can be built upon by future academics. These conversations often devolve into a sterile debate over definitions —this monograph aims instead to explore exciting and gratifying avenues of inquiry as we seek to better understand and acknowledge what the art-form of *contortion* really is all about.

CHAPTER 1: DEFINITION, THEORIES AND GLOBAL DEVELOPMENT OF CONTORTIONISM

The practice of body flexibility can be found in many cultures and often dates back thousands of years. In this concise overview, some of the various cultures that practiced body flexibility will be discussed to define the development of contortion more distinctly. Examining forms of body flexibility in other cultures helps to distinguish between the performance art-form contortionism and the manifold practices that share the same trait: extreme physical flexibility. This review will begin with the etymology of contortion in the English language and ancient records found in tombs, documenting up to its popularity on televised talent shows in the 21st century.

Etymology

The English roots of the word *contortion* trace back to 16th century French language when the Latin word *contortiōn-em* (a noun describing action) was derived from the French word contorsion. It describes "the action of twisting or writhing, as well as the fact of being twisted and the distortion by twisting" (Oxford, 2018: A). The first recorded use of the word *contortionist* in the English language to describe someone who professes and practices contortion was in 1859 in the book *A Panorama of the New World* by Sir Kinahan Cornwallis, a British diplomat and author.

He narrated an event with "male and female Equestrians, Tumblers [and] Acrobatic Performers, Contortionists" (Oxford, 2018: B). Throughout this monograph, the term *contortion* refers to the acrobatic discipline as defined in the introduction and the term *body flexibility* will be used to describe various practices in different cultures that are in appearance and execution similar to the acrobatic discipline. The term contortion is often used widely in Western literature to describe any kind of body flexibility, as used in yoga, dance, martial arts etc., which why it is important to establish the appropriate use of the term *contortion* as it is not representative for each practice of body flexibility in its respective discipline, culture, sport, and other related activities. This also prevents confusion among aspects of art-forms, cultural practices, and acrobatic disciplines.

The word *contortionism* was first printed in a 1927 article in the British newspaper *The Daily Telegraph*, describing the profession of a contortionist as "[...] an idealization of contortionism, twist their lithe bodies into all manner of graceful poses" (Oxford, 2018: C). Seeing evidence of how these words were first used in print, and understanding that the first (equestrian) circus was founded by Philip Astley in 1768 in England, we can begin to see when the first "contortionists" might have performed in European circuses. The aforementioned advertisement from K. Cornwallis in 1856 illustrates the demand for contortionists at the time. The Victoria and Albert Museum (V&A) in London describes the establishment of the circus in England by Philip Astley as followed:

> Philip Astley (1742 – 1814), a six-foot tall, ex-cavalry man, is often credited as the 'father of the modern circus'. In 1768, he and his wife Patty established Astley's Riding School in London, where Philip would teach in the morning and perform equestrian tricks in the afternoon. [...] Philip's most famous act

and widely considered to be the first circus clown act, was 'The Tailor of Brentford' or 'Tailor's Ride to Brentford', in which he acted out a comic journey on horseback. [...] Astley is also credited with discovering that the ideal size for a circus ring is 42 feet in diameter. [...] Astley quickly began to incorporate other acts from the fairs and pleasure gardens of London and Paris into the performance. These were acrobats, jugglers, rope dancers, clowns and strongmen. By 1780 he had built a roof over the entire arena so that his audiences could enjoy performances throughout the whole year. Astley may have been credited as the 'father of modern circus' but it was his rival Mr. Charles Dibdin (1745 – 1814), British composer, musician, dramatist, novelist and actor, who first coined the word 'circus'. Dibdin copied Astley's formula of dramatic equestrian entertainment by opening The Royal Circus a short distance from Astley's Riding School (V&A, 2021).

Based on this testimony, I conclude that contortionists were first "invited into the circus ring" and established as a "staple" circus discipline in the West sometime between 1768 and 1859. Being specifically named in print indicates that contortion was gaining name-specific familiarity and that it was sought-after by audiences in the Western entertainment world, as evidenced by casting calls in trade magazines. Although there is no hard evidence, it is possible that, prior to this time, contortionists were part of traveling shows and exhibitions. To understand how contortion became a staple in Western circus establishments, one must consider the practice of body flexibility in ancient civilizations and analyze the developments of performing arts throughout the ages.

The Practice of Body Flexibility in Ancient Civilizations

Very little is known about the ancient history of contortion, but the depiction of flexible dancers and acrobats in statues, reliefs, and wall paintings demonstrates that the practice of body flexibility existed in various cultures around the world, carrying a variety of functions and values in each society. Identifying patterns and similarities by comparing the practice of physical flexibility in various cultures provides a better understanding of the developments, functions and theories of these practices. Artifacts that were preserved throughout past centuries, include wall drawings depicting flexible temple dancers in the pyramids of Egypt, flexible acrobats and dancers in paintings on ancient pottery from Greece, and clay statues in Mexico. A particularly vast array of images depicting body flexibility is displayed in temples and pyramids in Egypt.

Ancient Egypt

The acrobatic dance in Egypt, as archaeologists refer to it, is an ancient practice of body flexibility with advanced techniques and movement patterns that can be examined in vast reliefs in temple structures and pyramids. Havva Eva Seyberth is a choreographer, dancer, and editor of the book *Orientalischer Tanz-Folklore und Hoftänze (Oriental Dance, Folk and Court Dance)*. In her chapter *Egyptian Dance History and Pharaonic Dances,* she describes a wall painting that shows dancers performing *Hebu Dance* at the *Opet Festival* while executing acrobatic backbend poses. The wall carving, from the Karnak Temple Complex in Egypt around 2000–1700 BC, depicts four dancers (or a repetition of the same pose executed by one dancer) in backbend position with straight arms and later with bent arms with the chin touching the floor. The latter could be an early record of the pose known today as *chest-stand*, which is typical (but not exclusively) for contortion (see similar arrangement of performers in

Figure 8). During a *chest-stand,* the performing artist bends backwards as far as possible from a standing position in order to bring the chest to rest on the floor and to look at the audience through the feet, which are still touching the floor. Numerous depictions of body flexibility that are very similar can be examined in various tombs in Egypt. These examples include the burial chamber *BH4 Beni Hasan, Lightroom-1040087 (from 2055 until 1650 BC) (Figure 7), the tomb RoHa 2292, Karnak, Red Chapel of female pharaoh Hatshepsut (2055 BC) (Figure 8), the Feast of Opet Panel, Luxor Temple (approximately 1400 BCE) (Figure 9), and in the Limestone Ostracon from Deir el-Medina: Dancer/Acrobat in Backbend,* found at the Worker's Village Deir el-Medina near Luxor (1292 and 1076 BCE). (Figure 10)

German Egyptologist Emma Brunner -Traut examines in her paper *Tanz im Alten Ägypten (Dance in Ancient Egypt)* the various practices of dance and body flexibility and their transformations and developments throughout the old, middle, and new kingdom of ancient Egypt. The history of Ancient Egypt is divided into specific periods namely the Old Kingdom (OK) Age of the Pyramid Builders (c. 2686-2181 B.C.), the Middle Kingdom (MK): 12th Dynasty (c. 2055-1786 B.C.) and the New Kingdom (NK) (c. 1567-1085 B.C.). In her chapters *Altes Reich (Old Kingdom), Akrobatischer Tanz im Göttlichen Kult (Acrobatic Dance in the Divine Cult)* and *Neues Reich (New Kingdom),* she analyses depictions of dancers and acrobats in various tombs. These images depict body flexibility and dance performances which were presented during processions and banquets to entertain pharaohs and members of the court, during ritual sacrifices, funerals, and during the offering of sacrifices, as well as temple performances to honor Egyptian gods. In the following, Brunner-Traut analyses in great detail the elements and functions of various performances

Fig. 7 BH4 Beni Hasan, Lightroom-1040087: Female acrobats and girls playing with the ball – 15th Tomb of Beni Hasan. Photo credit: kairoinfo4u, 2009. Available at: https://www.flickr.com/photos/manna4u/4127122259/

Fig. 8 RoHa 2292. Karnak Egypt, Red Chapel of female pharaoh Hatshepsut, Exterior wall. Link: Photo credit: kairoinfo4u, 2007 (Flickr). Available at: https://flic.kr/p/FeVqo

Fig. 9 *Feast of Opet Panel*, Luxor Temple constructed approximately 1400 BCE. The Festival of Opet depicted on the western wall of the court. Photo credit: Ovedc. Link: https://commons.wikimedia.org/wiki/File:By_ovedc_-_Luxor_Temple_-_56.jpg

Fig. 10 Ostracon (limestone) from Deir el-Medina: Dancer/Acrobat in Backbend. Found at the Worker's Village Deir el-Medina near Luxor (1292 and 1076 BCE). *Tänzerin auf einem altägyptischen Ostrakon, gefunden in Theben, heute im Turiner Museo Egizio*; Malerei auf Kalkstein, 10,5x16,8cm, 19. Dynastie, um 1300 v. Chr. Photo credit: Public Domain/ Author unknown. Available at: https://commons.wikimedia.org/wiki/File:Female_topless_egyption_dancer_on_ancient_ostrakon.jpg

during the Old Kingdom, Middle Kingdom and New Kingdom (sections of the original paper translated from German to English by the author):

> The acrobatic dance, performed to honor the goddess Hathor and other gods, originated in the Old Kingdom, developed throughout the Middle Kingdom and reached its prime in the New Kingdom. Throughout these three major periods, the acrobatic dance changes its outer form but it remains an eccentric art-form, which demands extreme flexibility of the human body. [...] The dances of the Old Kingdom are community dances; they have a social function. A larger dance group can, however, also be arranged in pairs, but always in pairs of the same sex. Overall, the men play a very subordinate role in dance. - In the Middle Kingdom and New Kingdom, as well as the Old Kingdom, acrobatic-eccentric dances were performed at religious festivals, mostly during processions to honor the gods, and belonged to those ecstatic dances that "can become a symbol of the mystical union of Gods." Although they are later devalued to artistry, they are rooted in magical practices (Brunner-Traut, 1958: 13).

Brunner-Traut's research deepens our understanding of the acrobatic dance in ancient Egypt, its development through Old, Middle and New Kingdom and its value as a community dance with a social function. It presents us with important details regarding the gender roles and status of the female dancer and recognizes the core function of the dance as an "eccentric art form" that is rooted in magical practice. Its various transformations during the regime of the three Kingdoms further present details about certain acrobatic exercises and "tricks", and how they developed alongside changing trends in art and society:

A small dance performance in the coffin chamber of the Kai-em-anch from the late 6th dynasty is very unique. Three of the dancers move in the usual dance step, but a fourth goes beyond the scope of canonical dance, that in this late phase of the Old Kingdom was considered to be restricting, and provides the observer with a glimpse of later forms [of the dance]. She boldly turns her body back and swings her limbs lithely in a curve [known today as bridge] that contrasts with the angular, determined and moderate movements of the others. Her destiny as a soloist is emphasized by her nudity (p.:19). [...] The costumes of the dancers differed greatly from the usual women's clothing in that they emphasized the shape of the body to avoid covering its movements (p.:15). [...] The Middle Kingdom was surprisingly uncreative. Music and dance became of lesser importance. [...] A rhythmically emphasized, non-melodic and illogical character is distinctive for the dance of the Middle Kingdom. It is significantly reduced in favor of sportive and especially acrobatic exercises. Acrobatics have strongly influenced the dance forms [of the Middle Kingdom] and even penetrated the dance as an autonomous discipline, and in one case literally replaced the actual dance in its entirety (p.: 37) (Brunner-Traut, 1958: 19-37).

The development of acrobatic dance in the Middle Kingdom stands in stark contrast to the Old Kingdom as it transforms from community dance with social functions almost to a sportive exercise that emphasizes mainly its acrobatic elements. Moreover, this development sets the stage for further improvements and increased difficulty in the evolution of the Egyptian acrobatic dance in the New Kingdom:

The acrobatics of the dance are now expressed in the New Kingdom in the figure that we nowadays refer to as "somersault". The performer bends over backwards in a quick move. The acrobats are mostly shown in the final phase of the exercise, so the figure could be confused with the "bridge", which the girls in the well-known acrobatic scenes in Beni Hasan execute. However, based on the on the depictions, observing the individual movement sections of the exercises, we can say with certainty that the dancers perform the somersault. From the posture described here, the girls rise up again and in doing so gain new momentum with which they repeat the exercise in rhythmic succession (Brunner-Traut, 1958: 13-49).

Brunner-Traut's detailed analysis of the images left behind in ancient Egypt, gives insight into the development and functions of body flexibility within dance performances and as autonomous discipline. It describes the role of the female dancer as well as the aesthetic and costuming during those performances. It appears that what we know today as bridge or backbend, was performed during the Old Kingdom, technically developed during the Middle Kingdom and later, during the New Kingdom, further refined into a somersault. The physical flexibility shown in these temple structures in Egypt has a striking similarity to what would be considered "modern" contortion and tumbling. Yet, Egypt is not the only country where we can find ancient traces of body flexibility. Mexico has its very own history of physical flexibility that is represented in the so-called Tlatilco Figurines.

Mexico

In the early 20th century at an excavation site in Mexico, numerous figurines were discovered that depict practices of body flexibility in ancient Mexico. The figurines have been identified by archaeologists and anthropologists to be female performers that execute acrobatic skills. Fernanda Hernandez, anthropology intern at the LACMA's Art of the Ancient Americas department and the Department of Anthropology at California State University, describes the Tlatilco figurines in her article *Examining Tlatilco Figurines*:

Tlatilco, which is the Nahuatl word for "place of hidden things," is an Early Formative period (c. 1200–900 BCE) Mesoamerican site located in the western Valley of Mexico. It consists of three small villages and an extensive cemetery. In the early 20th century, the site was discovered by local miners and instantly attained recognition for its sophisticated archaeological materials. Tlatilco is known for its funerary practices, ceramic vessels, and figurines, most of which date to the site's apogee during the Early Formative period. Tlatilco's pottery vessels include a wide range of types, including animal effigies and many composite and inventive shapes. There are several similarities between Tlatilco materials and those of the Olmec archaeological culture located along the Gulf Coast of Mexico. For instance, a figurine known as "the Acrobat," found in the Tlatilco cemetery among other grave goods, exhibits a theme common in both Olmec and West Mexican art—acrobatic skill and yoga-like poses (Hernandez, 2021).

It is recorded that Mexican artists practiced considerable realism, not allowing much abstraction to influence their art, which suggests that the Tlatilco figurines were depicting realistic scenes (Barakat, 2021). The figurine called "The Acrobat" (Figure 11) depicts a typical "chest-stand" pose that is used in many practices of body flexibility and contortionism. The figurine is hollow and was probably used as a vessel to drink from.

Fig. 11 Tlatilco Figurine. Ceramic art recovered from Tlatilco, pre-Columbian village in the Valley of Mexico, commonly known as the "Acrobat", circa 1300 - 800 BCE. Photo credit: El Comandante. Available at: https://en.wikipedia.org/wiki/File:Acr%C3%B3bata_de_Tlatilco.JPG

Many statues found at the Tlatilco site depicted women either in various traditional dresses or performing body flexibility. These findings show the level of body flexibility and suggest a deeper tradition in this particular area. The ability to execute a chest-stand usually requires long and meticulous training. Preserved for eternity in clay figurines as tangible heritage, these practices must have been of particular importance to its peoples and suggest a certain status of the women who executed these practices. The illustration of physical flexibility in pottery and stone figurines can also be traced to Europe where similar poses have been chosen by craftsmen to be depicted in every-day utensils and architectural structures.

Ancient India

Various ancient temple structures in India display sculptures that execute different forms of body flexibility such as kamasutra, vedic rituals and yoga. The Achyuta Raya temple (1534 CE) for instance, illustrates sculptures and reliefs of yoga asanas (yoga postures), whereas the Khajuraho group of temples (950 to 1050 CE) illustrates erotic motifs of kamasutra practices that include body flexibility. The motifs of body flexibility in Indian temples are manifold and complex and sometimes show hundreds of sculptures in one temple alone. In his article *Sex, love, and Relationships: My Journey of 40 Years* for the *Indian Journal of Psychiatry*, Dr. Mrugesh Vaishnav of the Samvedana Happiness Hospital describes the illustration of kamasutra poses in temple structures and their function:

> The Kama Sutra [...] is an ancient Indian Sanskrit text on sexuality, eroticism, and emotional fulfillment in life. Kama Sutra is neither exclusively nor predominantly a sex manual on sex positions, but written as a guide to the "art of living" well, the nature of love, finding a life partner, maintaining one's love life, and other aspects pertaining to the pleasure-oriented faculties of human life. [...] These teaching in Sex and sexuality was not given in Private chambers or class rooms but were depicted openly in the ancient caves of Konark, Khajuraho & in many Hindu temples (Vaishnav: 2019).

Statues of kamasutra poses, therefore, served the purpose of teaching local communities about life, marriage and relationships. The temple structures that illustrate hundreds of statues not only show one aspect of a certain doctrine, but rather tell stories about the Indian culture and philosophies; passing on knowledge about various concepts that concern life such as spirituality, relationships, health and vedic rituals, yoga and the art of living. Anthropologist and mythologist Dr. Sadashiv Ambadas Dange, University of Bombay, describes the depiction of erotic temple sculptures in his article *Sex in Stone and the Vedic Mithuna* as followed:

> The erotic sculptures innovated many things; but the main source seems to be Vedic rituals, which were themselves influenced by folk-customs of sexy songs and rituals. The Indian erotic sculptures show the innovation of many details that answer to the development of art. But the motif of sanctified sex goes to the Vedic period, with the simple mithunas [sexual intercourse and tantric sex] formed from the various sacrificial ingredients accompanied by the ritual-coitus varieties (Dange, 1977).

These friezes, however, are not only illustrating erotic motifs. The temple structures often depict historical stories that include all aspects of life, using symbolism to express the ideas and beliefs of Hinduism, Indian literature and fine arts. In her article *Erotic Sentiment in Indian Temple Sculptures*, Indologist Rekha Rao describes the temple sculptures as followed:

Most of the Apsara sculptures are based on different aspects of Shringara rasa, adhering to the rules prescribed in the treatise of Indian theatrics-Natyashastra. Shringara is the rasa used to portray on stage mutual desire and romantic love as primary emotion between a man and woman. The permanent mood – Sthayibhava of Shringara is Rati, meaning physical attraction and pleasure. Shringara rasa – the sentiment of erotic love, and first of the nine rasas / navarasas as they are called are the natural states of mind experienced by humans. Of the nine sentiments -nava rasas, shringara occupies an important place in the history of ancient Indian literature and fine arts. Indian temples show the figures of apsaras depicting the sentiment of love, both in the theoretical aspects relating to theatrics (as described in Natyashastra by Bharata Muni around 2nd century AD [CE]) as well as in the practical side of life with Kamasutra of Vatsyayana (by sage Vatsyayana, around 2-3 century AD [CE]) as its base (Rao, 2018).

Rekha Rao then categorizes the sculptures as followed:

1. *Theatrical Depictions* (Based on Natya Shastra): Aayoga, Viprayoga and Sambhoga.

2. *Non-Tantric Depictions* (Based on Kamasutra): Sambhoga.

3. *Tantric Depictions* (Based on Tantra Yoga): Kundalini Yoga, Hatha Yoga, Nada Yoga (Rao, 2018).

Yoga in particular, as mentioned in Number 1 and 3 of Rao's categorization, is a doctrine of particular significance when considering the practice of body flexibility. Similar to depictions of kamasutra poses, yogic motifs and figures are represented in many Indian temples. The Ministry of External Affairs for the Indian government describes in the article *Yoga: Its Origin, History and Development* by Dr. Ishwar V. Basavaraddi, Director of Morarji Desai National Institute of Yoga, the complex connotations of the statues:

[...] Yogic motives and figures performing Yoga Sadhana suggest the presence of Yoga in ancient India. The phallic symbols, seals of idols of mother Goddess are suggestive of Tantra Yoga. [sic] Presence of Yoga is available in folk traditions, Indus valley civilization, Vedic and Upanishadic heritage, Buddhist and Jain traditions, Darshanas, epics of Mahabharat and Ramayana, theistic traditions of Shaivas, Vaishnavas, and Tantric traditions. [...] Yoga is essentially a spiritual discipline based on an extremely subtle science, which focuses on bringing harmony between mind and body. It is an art and scince [sic] of healthy living. The word 'Yoga' is derived from the Sanskrit root 'Yuj', meaning 'to join' or 'to yoke' or 'to unite'. As per Yogic scriptures the practice of Yoga leads to the union of individual consciousness with that of the Universal Consciousness, indicating a perfect harmony between the mind and body, Man & Nature. (Basavaraddi: 2015)

These sculptures are evidence for how advanced these practices of body flexibility in India were at that time and how physical flexibility is applied in three considerable areas of the Indian culture, namely vedic rituals, yoga and kama sutra. They are evidence for the significance of body flexibility in the Indian culture and in particular for the long-established tradition of yoga. Shared traits of these practices are their benefits to health and well-being, the erotic life and spirituality as they consider distinct aspects that foster harmony of the body and mind.

Europe

Many impressions of body flexibility can be found in architecture, paintings, pottery and sketches from the Middle Ages in Europe, around 1300-1600 BC. A limestone figure as portion of a pilaster (a part of an

Fig. 12 (left) (Front view) Portion of a Pilaster with an Acrobat. MET Museum. French; Pilaster; Sculpture-Architectural Date: circa 1150 –70, Medium: Limestone. Geography: Made in Lyonnais, France. Credit Line: The Cloisters Collection, 1947. Photo credit: Public Domain/Met Museum. Available at: https://commons.wikimedia.org/wiki/File:Portion_of_a_Pilaster_with_an_Acrobat_MET_cdi47-101-25.jpg

Fig. 13 (right) (Side View) Portion of a Pilaster with an Acrobat. MET Museum. French; Pilaster; Sculpture-Architectural Date: circa 1150 –70 Medium: Limestone. Geography: Made in Lyonnais, France. Credit Line: The Cloisters Collection, 1947. Photo credit: Public Domain/Met Museum. Available at: https://commons.wikimedia.org/wiki/File:Portion_of_a_Pilaster_with_an_Acrobat_MET_cdi47-101-25s4.jpg

architectural structure), made in Lyonnais, France from around 1150BC-1170 BC shows an acrobat or dancer performing a chest-stand (The Met: 2021). (Figure 12 & 13) Greek *pelikae*, vessels similar to an *amphora*, from the 4th century BCE show images of female acrobats and dancers in contortion-like poses. One *pelike* depicts a performer shooting an arrow from a bow that she is holding with her feet. (Figure 14 & 15) This is a trick that requires tremendous skill and control over the body which leads to the question about to what extent the training methods were already developed in 4th BCE Greece. Shooting an arrow with the feet is a popular trick that is still performed in modern day contortion routines

145

Fig. 14 (left) Female acrobat shooting an arrow with a bow in her feet; Gnathia style pelikai; 4th century B.C. Antikensammlung Berlin. Photo credit: Marcus Cyron. Available at: https://en.wikipedia.org/wiki/File:Antikensammlung_Berlin_525.JPG

Fig. 15 (right) Hydria Acrobat Vase. British Museum, Townley Collection, Upper floor, room 73: The Greeks and Italy. A female acrobat next to a potter's turntable. Detail from a Campanian red-figure hydria, ca. 340-330 BC. Photo credit: Jastrow. Available at: https://en.wikipedia.org/wiki/File:Hydria_acrobat_BM_VaseF232.jpg

Fig. 16 (below) Photo credit: Mongolian Contortion Center SF, Serchmaa Byamba. Contortionist: Khulan Myagmarsuren. Photographer: Robin Gee.

(Figure 16). Another insightful image of body flexibility is part of a frieze sculpture around 1410CE in the cathedral in Rouen, France. Here the dancer Salomé is depicted performing in a contortion-like pose before the banquet of Herod (Toepfer, 1999:105). These traces of body flexibility suggest a vast development of performing arts throughout Europe.

Author Travis Stuart (Trav S.D.), provides in his book *No Applause—Just throw Money* a concise timeline of the theatrical developments in various countries and eras, enumerating the Greek mimes who juggled and performed acrobatics, dance, and comical sketches during the Golden Age of Greece (500-300 BC). The Roman mimes materialized in the Republic at about 300 BC and were closely associated with the Atellan farce, ancestor to the Roman comedies of Plautus and Terence, the commedia dell'arte (16th to 18th century), the comic creations of Shakespeare (1564) and Molière (1622), and all slapstick straight through the vaudeville era (Paris: around 1750; US: around 1880) (Stewart: 2005). Stuart further provides an outline that highlights the developments of performing arts through the ages, focusing on early variety acts and presentations of dramatic literature. From 101-200 CE the *fabula raciniata* (an early form of variety theatre) incorporated tightrope walkers, trapeze artists, tumblers, jugglers, sword-swallowers, fire-eaters, dancers, operatic singers, and stilt-walkers. Throughout Euro-American history, the descendants of those mimes persisted. During the Middle Ages (500-1500 CE) itinerant bands of jongleurs, minstrels, troubadours, and similar entertainers would tramp from village to village with their exhibitions of juggling, fire-eating, magic tricks, little songs, and bits of clowning. They were then incorporated into the presentation of great works of dramatic literature in amphitheaters as preludes and entr'actes during the Elizabethan England from 1558 CE, and this tradition was perpetuated in America into the late nineteenth century from 1801-1900 (Stewart: 2005).

The examination of the practice of body flexibility in other cultures provides us in some instances with patterns and similarities with which we can compare the developments, functions and theories of these art forms and practices with each other. We discovered for instance, how important acrobatic dance in Egypt was during the reign of the three kingdoms and how it was transformed and utilized as magical and spiritual practice, and as a way to serve the rulers (pharaohs) of the country. This notion of using performing arts in political dynamics can be found as well in Chinese acrobatics that served the ruling party as court entertainment in ancient China and again from the 1950s onwards as a political tool in international diplomacy (as discovered in Chapter Four). Further, themes of spirituality are identifiable in Tlatilco figurines, in yoga practices, Egyptian acrobatic dance, and in Mongolian contortion. Yet, many of these ancient practices have died out, and only a very few cultures continue the century-old practice of physical flexibility today. Those that are continued today progress and evolve and oftentimes echo the changes in society, art, and politics. This can be observed, for instance, in China and Mongolia, where contortionism was commodified in the 1940s and where the artist's body was utilized as political tool in international diplomacy (as explored in Chapter Four), Learning from ancient cultures and their practices, therefore, helps us to deepen our understanding of the traditional art forms that are still carried out today and how they developed and evolved within distinct political, spiritual and cultural environments.

Nonetheless, despite the material evidence from different cultures throughout the ages, little is known about the postures and ancient training methods of the practitioners those reliefs, paintings, and statues depict. Apart from the practice of yoga, which is well-documented and researched, a very limited amount of literature about the practice of body flexibility in ancient cultures have been published. Online sources, especially those regarding the history of contortion, are scarce and oftentimes derived from apocryphal myths and legends. Further study would doubtless prove fruitful, but such research is beyond the scope of this monograph.

CHAPTER 1.1: DEVELOPMENT OF CONTORTIONISM IN THE WEST DURING THE 20TH AND 21ST CENTURY

This chapter considers early developments of contortion in the West, mainly throughout the 20th and 21st century. By creating a concise timeline, it examines contortionism as a circus discipline, the representation of contortion in Hollywood movies, the sexualization of body flexibility, and considers its popularity in televised talent shows and on social media. Tracing the early emergence of contortionism in the West, provides a crucial perspective for understanding current developments and how contortion was popularized in recent years. It further addresses common misconceptions that contortion, yoga and other practices of body flexibility are one and the same.

Early Emergence of Contortion in Print Media

From the 1800s, the modern entertainment industry began to emerge and expand across the world, and with it came an increase in print media as show businesses started to advertise their programs, with contortionists being more often mentioned in advertisements, reviews, and periodicals. As Dr. Robert A. Houston, Professor of Modern History at University of St. Andrews, discusses in his article *The Growth of Literacy in Western Europe from 1500 to 1800*: "Between the Renaissance and the age of Romanticism, Europe experienced the beginnings of a profound transformation from restricted to mass literacy. In 1500 very few people could read and write, but by 1800 a majority of adults in north-western

Europe were literate, some able to enjoy an unprecedented volume and variety of print and writing (Houston, 2018)." Education during the age of enlightenment (1650 to 1780) in Europe progressed steadily, and school became mandatory for children in the US in 1852 and in the UK in 1880. With this, print media became more and more commonplace in every level of society and was indeed used by show businesses to advertise their program. The promotion of contortion performances reinforces the aforementioned conclusion that contortionism was a profession in the 19th Century and regularly presented in the circus and vaudeville shows in the Western world. It comes as no surprise that contortion was soon discovered by the movie industry.

Colonial Exhibitions and the Golden Age of Hollywood

By 1940—the golden age of Hollywood—contortion had entered the movie industry. The era of early American film is known for frequent occurrence of exoticism and its fascination with "the other," whether it was the appropriation of ethnic groups or the exhibition of human beings with physical differences and abilities, often referred to as "freaks." In their book *Anthropology goes to the Fair*, anthropologists Nancy J. Parezo and Don D. Fowler analyze the emergence of colonial exhibitions and world fairs between 1810 and 1940 where thousands of people were exhibited in inhumane conditions:

> World's fairs began with London's Great Exhibition of the Works of Industry of All Nations (dubbed the "Crystal Palace" by *Punch* magazine) in 1851. From then until 1915 world's fairs sprang up like mushrooms to celebrate the heyday of European and American industrialism and imperialism. In Europe international exhibitions became grandiose stages on which nations bragged about their industrial, financial, technical,

intellectual, social, and scientific "progress," their ability to extract raw materials from their colonies, and their successes in "civilizing" their colonial subjects (Parezo, 2007: 107-110).

Nearly thirty-five thousand people were exhibited, and billions of visitors attended these fairs to get a glimpse of the "exotic other." Major exhibitions came to have standard features such as the display of machinery and technology, "cultural" exhibits, sculpture, painting, music, and other fine arts. Another feature was the establishment of permanent public institutions such as the Trocadero complex, which were initially funded by exposition corporation profits and given as gifts from private donors. Government funding also contributed as direct subsidies or supplemental monies to aid exposition corporations. These exposition corporations were used to amass archaeological and ethnographic collections to create a prehistoric and historic cultural heritage that supported current nationalist and colonialist ideologies. However, the main feature was the exhibition of human beings:

> "[The] feature of major expositions was extramural entertainment that included 'exotic' peoples. Fairs, held for many centuries in nearly all the world's trade centers, were mixtures of commerce, entertainment, and theater with dancers, musicians, actors, circuses, jugglers, food vendors, thieves, prostitutes, hawkers, and con artists. Similar congregations gathered at or near modern expositions and included displayed people, billed as 'savages' from Africa or Polynesia, who could be gawked at for a fee" (Parezo, 2007: 111-129).

This "fascination" with the "exotic other" evolved across entertainment mediums and a variety of societies. It was quickly adapted by the

Hollywood industry and became a profitable source for the entertainment industry. In today's age, these exploitative methods would generate a public outrage but in the 1940s it was common entertainment. Tod Browning's 1932 movie *Freaks*, to name one example, displays a human skeleton (portrayed by actor Peter Robinson), a female actor with congenital general hypertrichosis (also known as "bearded lady syndrome", portrayed by actress Jane Barnell), a microcephalic (portrayed by actress Shlitze) and a completely limbless actor (portrayed by actor Prince Randian). Despite its controversial and exploitative nature, the fascination of the wider public with the "exotic other" prevailed and did not diminish in popularity amongst mainstream Americans. It was marketable and so-called freaks were often hired for horror or comedic roles in Hollywood movies including *The Wizard of Oz* (1939) and *House of Horrors* (1946). A particularly famous contortion scene is *Solid Potato Salad* performed by the Ross sisters in the movie *Broadway Rhythm* from 1944 that was staged as comedic act. In addition to horror and comedic genres, contortion has also been perceived as erotic performance art-form with some contortion artists catering specifically to this particular image.

Eroticism and Contortion

Body flexibility has often been objectified and identified with erotic fantasies, and some female contortionists who used their skills to cater to fetish fantasies supplied the erotic niche driven by market demand—a trend which has continued through today. An erotic contortion performance is mainly created for entertainment purposes to meet the demands of the entertainment industry. An internationally well-known contortionist who specializes in erotic contortion performances is Russian born performer Julia Guenthel, better known by her stage name Zlata. She is the owner of the entertainment company *Fleximotion* in Germany and advertises paid memberships on her website, offering access to videos and pictures of female contortionists dressed up in fetish costuming and erotic poses. Other contortion professionals aim to make contortion a respected art form, and thus dislike this development for fear of being categorized as sex workers. It is evidenced, however, when looking at contorted bodies throughout history, that body flexibility has been subject to male fantasies for many centuries. In his publication *Twisted Bodies-Aspects of Female Contortionism in the Letters of a Connoisseur*, historian Karl Toepfer thoroughly examines the theory of eroticism in contortion practices and performances in the West, mainly between the 19th and 20th century. He also gives insight into historical recordings of sexual intercourse with flexible women as depicted in temple structures in India, dating back to the 13th century: "In India, Southeast Asia, and China, female contortionism has for an unknown number of centuries been associated with idealized expressions of erotic happiness. Some erotic sculptures in India explicitly represent female contortionism as sexual act, dramatizing the perception that 'since Desire permeates the entire body, contact at every point is pleasure-yielding'" (Toepfer, 1999:108). Despite this valuable source about body flexibility of the 13th century India, I challenge Toepfer's use of the term "contortionism" as it is not evidenced that the depicted woman in the wall carving from the 13th century is indeed a contortionist. The practice of yoga and kamasutra in India dates back thousands of years which leads to the possibility that the women depicted in those temple structures were kamasutra and/or yoga practitioners, equally capable of extreme body flexibility, but who train their discipline for personal and spiritual reasons instead of for public performance.

Toepfer's observations, however, give insight into the perception of male audience members and their fascination with women capable of extreme body flexibility: "It is not possible to place the feet next to the mouth without magnifying perception of the pubic zone, and of course, when the head moves very close to the genitals, the spectator observes a 'creepy' displacement of the 'proper' distance between the brain and the sex organ" (Toepfer, 1999:104). The fetishizing of body flexibility through "creepy" (as Toepher puts it) and erotically appealing movements and body positions, has changed the public perception of contortionism. Through the course of the 20th—and into the early 21st-centuries, the public's erotic perception of the art-form has allowed companies like *Fleximotion* to grow. Of course, contortionism didn't only find its way on the screen by catering to the erotic industry or by being appropriated in Hollywood movies. Contortionists have performed in a variety of capacities throughout the years, showcased for a number of reasons. With the rise of televised talent shows such as America's Got Talent, the art of contortionism experienced a new peak in popularity.

Televised Talent Shows and Social Media

In recent years, following the rise and popularity of televised talent shows and competitions, the demand for contortionists in the West has increased. In the late 20th and early 21st century, contortion was strongly associated with the circus all around the world but became very popular during the past decade of the 21st century. Online interviews on various news outlets with accomplished Western contortionists, such as Lilia Stepanova, Pixie Le Knot or Nina Burri, to name a few, have increased. They give insight into the contortionist's backgrounds, which is often in gymnastics or dance, prior to their specialization in contortion. However, these interviews reveal little, if any, information about the history or development of the artistic discipline beyond the practitioners' own experiences. Lilia Stepanova for example, is a former gymnast and reached fame through her appearance on *America's Got Talent*, Pixie Le Knot who has a background in gymnastics as well, was hired to display her contortion skills by playing an exotic prostitute with contortion skills in *Game of*

Thrones. Nina Burri has a background as professional dancer and was internationally recognized after becoming one of the finalists on the Swiss' television show *Die grössten Schweizer Talente*. In response to its growing popularity, the need for more information about contortion initiated a trend on social media where contortion practitioners share their training knowledge online.70

Content about body flexibility on social media platforms has multiplied over the past decade and aims to educate viewers through online tutorials or videos that are available to cater both the hobby and the professional contortionist. Statistics on *Google Trends*⁵ for example, show an increase in popularity for the term *contortion definition* between 2008 and 2021. Using 2008 as a baseline for reference, data shows that the term was at its ten-year high as a search term in 2016—the year contortionist Sofie Dossi became one of the finalists during that show's season—and 2017. In a second data set, using the terms *contortion* (blue) and the term *contortion poses* (red) in a comparing timeline between 2016 and 2021, one can see that many of the biggest spikes appear in and around May and September, which is when *America's Got Talent* broadcasts. April also shows an uptick, presumably as that is the month the TV show is most promoted (Google Trends, B. 2021).

With the popularity of contortionism as both a hobby and profession rapidly expanding comes the need for more information about this art-form. As more contortionists begin sharing their training and performance content online, it becomes difficult for the general audience to distinguish

70   Google Trends A, 2021, Contortion Definition. Available at: https://trends. google.com/trends/explore?q=contortion%20definition&date=2008-04-04%202021-05-04 ;
Google Trends B, 2021. Contortion & Contortion Poses (comparison). Available at: https://trends.google.com/trends/explore?cat=3&date=today%205-y&geo=US&q=-contortion,contortion%20poses

the difference between contortion and yoga – many contortionists share training videos in studios and gyms, rather than photos of them plying their craft on the stage. Both practices share the trait of physical flexibility and particularly when looking at contortion and yoga poses in pictures outside of a performance context; it is hard to determine which is which. Since it is hard to ascertain the difference between disciplines with body flexibility from the visual image only, contortion practitioners on Instagram started using the hashtag *#notyoga* to distinguish themselves from other disciplines.

The apparent interest in contortion initiated the founding of more centralized online platforms that offer video tutorials, often with a glossary for contortion students. *The Circus Dictionary*, for example, an online platform founded in the United Kingdom, has published a contortion glossary with a collection of the most important contortion postures divided into different levels of difficulty. In video tutorials, a professional contortionist performs contortion poses, with some of them unique to contortion and others used interdisciplinarily or in dance and sports genres (Circus Dictionary, 2018: A). These platforms can be particularly helpful for beginner contortion students, however, there are still widespread misconceptions about the difference between yoga and contortion.

In summary, considering the developments of contortion in the West, as contortion transformed from circus discipline to being featured in Hollywood movies and later becoming a staple in televised talent shows, this concise timeline provided a deeper understanding of the fascination with contortion and its popularity that we see today.

By addressing common misconceptions that contortion, yoga and other practices of body flexibility are one and the same, and with the emergence of the hashtag #notyoga, the demand for scholarly literature about this art-form was emphasized.

CHAPTER 1.2: DEFINITION ISSUES AND COMMON MISCONCEPTIONS ABOUT CONTORTIONISM

Contortionism is clearly a popular phenomenon. Despite its popularity as a performance art-form, however, many people still confuse contortion with yogic practices. Though they both deal with physical flexibility and range of motion, they are distinct disciplines. Yoga is a holistic practice that focuses on physical and mental well-being, while contortion is a circus discipline. Although Indian yoga practices (see comparison Figure 17 and 18) share similar movement patterns and poses with contortionism, the focus here is directed towards a holistic, spiritual, philosophical and healthful approach that balances exercises, meditation and nutrition, but

Fig. 17 (left) Yoga Pose *Ghanda Bherundasana* by Indian yoga practitioner ManinderYoga (Photo credit: With friendly permission from ManinderYoga, 2017)

Fig. 18 (right) Contortion Pose *Chest Stand* by Mongolian contortionist Urnaa Uranbileg. (Photo credit: With friendly permission from Uranbileg, 2017)

without any consideration that contortionism gives to an audience or spectators. Moreover, yoga training and contortion training differ greatly as contortionists will undergo active stretching that is executed by their coach, whereas yoga practitioners work on their poses and exercises mainly alone and without pressuring the limbs or the back into extreme positions. To give an example of yoga and contortion poses see images 17 and 18, which appear very similar in direct comparison. Both practitioners execute the so-called *chest-stand,* called *ghanda bherundasana* in yogic practice, where the feet are being placed right next to the head. The spine is bent so that the buttock is placed close to the performers head. The execution of both the *ghanda bherundasana* and the *chest-stand* are similar, but the training process and purpose are different. Physical benefits of the *ghanda bherundasana* are believed to reduce stress and activate three chakras. The *chest-stand* in contortion, depending on the cultural context that it is performed in, can have a deeper, symbolic meaning. In Chinese contortion, the circle that is ultimately depicted in the bending of the body, symbolizes perfection and is rooted deeply in Chinese philosophy (as explored in Chapter Three).

In China and Mongolia, contortion is a performance art-form that stems from folk dance and folk acrobatics and is considered "intangible cultural heritage" as it traditionally depicts labor, spirituality, the relationship between man and nature and other aspects of daily life. Yoga, on the other hand, is executed to increase physical and mental well-being. Dr. Ishwar V. Basavaraddi describes yoga as a method to create harmony between body and mind:

Yoga is essentially a spiritual discipline based on an extremely subtle science, which focuses on bringing harmony between mind and body. [...] One who experiences this oneness of

162

existence is said to be in yoga, and is termed as a yogi, having attained to a state of freedom referred to as mukti, nirvana or moksha. Thus, the aim of Yoga is Self-realization, to overcome all kinds of sufferings leading to 'the state of liberation' (Moksha) or 'freedom' (Kaivalya). Living with freedom in all walks of life, health and harmony shall be the main objectives of Yoga practice [...] Yoga is also commonly understood as a therapy or exercise system for health and fitness. While physical and mental health are natural consequences of yoga, the goal of yoga is more far-reaching. Yoga is about harmonizing oneself with the universe. It is the technology of aligning individual geometry with the cosmic, to achieve the highest level of perception and harmony (Basavaraddi: 2015).

Thus, yoga is a lifestyle and holistic exercise to increase physical and mental well-being, and differs compared to that of a contortionist whose training intensity is comparable to that of an athlete that practices extreme flexibility, "tricks," and sequences with the goal of performing on stage for an audience.

Furthermore, a yoga practitioner allows the body to become "comfortable" during the exercise and within the pose. Breathing is an important part of the holistic yoga practice. While holding the yoga position, the practitioner breathes calmly and when they feel that the muscle softens and expands, they inhale and exhale again and at the same time allow the body to go slightly deeper into the stretch. The contortion training, in contrast, aims to push the body into extreme positions that are desired for entertainment purposes (see Figures 42 and 43). Both in yoga and in contortion, maintaining a stretch through discomfort is part of the training, however, a contortionist is used to a certain level of pain to achieve extreme flexibility, as the training is more forceful, to achieve the desired results faster. As contortion is a performance art-form, the entertainment element is an important entity, and during a performance the contortionist has to execute the poses in quick succession according to the tempo of the performance music, while executing smooth transitions between the contortion poses and controlling the facial expressions. However, cultivating bodily flexibility, regardless of the intent, requires a singularly dedicated lifestyle. This applies to both yoga and contortionism.

Definition Issues in Literature

Body flexibility is an interdisciplinary concept that relates to different disciplines with a wide-ranged glossary of exercises that are applicable to a variety of performance art forms or sports. It is important, however, to distinguish between the disciplines to avoid misconceptions. In his book *Science of Flexibility* (1952), former gymnast, coach and men's gymnastics judge Michael J. Alter argues that contortionism is used in different art forms and disciplines, such as Hatha Yoga, rhythmic gymnastics, martial arts, and ballet: "Contortionism can be seen in many arts and disciplines, especially in circus and variety show acts. Hatha yoga, because it incorporates countless a*sanas,* or postures, many of which include extreme degrees of flexibility, is perhaps the best-known discipline that features 'contortionism'" (Alter, 1952:95). However, based on my research and lived understanding, as well as the prior discussions of language, history, and practice, I find this definition lacking. It reduces *contortionism* solely to its aesthetic value rather than acknowledging it as a discipline that is lived. It is therefore imperative to distinguish between the performing arts discipline of contortionism and the simple cultivation of body flexibility: The first, *contortionism,* is a profession and autonomous art form, and the latter, *flexibility,* is a technical *ability* of many sport and art forms such as martial arts, ballet, rhythmic gymnastics, pole dance and more. I argue that contortionism is a profession with a complex variety of theories that should not be confused with other professions, sports, or art forms. Alter's examples relate to extreme body flexibility that is *applied* to different disciplines. I further contend that extreme body flexibility does not automatically identify someone as a contortionist. Contortionists are defined by the showcasing of their abilities. The contortionist is steeped in a training practice, and oftentimes within a distinct cultural context and artistic framework that allows them to use their flexibility to create choreographies and build a self-contained act. A contortion act has very specific aspects that make it unique, despite its feature of presenting body flexibility, for example in the succession of poses, the transitions between postures, even the tempo in which certain tricks are presented. It is, therefore, rather misplaced and confusing to describe something as "contortion" when it is a remark about "flexibility". This example displays the necessity for more education regarding this art form, especially since the art of contortionism has gained new popularity worldwide through televised talent shows.

Despite the aforementioned conflation between disciplines, some poses are unique to contortionism. A world-renowned and exclusive contortion trick, for example, is the Marinelli bend, named after H.B. Marinelli (1864-1924), who was a male contortionist of Italian descent who grew up in Germany. He performed internationally under his stage name "The Boneless Wonder." The Marinelli bend is considered as one of the most extreme and difficult contortion tricks. It is performed only by professional, experienced contortionists and is executed by using a short metal cane that is anchored on stage with a mouth grip/bit on one end. The contortionist bends backwards to bite into the mouth grip, then lifting both hands and feet off the floor. The entire body weight is now resting only on the upper jaw and folded spine of the performing artist. It is presented as a highlight in contortion performances and is usually executed during a solo act. However, only one person in history, female contortionist Wang Xiaoqian from China, was able to perform a triple Marinelli bend between the years 2004 and 2009. On top of her own body weight, she was able to balance two more contortionists with only the strength of her upper jaw. The two flyers performed handstands on top of her body while holding onto her hip bones.[71] Some have asserted that she stopped performing after suffering a fatigue break of her waist due to heavy pressure, though there is no information available to confirm or deny the rumor.

Chapter Two will further explore the historical context that has led to the extreme performance levels and training methods in Chinese circus that we see today. Extensive international research is needed to collect sufficient data to illuminate the art of contortion and its history in different countries, eras, and contexts. However, the authors' research, while studying contortion in Mongolia and China, revealed that although the traditions of contortion were passed on through practice from one generation to the next, the cultural understanding of what the essence of contortion is varies from country to country. Across these cultures, contortion is nowadays understood to be a form of performance art or entertainment. However, the perception of contortion, its origins, and its performance contexts remain very diverse. With this mixture of information, as explored throughout Chapter One, it is a difficult task to verify the authenticity of each source of knowledge in defining the notion of contortion in a variety of contexts.

---

71   Triple Marinelli performance" Wang Xiaoqian's triple Marinelli bend at Chinese Henan TV channel": https://www.youtube.com/watch?v=mrc103vjWeA&ab_channel=Marinellibend (by Marinelli bend)

When identifying the theory of contortion in a historical context, it is clear that it underwent numerous transformations in past centuries. The available evidence reinforces that contortion is a folk art that stemmed from practices of body flexibility in different cultures and that was later adapted, stylized, and commodified into a circus discipline. I therefore argue, that contortionism is an autonomous performance art form and movement pattern, that has been executed in various cultures, societies, and political contexts. Questions regarding the origins of contortion and acrobatic performance tradition anchored in Chinese performance history are still relevant, together with numerous hypotheses about its evolution in East Asia, which needs clarification. Each country mentioned in this chapter has inherited its own contortion culture, tradition, and society, and as a result the function and theories of contortionism vary tremendously from region to region. Body flexibility was representative in ritual practices such as the temple dance in ancient Egypt, as comedic acts in Hollywood movies, as part of vaudeville, circus and freak shows, and as an object onto which to project erotic fantasies. The complexity of contortionism seems to have evolved even in recent years as a result of the influence of TV and social media platforms. Therefore, traditional institutions with a long history in contortion practices, such as the *Beijing International Art School*, have to adapt to meet the needs of this fast-paced industry.

CHAPTER 2: GENESIS AND DEVELOPMENT OF CONTORTIONISM IN CHINA

Chinese acrobatic theatre dates back over 2000 years, to at least the Qin Dynasty (221-206 BC). This dynasty marked the beginning of the Chinese Empire, and it is where we find the first records of acrobatic performances. Depicted in wall carvings and mural paintings, acrobats have been found in numerous tombs. Writer, editor, and scholar of the history of Chinese acrobatics Fu Qifeng discusses the genesis and developments of Chinese acrobatics in her book *Chinese Acrobatics through the Ages.* Fu Qifeng's family has pursued magic and acrobatics as a profession for three generations. She has been with the *China Acrobatic Troupe* of Beijing as a performer, coach, and researcher, and she is currently the Deputy Director of the *Chinese Institute of Acrobatics Theory* and is a member of the *China Association of Magicians.* It should be mentioned, however, that her publication *Chinese Acrobatics through the Ages* offered only a few references to support her findings. This leads one to the assumption that the data presented is based on oral history that was passed on from one generation to the next, the same way acrobatic skills were passed on. Nonetheless, the display of artifacts from various tombs of ancient China that she presents in her literature as material evidence underpin her research. Fu Qifeng's book includes various images of material evidence in form of tomb artifacts, wall carvings, and paintings that depict the rich history of Chinese acrobatics. Here, we can see that folk arts such as dance and acrobatics were often performed alongside musicians, singers, actors and other art forms. Her catalog offers images of body flexibility performed next to other performative acts at small venues and large-scale events.

Fu Qifeng analyses the genesis and developments of Chinese acrobatics as follows:

> World-famous for its distinctive national style and superb skills, Chinese acrobatics is one of the world's earliest performing arts making use of gymnastic skills. We may trace its history back to primitive society. Counting from the time when it gradually became a fairly integrated performing art, it has a history of more than 2,000 years. During this long period, it has gone through many vicissitudes and has been persecuted by the feudal ruling class on many occasions. But, taking root in the fertile soil of the people, it has consistently retained its vitality handed down from generation to generation. Several thousand years ago, the forefathers of the Chinese nation, inhabitants of the Yellow River Valley, created the acrobatic arts, drawing examples from labour, fighting, religious sacrifice and other aspects of daily life. In feudal society, Chinese acrobatics traversed a course from the commoners to the court and back to the commoners (Fu, 1985: Preface).

During the Han Dynasty, the acrobatic performances that consisted of simple skills developed to an extraordinarily high level of artistry with a varied repertoire that included pole balancing, plate spinning, and tumbling.

Throughout her book, Fu Qifeng does not use the terms *body flexibility* or *contortion* but instead the terms *calisthenics* and *backward waist-bending calisthenics* to describe performances of body flexibility and contortion. This includes performances nowadays known as *Rolling Cups* or *Rolling with Cups* which are distinctly contortion performances. This might be due to the fact that in 1985, the publishing year of the book, different terminology was used as the book was translated from Chinese into English. In her book, the contortion act *Rolling Cups* is called "calisthenics performance *Rolling with a Cup of Water*" (Fu, 1985: 123). Fu Qifeng's research provides an important opportunity to advance the understanding of the development of contortion in ancient China, as numerous artifacts depict physical flexibility. The observer can identify how body flexibility can be performed as its own discipline or married with another discipline, such as while balanced on a pole or in the context of a hand-balancing performance. A prominent example is the 2000 years old artifact, a tray with clay figurines, from the Han dynasty that was unearthed in Jinan of the Shandong province, and that is depicted on the front cover of Fu Qifeng's book (Figure 19):

People in the Han Dynasty were very fond of recreation so there were often performances of the "Hundred Entertainments[72]" at festivals and celebrations. At banquets and gatherings, the families of nobles and wealthy people also frequently used performances presented by musicians, dancers and actors to entertain guests. Two-thousand-year-old pottery figurines of musicians, dancers and acrobats [...] unearthed on Jinan's

72   The Han Dynasty consisted of two dynasties in Chinese history: The Western Han Dynasty (present-day Xi'an in Shanxi Province) and the Eastern Han Dynasty (present-day Henan Province). As acrobatics flowered in both the Western and Eastern Han dynasties, they were called the "Hundred Entertainments" of the Han Dynasty (Fu, 1985: 13).

outskirts in Shandong Province depict in a concise and vivid manner the folk acrobatic performances of the Western Han Dynasty. Fourteen acrobats are shown in a performance of the most essential acrobatic skills such as handstands and backwards waist bending in calisthenics (Fu, 1985: 14)

Fig. 19 Clay figurines on a tray: Music, dancing and acrobatic figurines from the Western Han Dynasty, unearthed from a Han tomb, Jinan, Shandong Province. Photo credit: Yargai Galtat.

A very detailed analysis about each figurine and discipline of this scene is provided by the Jinan City Museum. In an animated video, the figurines are brought to live and are discussed in great detail.[73] Here, a group of four acrobats, two of them performing handstands while bending their hips and legs forward and two of them performing contortion. They are presented in the video from multiple angles, and their movements,

---

73   Jinan City Museum, animated video: https://www.bilibili.com/video/av200935105/

purpose and functions are analyzed by the scholars of the museum in an attempt to explain why these art-forms were so popular during that time (translation from Chinese to English by Yargai Galtat):

> The four acrobats are all male. Two of them are wearing a pointy hat and they are executing a trick called NaDaDing, which is a basic skill in the handstand discipline, presenting strength and stealth and a strong posture. They are walking on hands with the head facing down, but still able to see the world. At that time this was a new skill and ordinary people were in awe and astonishment of witnessing such artistry. The handstand represented a new point of view at the world for the ordinary people. Handstand was symbolic for changing/turning the body upside down and it presented the possibility to change the mind as well (Jinan City Museum, 8:31).

> The other two acrobats are displaying contortion, a practice of extreme body flexibility, presenting a human's physical ability of extreme body shapes. One acrobat appears to either shape his body into a bow in order to shoot a very strong arrow, or another possibility would be that the contortionist is trying to create a shape with his body similar to that of a jade bracelet [called Yu Huan] meant to be given to a lover to hold them forever (Jinan City Museum, 9:26).

Scholars of the Jinan City Museum provide with their analysis an exciting opportunity to advance our knowledge of the aesthetics and functions of acrobatics as well as of contortion in ancient China. The reference to a circular shape, in this case the jade bracelet, gives insight into the aesthetic aspects of contortion performances and possible symbolism in Chinese contortionism and suggest a deeper meaning of the movement repertoire (Figure 20).

Fig. 20 Clay Figurine from figurine tray *Contortionist*: Music, dancing and acrobatic figurines from the Western Han Dynasty, unearthed from a Han tomb, Jinan, Shandong Province. Photo credit: Yargai Galtat.

In addition to the artifacts presented in Fu Qifeng's literature, the depiction of body flexibility can also be identified in numerous other artifacts:

The *Stone relief Hundred Entertainments* depicts a juggler (right), a Dancer performing the *Qipanwu* "Seven Plates Dance" (center), and an artist performing a contortion-like trick while balancing on stacked benches (left). The relief is from Szechuan, China and originates in the Qin or Han dynasty. (Figure 21)

Fig. 21 Stone relief with "Hundred Entertainments" depicting a juggler (right), a dancer Qipanwu - Seven Plates Dance (center) and an artist performing a contortion-like trick while balancing on stacked benches (right). Relief from Szechuan, China. Han or Qing dynasty. Photograph: Courtesy of Prof. Arthur Lewbel.

Fig. 22 *Figurines of Entertainers.* Han Dynasty (206 BCE–220 CE). Front and center, acrobat in contortion-like posture. Henan Provincial Museum, Zhengzhou Ceramic tomb figurines of jugglers, dancers, acrobats, and musicians provided entertainment for the afterlife, and allow today's viewer to imagine scenes of everyday enjoyment in the world of the Han. Photo credit: G41rn8. Available at: https://commons.wikimedia.org/wiki/File:China_2006_8-70.jpg

The *Figurines of Entertainers* from the Han Dynasty (206 BCE–220 CE) are arranged around an acrobat (front and center) in a contortion-like posture. The ceramic tomb figurines of jugglers, dancers, acrobats and musicians were believed to provide entertainment for the afterlife, and allow today's viewer to imagine scenes of everyday enjoyment in the world of the Han. (Figure 22)

The *Han Pottery Acrobats* (Han Dynasty 206 BCE–220 CE) present in the front left corner an acrobat executing a handstand while bending the hips and legs forward. (Figure 23)

Fig. 23 Han Pottery Acrobats. Han Dynasty (206 BCE–220 CE). Left and front: Acrobat executing a handstand while bending the legs forward. Han Gallery, Henan Provincial Museum, Zhengzhou. Photo credit: Gary Todd. Available at: https://commons.wikimedia.org/wiki/File:Han_Pottery_Acrobats_(10340375955).jpg

The *Stone Brick displaying Acrobats* from the Han dynasty shows an acrobat in contortion-like posture while balancing on stacked tables/ benches. (Figure 24)

Fig. 24 Stone Brick displaying Acrobats. Second from left: Acrobat in contortion-like posture balancing on stacked tables/benches. Eastern Han Stone Tomb Brick 21. Nanyang Museum of Han Dynasty Stone Carving, Henan Province, China. Photo credit: Gary Todd. Available at: https://commons.wikimedia.org/wiki/File:Eastern_Han_Stone_Tomb_Brick_21.jpg

Fig. 25 Body Flexibility on Pole. *Acrobats. Northern Wei. Datong City Museum.* Image description: File: Datong 247. In this lively painted-pottery composition, two children spin and balance on a pole that is supported by a strongman on his forehead. To the left, another member of the troupe bangs a pair of cymbals. Such performances are documented as early as the Eastern Han Dynasty, for example in tomb bricks from Henan. Photo credit: G41rn8. Available at: https://commons. wikimedia.org/wiki/File:Datong_247.jpg

The figurines that depict body flexibility on the pole from the Han dynasty, show two children spin and balance on a pole that is supported on the forehead of a strongman. (Figure 25)

It is apparent from this substantial amount of material evidence that the practice of physical flexibility was a staple in acrobatic performances already in ancient China. The vivid imagery evidenced in the figurines and reliefs provides the observer with an intimate glimpse into ancient Chinese society and its world of entertainment.

Categorization of Contortion in China

As these artifacts presenting body flexibility are dated to the Qing and Han dynasty, another source, Chinese cultural encyclopedia *WapBaiKe*, asserts that the history of contortionism in China dates back even further than the Qin and Han dynasties to around 771 BC (around 450 years prior to Qin and Han dynasty), the Spring and Autumn and Warring States period:

> Contortion, known as *Body Art beyond the Limits,* is a unique art form that was formed in the Spring and Autumn period [770-ca. 475 BCE] and the Warring State period [ca. 475-221 BCE]. It developed during the Sui Dynasty [581-618 CE] and entered the court during the Tang Dynasty [618-906 CE]. Unlike general acrobatics that aimed to appear of high difficulty, contortion was designed to engage with human emotions and to let the human body appear limitless and the movements effortless. The murals of the ancient tomb of Liaoyang Bartaizi depict a girl performing a backbend on a black lacquered type of wooden platform. The little acrobat stands on the side of the small table, leaning back, her hands flipping backwards, and supporting her hands on the small table, creating the form of the backbend. When China became the *Peoples Republic of China*, first premier Zhou Enlai officially renamed contortion from *Body Art beyond the Limits* to *Rou Shu* and categorized contortion within the traditional acrobatic family (Wapbaike, 2018).

The accuracy of the article cannot currently be validated as the author is not located in China to confirm and compare the data with local literature. It could be argued that it draws on an idealized image of the history of contortion and, therefore, further research would be needed to confirm this statement. The text however, if proven to be accurate, could reveal important details regarding the history of contortion, its genesis and development in ancient China. It informs us about the early aims of the training methods, the desired image, and aesthetics of contortionism, as well as the distinction between contortionism and other acrobatic acts. The question remains to what extend the development of contortionism considers aspects of daily life and human emotions, for example, in choreographies or particular movements that would have depicted ancient myths or legends. Further research could aim to illuminate a linkage between ancient practices by examining evidence of these notions in current practice.

The text furthermore labels contortion as unique and identifies it therefore as an exclusive art form since its establishment, while the categorization of contortionism in the text further reveals how it was perceived in ancient China. Based on this information it appears that contortionism, first referred to as *Body Art beyond the Limits* in ancient China, was categorized as an art form and had somewhat of an autonomous position compared to other acrobatic acts, by distinguishing it as its own performing art. It was only after it was renamed by Zhou Enlai to Rou Shu during the founding of the People's Republic of China in 1949 that it was categorized along with acrobatics.

An artifact of significant importance is the礼仪之邦 *State of Etiquette* relief made of gray pottery portrait-tiles with acrobatic patterns, which is currently on display in the *Quzhou Museum*. In an article of the *Yudon*

Observation about the exhibition of artifacts at the *Quzhou Museum,* the relief is described as followed:

> The front is decorated with 14 vivid and lifelike acrobats, who could be ethnic or foreign artists; the edges are decorated with dragon, phoenix, tiger, and hunting patterns. There are four characters in the middle part of the upper side of the frame of the portrait bricks, such as carriages and horses. Local folklore, cultural and historical experts believe that this "State of Etiquette" relic with acrobatics from the Han Dynasty not only has unique significance in the history of art, but is also useful for studying the social and economic life, rules and regulations, customs, and artistic ideas of the Han Dynasty (Yudon Observation, 2020).

In addition to this description, this relief shows the acrobatic disciplines divided, and each artistic discipline has been assigned its own space as if they were categorized. Jugglers, acrobats, and musicians are depicted in 14 squares alongside each other. On the top row, in the square fourth from the left, an acrobat performs a chest-stand and looks at the audience through his legs. This particular pose is the same as depicted on the tray of clay figurines from the Jinan-Shandong province and it indicates that the performer here is a contortionist. The particular separation of each artistic discipline in this artifact leads to the theory that contortion indeed has been an autonomous art form already during the Han dynasty. The depiction further suggests that body flexibility was not only utilized in other disciplines, but performed as an autonomous specialty (Figure 26) and that the disciplines *theatre, music, dance* and *acrobatics,* as they are often depicted at venues together, are of equal value.

Fig. 26 The rare relief from the Han Dynasty *State of Etiquette* made of 14 pottery portrait-tiles depicts various acrobatic disciplines and is currently exhibited in the Quzhou Museum (2021). Photo credit: Thom Wall.

An archaeological study that focuses on folk and spiritual dance and its functions and theories in ancient China, provides a similar theory by examining artifacts found in tombs from the Han dynasty. Archaeologist Marta Zuchowska from the Faculty of Archaeology at the University of Warsaw analyses in her chapter *Dancers' Representations and the Function of Dance in Han Dynasty (202 BC – 220 AD) Chinese Society* some of the same motifs in Han dynasty funerary reliefs as Fu Qifeng in her book *Chinese Acrobatics through the Ages*. Dancers and acrobats were oftentimes depicted performing alongside one another in life on funerary reliefs. Here, she analyses the *Qipanwu - Seven Plates Dance* (see figure 21) depicted in a relief from Peng county, Sichuan province from the Han dynasty, and a relief from Beizhai:

> Generally, the line between dance, acrobatics and martial arts during the Han dynasty was blurred. For example, the qipan dance is usually represented as part of a group, along with performing flying swords artists and jugglers. All activities represented on the Beizhai relief are included, in Chinese

nomenclature, under the common term of baixi, which is usually translated as 'acrobatics'. Even if represented in a funerary context, they seem to be entertainment rather than ritual or ceremony. In fact, it looks like most of the performing arts developed from old forms of ritual dances, but we rarely find dancers in ceremonial contexts represented in Han dynasty iconography (Zuchowska, 2014: 71).

The funerary reliefs depict how different art forms were arranged in various settings, indicating their significance in society, but as Zuchowska pointed out, their functions in ritual and spiritual context needs further investigation. An interesting aspect of future research could be how body flexibility and contortion were deployed in ancient Chinese ritualistic and ceremonial practice.

In her chapter *Constantly Improving Skills*, Fu Qifeng describes how contortion (Fu's *calisthenics*), evolved from the traditional Chinese skills of soft-intrinsic exercises by referencing a stone carving from the Han dynasty in Anqui, Shandong province: "Relying on her skill in using her waist and legs, a performer can bend her body into the shape of a ball or ring. She can also do handstands on a flower-shaped stage prop and bend her body into three twists as if her bones were soft as cotton. These acts are evolved from the traditional Chinese skills of soft-intrinsic exercises" (Fu, 1985: 114). The relic described here depicts multiple contortionists performing backbends, with three of them on top of a high pole that is constructed like a stage that can be lifted up high in the air, balanced by only one performer. The "pole-stage" elevates the contortionists high above ground. These particular details of "bending the body into the shape of a ball or ring and into three twists" while executed on a high pole, provides information about how advanced and complex the performances and the training were at that time. The scene depicted in the relief takes place in a large square, possibly a market square, and the contortionists are surrounded by other acrobats who present their tricks at the same time. Elevating the contortionists on a pole could be evidence that this performance was something to be seen by a large crowd of people.

There is abundant room for further progress in determining how these performance art-forms developed and transformed through the ages, from representation of daily life aspects to court entertainment to spiritual practice.

Silk Road

To further explore the development of ancient Chinese acrobatics, it is important to discuss the country's early trade routes. The Chinese art sector developed greatly thanks to the Silk Road (114BCE – 1450CE), which connected China with the West. The Silk Road was a network of multiple ancient trade routes that encompassed land routes and sea routes connecting multiple locations from East Asia, South Asia, Persia, East Africa, the Near East and Southern Europe. It established foreign trading which subsequently led to cultural and remarkable artistic exchange, as described by Fu Qifeng:

> During the rule of the emperor Wu, named Liu Che, (140-87 B.C.) economy thrived, the country became a mighty power, people lived in peace and stability, and civilization flourished. The emperor used diplomacy and military force to expand his territory. He sent Zhang Qian as and envoy to the Western regions (a general reference in the Han Dynasty to areas beyond present day Yumen pass in in Gansu province) to promote cultural exchange and enhance the friendship between the

people of China and the people in Central Asia. With this exchange, Chinese acrobatic art also made great progress and flowered. [...] During his rule, he [emperor Wu] established *Yue Fu* – the office in charge of music – and ordered the performance of "Hundred Entertainments". He sent Zhang Qian as an envoy to the Western regions and opened the famous "Silk Road". He promoted economic and cultural exchange between the East and the West, and used acrobatics as a form of diplomacy to meet the needs of certain political conditions (Fu, 1985: 13 and 16).

Circus historian Dominique Jando further summarized the development and the impact of foreign influence on Chinese acrobatics and analyzed some of the characteristics of the Chinese acrobatic theatre:

Over several millennia, its peoples have created many forms of performing arts, each of them characterized by a host of schools and styles. They have followed, for centuries, a linear evolution aimed towards the extreme refinement of the skills involved in a particular art form. Although China started contacts with non-Asian countries more than two thousand years ago, foreign influences were absorbed and rendered with a Chinese flavour for the sole benefit of that evolution. In this peculiarity lies the most important difference between Chinese and Western cultural traditions: The latter is more organic and open to new components, while the Chinese tradition aims towards the perfection of already known elements, and the integration of new elements into an existing mould (Circopedia, 2018).

Jando's statement aligns with the earlier statement about the ambition to reach flawless excellence – the record-breaking triple Marinelli bend, for example. This search for perfection was apparent as well in the classroom of the *Beijing International Art School*, as the author could observe first-hand during her training in China. At the heart of many Chinese performing arts is the aim of setting benchmarks on the international stage through technical perfection, extreme discipline, and strong aesthetics.

Cultural Revolution and the Reformation of the Acrobatics Sector

After the founding of New China in 1949, the acrobatics sector experienced great changes under Mao Zedong's rule, and new policies were established to enforce a reformation so that acrobatic acts could be utilized for the political agenda of the People's Republic of China (PRC):

> Chinese acrobatic arts have been marked by vicissitudes for over 2000 years, gradually changing form court entertainments into itinerant shows. [...] A lot of feudal superstition, vulgarity, cruelty and horror have been mixed into an abundantly artistic acrobatic heritage. In the early 1950s Premier Zhou Enlai said: "Acrobatics should give people an aesthetic appreciation and pleasant sensation. Neither deformity nor excessive stimulus should be used to attract the audience" (Fu, 1985: 105).

In an effort to reform the acrobatics sector, certain performances that were considered harmful to the mental and physical health of the performer and unworthy to represent China, were banned. Performances that displayed "deformity or excessive stimulus" such as "Eating an Electric Light Bulb", "Swallowing Five Poisonous Creatures" (scorpion, viper, centipede, house lizard and toad), "Dwarf's Comic Acts" (where a person's physical defects were exploited to attract spectators), "Swallowing a Sword" and many more, were prohibited. Instead, acts that were considered fine traditional presentations were improved: "Jumping through Hoops on the Ground", Handstands on a Pyramid of Chairs", "Juggling with the Hands", and "Cycling" among others (Fu, 1985: 105). However, these were only the first steps that were taken. After the founding of New China, the policies "Let a Hundred Flowers Blossom and Weed through the Old to bring forth the New" and "Make the Past serve the Present and Foreign Things serve China" were introduced by the Party Central Committee to make significant changes in the acrobatics sector. A performance with *fine traditional* acrobatic acts was planned to be presented to the leaders of the Chinese government:

> In October 1950 outstanding acrobats from Shanghai, Tianjin, Beijing, Wuhan and Shenyang presented a performance in the Huairen Hall in Zhongnanhai, Beijing – the political centre of New China. [...] This was the first acrobatic performance in New China and also the first step Chinese acrobatic arts had taken in weeding through the old to bring forth the new. The items presented were wholesome, possessing simplicity and grace, and richly tinged with national characteristics. They reflected the Chinese people's new mental outlook. The late chairman Mao Zedong [...] and other party and government leaders attended this performance and gave it high praise and encouragement. They decided that these acrobats should form a troupe as a cultural delegation of New China to tour European countries (Fu, 1985: 99).

In 1950, shortly after the *First National Congress of Writers and Artists*, the *Ministry of Culture of the Central People's Government* set about establishing an acrobatic troupe to prepare organizationally for the revival of the traditional acrobatic arts. The late Premier Zhou Enlai summoned competent functionaries on art work and administration to engage in preparations for this task. He personally attended to the selection of the acrobatic acts as well as to the ideological style, previous artistic training, and living conditions of the performers, and certain policies were established to secure his agenda and ideologies (Fu, 1985: 98). The policy "Let a Hundred Flowers Blossom and weed through the Old to bring forth the New" was established to transform and develop theatrical art including traditional circus.[74] Due to the reformation of Chinese traditional circus under the policy "Let a Hundred Flowers Blossom and weed through the Old to bring forth the New" contortionism, based on its attributes, was categorized within the acrobatic family and enjoyed a countrywide revival. The policy brought about a spectacular renaissance of the old acrobatic theatre; acrobatic troupes were created in each province and every major city, and were given their own theaters. The teaching was (and still is) done within the troupe, with experienced performers training the new generation (Circopedia, 2018). As part of this new policy, first Premier Zhou Enlai then renamed the art of contortionism from Body Art beyond the Limits to Rou Shu, with Rou standing for "soft" and "flexible" and Shu standing for "technique". (Figure 27)

柔 Rou = soft/flexible 术 Shu = technique 软功=soft work > Rou Shu (Contortionism)

Fig. 27 Illustration of Chinese Characters for Rou Shu. Photo credit: Mariam Ala-Rashi

---

74   The sentence *Let a hundred flowers blossom and weed through the old to bring forth the new (bai hua qi fang tui chen chu xin)* was written by Mao in 1942 for the founding of the Yan'an Institute of Beijing Opera (Ban, 2010:221).

The strategy to utilize acrobatics to demonstrate China's power, strength, and prowess in international diplomacy stems from Mao Zedong's ideology. The Cultural Revolution (1966-1976), a brutal sociopolitical movement to preserve Maoism initiated by Mao Zedong, signaled his return to a seat of power after a less extremist period. This violent movement purged opponents that did not agree with his ideologies and aimed to preserve Chinese communism by eliminating capitalist and traditional theorists. The article *Power of Symbolism: The Swim that changed Chinese History* by James Carter reflects on Mao's Cultural Revolution. In a public demonstration to prove his physical strength, Mao Zedong swam in the Yangtze river to set the stage for the launch of the *Great Proletarian Cultural Revolution*:

> The point of Mao's swim was to demonstrate his physical prowess and good health, defying rumors that his age and time out of the spotlight suggested he was anything less than a capable leader. The emphasis on physical fitness had deep roots. One of his very first pieces of public writing was "*A study of physical education*" an essay in the celebrated magazine *New Youth*, published in 1917. Written long before the Cultural Revolution or the People's Republic — several years before even the founding of the Communist Party — Mao revealed the link between the physical and the intellectual that would guide his actions. "Because man is an animal," he wrote, "movement is most important for him. And because he is a rational animal, his movements must have a reason." Throughout his life, these principles applied: Mao valued action above all, and those actions were always based on a principle. More often than not, the principle was what he deemed to be strengthening China (Carter, 2021)

Moreover, this development of competitive practice can be found in examples of the aesthetics, training methods, and the political context of the educational art institutions, such as the *Beijing International Art School*. The expansion of art departments within larger circus schools increased, especially since the founding of the largest theatrical company in the world *Cirque du Soleil* in 1984. *Cirque du Soleil* is part of the new generation circus of the late 20th century, also known as *cirque nouveau* or *cirque contemporain,* and conveys traditional circus skills with a theme or a story instead of just tricks for the sake of spectacle. In her article *From China to the Big Top: Chinese Acrobats and the Politics of Aesthetic Labor, 1950–2010,* scholar of media and film at the Queens University, Canada, Tracy Ying Zhang estimates that between 1987 and the 2000s various entertainment companies brought more than a thousand Chinese acrobats to North America:

> The incorporation of acrobatics from the PRC into North American entertainment began in the mid-1980s. Since then, Chinese acrobats have performed in diverse venues, including circus tents, theaters, arenas, theme parks, high-end nightclubs, and cabarets. Founded in 1984, the Cirque, currently the largest North American circus company, and one of the main employers of circus artists, started to hire Chinese acrobats around 1987. A news article in The Globe and Mail (2010) states that twenty percent of Cirque's 1,500 performers worldwide are Chinese (Zhang, 2016:41).

Despite its seemingly late emergence into the West, the staples of Chinese acrobatics have remained the same for centuries. However, Chinese circus and acrobatic theater started incorporating other performative genres, such as dancing, singing and acting which became increasingly important elements, in response to the demands of the late 20th and early 21st century entertainment markets. Chinese classical dance and Chinese acrobatic theatre are both categorized as traditional art forms and taught at large art institutions and state supported schools such as the *China Wuqiao International Acrobatic Art School,* the *Shanghai Circus School* and the *Beijing International Art school.* Both the *China Wuqiao International Acrobatic Art School* and the *Beijing International Art School are* of the very few acrobatic institutions that offer student visas for international students, as they are supported by the Chinese government.

The *Beijing International Art School* (BJIAS), offers full-time education in Chinese classical dance and circus students are obliged to take part in the dance classes at least twice per week on Wednesdays and Saturdays. As the largest employer of acrobats in the world, *Cirque du Soleil* has influenced circus productions worldwide, and Chinese circus performers are trained in dance as an addition to their acrobatic practices. Leading circus schools in China therefore often administer a dance department to maintain a competitive variety in their show program. Since then, the emphasis on musicality for performing acrobats has gained importance. Music in traditional circus shows was primarily to create an atmosphere in the background, and acrobatic routines were not tightly coordinated to match the rhythm. It was, and still is often, part of a traditional circus routine to pause after a very difficult trick to give the audience time to show their appreciation to the artist through applause. Especially in Western traditional circus, to name one example, the live orchestra often interrupted the music to herald highlights of a performance with a drum roll. In the early 2000s, transitions between tricks and musicality seemed to be of lesser importance than the physical skills they demonstrated, and acrobats often simply walked from one spot to the other to mentally prepare for the next trick. In the years that followed, however, presumably through the influence of the media and the development of contemporary circus which raised the benchmark internationally, circus acts were choreographed with musicality in mind, instead of simply focusing on the tricks themselves. The transitions between movements have become of equal importance. By educating its acrobats in musicality and dancing, the Chinese circus successfully catered to the global entertainment market's demands while staying true to the roots of Chinese circus training by offering a well-rounded performance program in both the traditional and contemporary categories.

In conclusion, this chapter illuminated the genesis of Chinese circus and how it is rooted in labor, fighting, religious sacrifice, and other aspects of daily life around 2000 years ago and explored the connection to the simultaneous development of contortionism during that time. Artifacts from various tombs of different eras demonstrated the significance of acrobatics, and contortion in particular, in ancient Chinese society. Tracing the timeline from ancient China all the way to the founding of the People's Republic of China in 1949, considering the influence of the Silk Road and the recategorization of contortion during the Cultural Revolution, allows us to understand current developments in the Chinese acrobatics sector. Setting new benchmarks on an international level through aesthetics of extreme discipline and technical perfection is at the heart of the evolution of Chinese circus and dates back, without doubt, to the era of international expansion of the Silk Road. Through the remarkable evolution of Chinese traditional circus as a result of international cultural exchange, the influence of the cirque nouveau and the intertwining of other art forms such as dance, Chinese circus became a recognizable export in circuses and theaters around the world.

CHAPTER 3: AESTHETICS AND PERFORMANCE ANALYSIS

This chapter analyses the aesthetics of extreme discipline during a traditional Chinese contortion routine that includes the use of glass chandeliers as props, called *Rolling Cups,* to heighten the level of difficulty (Video: Cb3815, 2007). It is a remarkably challenging performance unique to Chinese contortion (see examples from various Chinese acrobatics troupes: Figures 28, 29, 30). One of the most important elements in Chinese contortion is the circle. It is not only reflected in the movements of a contortion performance where the artist is creating circle-like shapes with the body to showcase extreme flexibility. The meaning of the circle is deeply rooted in Chinese philosophy and illustrates the aim for perfection in crafts, painting and calligraphy, music and theatre, including contortion. The aesthetics in Chinese contortion in particular revolve around the shape of the circle that is not only reflected in deep backbends and circle shaped movements, but also in smooth transitions between poses and the use of intricate props to heighten the level of difficulty. All in the effort to create the perfect contortion performance. In her chapter *Rolling with Cups and the Chinese Tradition of the Circle* of her book *A Primer of Chinese Acrobatics* (2003), Fu Qifeng provides details to symbolism in Chinese contortion performances and a definition of the movement repertoire:

Fig. 28 Troupe de Fujian, China, performing the contortion act "Rolling Cups" for the 16th Festival Mondial du Cirque de Demain, 1993. Photographer: Bertrand Guay. "Festival Mondial du Cirque de Demain-Paris". Courtesy and Copyrights: Association Française pour le Cirque de Demain. Available at: https://www.cirquededemain.paris/en/medias/galleries/gallery/16

Fig. 29 Dai Wenxia from China performing the contortion act "Rolling Cups" for the 5th Festival Mondial du Cirque de Demain, 1981. Photographer: Paul de Cordon. "Festival Mondial du Cirque de Demain-Paris". Courtesy and Copyrights: Association Française pour le Cirque de Demain. Available at: https://www.cirquededemain.paris/en/medias/galleries/gallery/5

Fig. 30 Shanghai Acrobat performing "Rolling Cups" Contortion Act. *Contortionist Shanghai Acrobatic Troupe.* Available at: https://commons.wikimedia.org/wiki/File:ContorsionistShanghai.jpg

Rolling with Cups is a highly popular traditional Chinese acrobatic act. Atop a small round platform, the acrobat, in most cases a woman, balances towers of glass cups on the limbs, forehead, and mouth while fluidly moving through a series of graceful postures and contortions. Most impressive is when the performer arches into a constantly revolving circular backbend, the crystalline towers of cups remaining perfectly balanced through every changing angle and motion. Another stunt of this type is *Rolling with Lights,* identical to *Rolling with Cups* except that the cups hold lit candles. *Rolling with Cups* has its origin in ancient sacrificial ceremonies in which priests manipulated ritual objects in various patterns to invoke the deities. Gradually, these rites came to be used to entertain the people rather than to entreat the gods, and a number of ritual movements and gestures evolved into acrobatic stunts. Each type of Chinese acrobatic act relies on specific basic movements. Fundamental to *Rolling with Cups* is contorting the body into a circular form (Fu, 2003: 29).

This analysis of the *Rolling Cups* routine, and the examination of the meaning of the circle, explore the difficulty of the movements and tricks that are used during the performance. It illuminates the level of endeavor and discipline that goes into a routine, which aims to appear smooth, easy, and effortless. Furthermore, this analysis will examine the facility of the performers' body and the function of the performance, for which this level of discipline is needed to create the desired image. The performance analysis will further demonstrate that one of the targets of Chinese training methods, as aforementioned in Chapter Two, is the desire to consistently set new benchmarks in order to be at the top of the performance industry. Particularly in the context of Cold War China, performing arts, served the purpose of illustrating notions of socialist culture and to create a collective sense of Chinese national identity and to demonstrate the efficiency of a socialist production system (Zhang, 2016:408). The *Rolling Cups* performance unmistakably embodies these ideologies.

The *Rolling Cups* routine involves two contortionists who balance and manipulate a series of glass chandeliers, one of which is held in between the teeth – supported only by a long pipe with a mouthpiece on the end. The glass chandeliers consist each of a handle with a small glass tray that carries four glasses, each about 4 cm across. On top of the four glasses lies another glass tray of slightly smaller size, with again four small glass cups narrowing to the top which altogether create a fragile glass pyramid. These glass pyramids carry up to sixteen small glasses in total and can weigh up to one kilogram each. (Figure 31) Chinese contortion – as is the case with contortion styles in surrounding nations – aims to display extreme physical flexibility in harmony with strength and absolute control over the human body to let the performance appear effortless through smooth transitions between poses. This level of proficiency can only be achieved through years of discipline and strict training from a very young age.

Fig. 31 Glass props for mouth (left), hand and feet (center and right). Photo credit: archive Mariam Ala-Rashi.

The performance can be best discussed through video analysis of a performance that aired as part of a cultural program in 2007 on China Central Television 4 (CCTV4). CCTV4 is the leading state television broadcaster in the People's Republic of China, with its broadcasts reaching millions of viewers inside and outside China. The performing contortion duo belongs to the *Zhejiang Acrobatic Troupe*, located near

Shanghai and performs a traditional routine using *Rolling Cups.* The *Rolling Cups* routine has been showcased by numerous generations of contortion duos and is only performed by the most skilled contortionists. No choreographer is named in reference to the act. However, as contortion skills are traditionally passed down from one generation to the next, it is possible that this routine has been performed for decades (or longer!) and is not the artist's own.[75]

The performance takes place on a spacious TV studio stage in front of a live audience and cameras with large paper fans as background decoration. Four female background performers of the same height and body shape, dressed in golden robes are seated behind a large and elevated contortion table in the middle of the stage. Their role is to assist the contortion duo during the routine by handling the glass props and to walk around the table reverently with folded hands, which gives the performance a spiritual atmosphere. For the untrained eye, it is not explicitly clear however, if the notion of spirituality is for entertainment reasons only or if it contributes to the context of the cultural program. The contortion duo consists of two female acrobats dressed in shiny, skin-tight body leotards with snakeskin print with the taller and presumably older girl wearing a blue leotard and the smaller girl wearing a white leotard. Both girls are wearing gymnastic shoes with a firm rubber sole, which is still soft enough to allow them to hold on to the glass props with their toes. Duo contortion routines consist of one performer, usually the stronger and taller person, being the so-called "base" and the other, smaller performer being the "flyer". The base, in this case the girl in blue, has to lift the flyer, the girl in white, who then executes contortion tricks while balancing on top of the bases' body.

---

75   During my studies at the Beijing International Art School I was able to observe the training for a similar version of this routine as it was practiced by two of my classmates Lan Lan and Wei Wei and taught by my coach Teng Li.

In this nine-minute routine, both girls start out in a Z-shaped hand- and chest-stand, facing each other while traditional Chinese music of an ethereal choir accompanied by Chinese musical instruments, such as the flute, starts to play. The Z-shape is achieved during a balancing position such as the handstand or chest-stand and where the back is arched so that the buttock is located above the contortionist's head while the knees are bent and the toes are pointed. The head, buttock, knees, and toes of the contortionist should be perfectly aligned to achieve the desired Z-shape (Circus Dictionary, 2018: B). Since the contortionist is in an upside-down position of a handstand or chest-stand, she is not able to see herself to correct her posture. Extreme discipline is needed to develop awareness for the correct placement of each body part. Furthermore, a "simple" contortion handstand such as the *bendy handstand Z* (also known as Z-bend handstand) as performed in the opening scene by the contortionist with the blue leotard, requires years of practice, absolute balance between a controlled muscle tension and the "relaxation" of certain muscle groups in the back. Specific muscle groups in the neck, back, and legs must be isolated to achieve the extreme Z-shape, which demands the performer to point their buttocks and ribcage in different directions. Here, the ribcage is pushed back, allowing the lower back to bend forward in order to place the buttocks above the contortionist's head. This requires absolute muscle control throughout the body to balance the entire pose, not only the flexibility to bring the body into position, but also the strength to hold the limbs in "unnatural" poses, all while remaining inverted, balanced on the hands. The bendy handstand Z alone needs years of professional handstand and contortion practice but is used in this routine as the very first pose of the performance, which displays already from the very beginning the high level of difficulty of this performance.

The aesthetics of the performance is one of extreme focus, and it is dramaturgically structured by presenting seemingly easy and elegant poses in the beginning, to then increase the level of difficulty by presenting two of the most extreme tricks of the contortion discipline as highlight of the performance. The choreography starts with simple and elegant contortion poses and the presentation of two glass pyramids while the artists are executing backbends and oversplits (splits that exceed the 180-degree "floor split", see Figure 40) alongside one another in perfect synchronization. Towards the middle of the performance (Cb3815, 3:32), the two contortionists start to engage in acrobatic partner combinations. The girl in white executes different handstand combinations, perched atop the pelvis of the base (who is, herself, contorted in a bridge pose).

To perform a simple, straight handstand on an even surface such as the floor requires months of training, but executing a handstand routine on top of the hipbones of the performance partner requires tremendous discipline: the human hipbones are slim and pointy and the attached skin and muscle structure constantly shifts and moves under pressure, which makes it difficult to find stability and grip when performing a handstand on top of it. The flyer's body needs to adjust constantly in response to the slight shifts during the performance. Furthermore, this particular area of the body is very sensitive and holding onto the bones with a firm grip and placing weight on them can cause pain or discomfort. That the two performers trust each other is therefore of utmost importance. The handstand routines executed on top of the base's body also require that the flyer place their foot on the base's pubic bone or in the area where the stomach and sternum meet, which are again both very sensitive areas of the human body (Cb3815, 3:58 and 4:19). The base therefore needs a well-conditioned muscle structure and a high threshold of pain, and the flyer needs to be in absolute control of her balance to avoid injuring the base's internal organs. Clearly, an artist must be incredibly disciplined to subject themselves to such a painful and dangerous discipline. The level of control over the body displayed in this performance highlights the level of deep trust between the performing girls—a trust that has been built over years and all culminates in a sensational, final sequence. The highlights of the choreography are two complex poses where both of the contortionists are balancing the glass chandeliers with their hands, feet and mouth simultaneously time while slowly moving from one position into the next.

For the first highlight near the end of the performance, two assistants enter the contortion table (Cb3815, 5:33) to place the glass props into the hands and mouths of the performers while they remain in a contorted, balanced posture. Every move in this exchange between performers and assistants needs to be carefully choreographed to maintain the balance of the pose while handing over the props in time. The placement of the mouth piece needs to be executed particularly carefully, as the flyer already holds two glass figures in her hand while leaning in a backbend position on her partner's leg. The flyer depends entirely on her assistant to adjust the mouth piece with great care. If the assistant places it too deeply into the mouth of the performer, the flyer's breathing might be affected (at best) or trigger her gag reflex (at worst). If she places the mouth grip too shallowly in the performers mouth, the performer cannot hold and control it properly and it might fall and cause the entire construct to collapse. Beyond the pressure of their grips on one another as they balance, no communication is possible between both artists since the flyer is leaning far backwards without being able to speak to the assistant. This handling of props alone, which only takes twenty seconds on stage, requires absolute control and focus from every person involved.

The girl in the blue leotard is lying on her back with both legs pointed straight in the air (Cb3815, 5:45). The flyer climbs up to sit on top of the bases' right foot after having received the big chandelier with the mouth grip and two smaller glass props to hold in her hands while balancing another glass figure on her left leg that is pointed to the roof as well. The base received the remaining glass chandeliers and balances one on top of her right foot and one with her right hand. Both contortionists are balancing now a total of six glass pyramids while executing a complicated contortion routine on top of each other. The base now grips her partner's shoulder in her right hand, slowly turning the entire construction and moving from lying on her back over to lying on her stomach while maintaining an extremely arched back. At this point, the base is controlling the entire position, including her own and the flyers body. Both contortionists perform minute corrections, carefully maintaining the glass props (and themselves) in perfect balance, as well as keeping their bodies in maximum stretch. The energy required to perform this trick is tremendous and can easily exhaust the contortionist's energy, which is why in her final pose after completing the turn, the base "only" lifts her arm for five seconds to bring her entire body into full stretch.

The second climax of the choreography (Cb3815, 5:45) shows the flyer performing a handstand on the sole of the base's foot, who is lying on her stomach with her back arched while holding a glass chandelier with her mouth and balancing another glass prop on her forehead. For safety reasons, and to stabilize the lower legs of the base, the assistant places a rope around the base's calves so that the flyer can execute the handstand safely. However, while trying to find stability during the transition into the handstand, flyer and base struggle to prevent the lower legs of the base from tilting to the side, and the flyer needed another two attempts to achieve the final handstand pose (Cb3815, 8:25). Despite this small error,

I argue that this imperfection helped the audience grasp of the amount of effort that goes into a contortion routine so that it appears light and easy. Furthermore, it displays the level of control a contortionist has to apply to overcome difficulties in order to perform at the level needed to represent China on TV.

The discipline and skill analyzed in this performance is rooted in Chinese philosophy and cultural practice, as well. The circular shape is synonymous for perfection and proficiency in Chinese society and the arts, and it represents an incentive for discipline and hard work:

> In traditional Chinese culture and philosophy, the circle represents moral integrity, and is often equated with beauty. The Chinese words for "perfection" and "proficiency" are both based on the character for "circle". Achieving these attributes (becoming "well-rounded" as we would say in English), is considered to be one of life's highest goals. All types of Chinese art, including architecture[76], crafts, painting and calligraphy, music and theatre, incorporate the circle as a symbol of perfection. The acrobatic act Rolling with Cups gives expression to the concept of the circle both physically and conceptually. Physically, the performer's body serves as a central axis which gives rise to a series of circular movements throughout the performance. Conceptually, the performer must attain "well-

---

76   An architectural masterpiece that represents the philosophy of the circle, and ultimately perfection, is the Temple of Heaven. The Temple of Heaven (Figure 32) is a sacrificial altar from the 15th century, conveniently located in the Tiantan park in a neighboring district of the Beijing International Art School and is a popular sight-seeing spot for students from BJIAS who often visit the temple on their days off. The temple was inscribed as a UNESCO World Heritage Site in 1998 and described as "a masterpiece of architecture and landscape design which simply and graphically illustrates a cosmogony of great importance for the evolution of one of the world's great civilizations." (UNESCO, 1998).

rounded" perfection and proficiency through arduous effort and practice. Various rolling movements expressing the circle, such as *Left-Right Revolution, Precious Round and Through the Moon Gate* are crystallizations of the wisdom and toil that acrobats invest in their art (Fu, 2003: 29).

Fig. 32 (footnote) Temple of Heaven. Title: Teil des Himmelstempels. Built in 1420 by Emperor Yongle. Available at: https://commons.wikimedia.org/wiki/File:Teil_des_Himmelstempels. jpg?uselang=de

As the circle is synonymous for perfection in Chinese culture and society, it appears that contortion with its rolling movements and shapes is indeed a discipline most suited to represent flawless aesthetics in the performing arts. The aim for perfection, as it is rooted in Chinese philosophy, is aesthetically reflected in contortion and illustrates why it is used as political vessel: to convey the image of perfection and strength.

The aesthetics of the performance as explored throughout this chapter were of extreme discipline and displayed extraordinary contortion abilities. Moreover, the televised performance mainly functioned as an entertainment focus and gave detailed insight into the execution of complex contortion poses and the use of certain muscle groups. The extreme discipline, as explored throughout the analysis, illustrates the level of skills a performer can achieve when trained rigorously for years. When considering the complexity of skills and the trust between the training partners and assistants, as well as the absolute synchronization during performances, the question arises as to how these aesthetics and disciplined bodies in Chinese contortionism are produced. As a former student of the *Beijing International Art School,* the author was able to experience the rigid training methods and living environment first hand, and they will be analyzed extensively in Chapter Five. However, in order to comprehend the parallels between the Chinese acrobatic training methods and its striking similarity to military drill, it is important to first investigate how these methods are rooted in China's political history.

CHAPTER 4: THE DISCIPLINED BODY AS A POLITICAL INSTRUMENT

This chapter will extend aforementioned aesthetics of extreme discipline by examining the use of Chinese acrobatics in political campaigns initiated in 1949, the founding of the People's Republic of China. It will further explore how the political influence accelerated already rigid training methods to a military level, in order to produce the desired disciplined body.

As explored in Chapter Two, the aesthetics of extreme discipline in Chinese circus have gradually developed during the past centuries with the aim to achieve world-class level. However, since the founding of the People's Republic of China in 1949, the arts sector had become a vessel for political campaigns and particularly the acrobatics sector had to undergo institutional reformations. Between 1949 and 1965, policies and campaigns initiated the institutionalization of acrobatic troupes, which became instruments of cultural exchange with China's neighboring countries and the West up until today.

To demonstrate strong political bonds with the neighboring countries such as Taiwan and Cambodia, or countries that were in political negotiation with China, the Chinese government made cultural exchange a common practice. The concept of cultural exchange as an instrument for political communication and the incorporation of performing arts as a contribution to an understanding of international diplomacy occurs across ages and cultures. It includes the incorporation of messaging in art, for example through music and dance, as state-trained artists are "utilized" by their governments. Governments recognized the impact that cultural activities had on how their countries were perceived abroad and started to sponsor cultural institutions. After the successful exchange in 1971 of the US and Chinese table tennis teams, which initiated the Sino-US rapprochement, the *Shenyang Acrobatic Troupe* and its seventy-eight members were sent on a four-month long tour through America. In her article *Bending the Body for China*, scholar Tracy Ying Zhang states:

> [...] In Cold War China, acrobatics was identified as "proletariat performing arts" and used to envisage the abstract notions of socialist culture. Onstage, acrobats' coordinated movements aimed to create a collective sense of Chinese national identity and to demonstrate the efficiency of a socialist production system. Meanwhile, the Chinese diplomats advocated the principle of "uniting the peoples" to facilitate Beijing's varied engagements with the superpowers, socialist allies, as well as non-allied countries, and they recognized that acrobatics' entertaining and folk qualities could appeal to a wide range of spectators in a diplomatic context (Zhang, 2016:408).

Here, Tracy Ying Zhang describes how acrobatics evolved as both an institution and an artistic medium to accommodate the PRC leader's agenda of building a socialist non-state (Zhang, 2016:408). The exchange of different art forms such as acrobatics, dance, music, and opera, was an often-used instrument in diplomatic negotiations between countries. The success of this political concept, however, was not only limited to an exchange of performances and shows but also permeated the educational system and initiated the exchange of teaching staff between art institutions, among other professional and artistic exchanges. Alexandra Kolb, Professor of dance anthropology at the University of Roehampton and author of *Dance and Politics in China,* examined Chinese intercultural crossovers and encounters with the West in modern dance. Here, US dance teachers in association with the *American Dance Festival in* Durham, California, visited the *Guangdong Academy* in Guangzhou with the aim to introduce and establish the genre of modern dance. They visited the academy for several months to teach a range of modern dance styles and compositional methods. As a result of the success of the project, the world-renowned *Beijing Dance Academy* initiated new dance classes and started to enroll students in 1993 (Kolb, 2017:356).

This arrangement worked the other way around as well. Students of foreign art schools, whose governments were in negotiations with China, were often enrolled for several months (or even years) to study at Chinese art institutions. When looking at China's offerings, which included performing arts like dance and opera, why would traditional Chinese acrobatics have been the first choice for international cultural exchange? The decision to send an acrobatic troupe overseas reflected the Chinese government's ideas about how to communicate 'Chinese-ness' to the US audience through the acrobatic body. From the perspective of Chinese diplomats, this 'traditional acrobatics' was an ideal cultural tool to invite the US audience to appreciate China's heritage as well as modern physical culture (Zhang, 2016:418). First Premier Zhou Enlai, a skilled diplomat in charge of the Foreign Ministry from 1949 to 1976, understood the power of acrobatics very well and famously stated in 1960: "The acrobatic art is different from Model Works (revolutionary operas) and other folk operas. The Left, Middle and Right can all appreciate [acrobatics]" (Zhang,

2016:416). His statement points out why Chinese circus has been used politically with great effect as a culturally unifying art-form.

The process of establishing state-run acrobatic troupes to serve a political purpose began in 1949 with the founding of the People's Republic of China, at the same time as the sino-soviet alliance took place. Professor Sergey Radchenko form the International Relations department of the University Cardiff asserts in his article *The Sino–Russian Relationship in the Mirror of the Cold War*:

> On July 1, 1949, in a Renmin Ribao editorial, Mao Zedong famously proclaimed that Communist China would henceforth lean to one side—the Soviet side. The CCP [Chinese Communist Party] had by then practically won the civil war. Mao's rival, Chiang Kai-shek had fled to Taiwan. The Chinese leader was now looking to position China in a world overshadowed by the political, economic, military, and ideological confrontation between the Soviet Union and the United States. In a sense, his choice—seeking alignment with the USSR—was a natural one. The CCP itself had been founded with Soviet involvement, and was ideologically affiliated with the world Communist movement, centered in Moscow (Radchenko, 2020. 270).

The similarities between the two neighboring countries -- China and the Soviet Union -- of using artists as political vessels in international relations are evident in their approach and execution (the USSR had actually nationalized circus in 1919, long before the country nationalized the cinema!) Enkhbold Chuluunbaatar, assistant professor for business administration and strategic consultant who focuses on management issues of state-owned enterprises in Mongolia, including cultural and creative industries, examines in his article *Mongolian Circus Industry in the Post- transitional Economy* the spillover-effects of the Soviet Union on its neighboring socialist countries:

> Soon after the Soviet government established the world's first State College of Circus and Variety Arts in 1927 (the school was also known as the Moscow Circus School), the Russian circus emerged as the benchmark of circuses worldwide [...], resulting in the supremacy of Russian circus in the world's stage. Circus became an even more prominent piece of culture and a point of pride; it played an important role in the development of cultural policy in the Soviet Union. Not long after Russian circus rose to the world's acclaim, the spillover effect was strongly felt by Mongolia—the neighboring socialist country —leading to the birth of Mongolian circus. Mongolia was a satellite state that was closely aligned with the Soviet Union since 1921 (Chuluunbaatar, 2014. 70).

The success of the Soviet circus model proved to be a beneficial element in international diplomacy, and heightened the status of the USSR and Mongolia in the West. Similar developments could soon be observed in the Chinese circus sector with the establishment of state-run acrobatic troupes in 1949, when communist leader Mao Zedong declared the creation of the People's Republic of China.

The first state-run troupe was the Beijing-based *China National Acrobatic Troupe (CNAT)* founded in October 1950, after a three-month long recruitment effort by artist-officials who assembled acrobats from cities and regions known for acrobatic excellence (Zhang, 2016:410). The recruited acrobats became salaried government employees, or "socialist cultural workers". Meanwhile, acrobatics was rendered with new political significance: the agile acrobatic body was used to display socialist China's ideal citizen subjects and national character (Zhang, 2016:413). The government's aim was to modernize acrobatics, which meant making changes on an institutional and aesthetic level, as well as improvements to the training methods used by their instructors. The military-like training methods developed during that time show similarities to recruitment and selection procedures of soldiers in the 17th century, as described by Michel Foucault in his book *Discipline and Punish-The Birth of the Prison*. Utilizing the human body as instrument to cater to a political agenda has been a tried and tested method for centuries, and it appears that the military drill that we can see in today's training methods is rooted in Mao Zedong's socialist China. In his memoir *Shanghai Acrobat – A True Story of Courage and Perseverance from Revolutionary China*, Jingjing Xue describes his rise from being an orphan who lived in poverty to becoming a praised performer in China and beyond—at times touring both communist and capitalist nations. As he represented China in the Shanghai Circus, he rubbed shoulders with key political leaders, while at other times endured countless threats and privation at the hands of the anti-intellectual and anti-artistic Maoist regime that included interrogation, forced labor, and detainment (Jingjing, 2021: Cover Copy-Apollo Publishers).

Jingjing Xue, who was recruited from an orphanage in China at the age of nine, gives insights into the life as a student at the *Shanghai Acrobatic Troupe*. Part of the curriculum were general subjects such as math, geography, Chinese, and history. Political education– including revolutionary ideology into the minds of future proletarians– was the objective in class across all curriculums. Here, he recalls a history lesson with his teacher Xu who told the students the history of the *Shanghai*

Acrobatic Troupe and how it was utilized and funded to serve the political agenda of the Chinese Communist Party CCP:

> She said that in October 1950, Chairman Mao Zedong, Premier Zhou Enlai and other leaders viewed performances by the best acrobats in China and, based on that night's performance, Premier Zhou proposed that a national acrobatic troupe be founded. The name-change from "trick players" to "acrobats" was a first sign of improved status. The government saw a political use for us: this troupe, the first of its kind in China, had visited the Soviet Union and set a precedent for artistic groups to travel abroad to perform and spread the message of the new China and become an avenue for cultural exchange with the outside world. [...] Starting in 1956, a five-year acrobatic program was taught at the troupe. The program broke the thousand-year-old Chinese tradition in which one master single-handedly taught his students, and replaced it with an educational scheme based on the Soviet model. Staff included professional acrobats, and cultural, dance and music teachers. We received training in all of these areas, laying the foundations for us to become skilled acrobats who would make our names throughout the world. All costs for education, food and board were covered by the government (Jingjing, 2021: 20 & 21).

For this political agenda, theatre-style performances were developed that "entailed designed lighting, stage sets, handheld props, costumes, and live music [...] and these acrobatic shows traveled internationally for cultural exchange" (Zhang, 2016:413). However, performing amidst this political-cultural climate was challenging for the artists as the acrobatic body was loaded with political messages. Furthermore, the pressure for acrobats was high and technical errors or accidents during performances were not tolerated. If performers made technical mistakes during a "revolutionary" show, then the performance failures were not considered random technical problems but signs of political subversion. As a result, the performers would be punished by the revolutionary committee: "At one point [the] Shenyang [Troupe] had to close down for a few weeks after an acrobat fell during a public performance, as radicals regarded this performer's technical error as an anti-CCP political statement" (Zhang, 2016:416). The image of discipline and perfection was given great importance and up until the early 1970s, most acrobatic troupes across the country still dressed their performers in army uniforms (Zhang, 2016:416).

These cultural exchange programs, that run through *Beijing International Art School* and the *China National Acrobatic Troupe*, have allowed China to "produce" disciplined, politically subservient bodies for decades – and continue today. From 2011 through 2014, the author shared the classroom with Cambodian and Taiwanese acrobats who entered the *Beijing International Art School* on an exchange program. The Cambodian students enrolled for a duration of 2 years of full-time study, while the Taiwanese students were visiting every summer for about 2 to 3 months. Since the complex transfer of Taiwan from the Japanese administration to China after the Second World War, the relations between China and Taiwan were tense, resulting in civil wars and uprisings regarding the independence of Taiwan and the policy "Unifying Taiwan by Force" was set in place under Mao Zedong's rule. Additionally, political tensions overshadowed the relations between Cambodia and China. The Chinese Communist Party (CCP) and chairman Mao Zedong supported the communist party *Khmer Rouge* and its brutal leader Pol Pot who tried to force Cambodia towards communism, which ultimately led to the genocide of 2 million Cambodians. Hence, the relations between China, Taiwan, and Cambodia have been uneasy for decades. To overcome difficulties and to display the "strong bond" between these three countries, the circus was utilized in China's propaganda. The *Beijing International Art School* had become an instrument of the Chinese government to promote international democracy by inviting young students to participate in the arts program. The annual visit of the Taiwanese acrobatic troupe during the summer term, therefore, aimed to strengthen the bond between both countries and possibly heal wounds between them. The progress and wellbeing of the students would be recorded through regular visits of Chinese and Taiwanese TV teams.

A similar concept was again applied with the invitation to a two-year exchange program of the Cambodian acrobatic troupe and resulted in the full-time education of a group of fifteen students between the age of six and seventeen. Two Cambodian or Taiwanese "life teachers", who often functioned as translators in addition to their role as motherly figure, accompanied the children for the duration of the course. However, the training program was entirely controlled and executed by teachers of the *Beijing International Art School*. Both countries benefit from this arrangement: while the Chinese and foreign governments used the students as a medium to accommodate their political agenda, the acrobats had the opportunity to train with some of the world's top coaches and therefore enhanced their chances of future employment in the entertainment industry.

However, China's use of the circus as a political tool was not limited to its geographic neighbors. In the May of 2012, the city of Beijing funded the production of *Tiananmen* – a music and dance show that features incredible scenery –to celebrate the capital's history. The production was advertised as *'Performance that presents the Capitals' Elegance. Tiananmen*

- Where the Five-Star red Flag is raised. Listen to the Ancient City's Echo. Feel the Beauty of the Capital'. It depicted the gate of the *Forbidden City* decorated with a portrait of former Chairman Mao Zedong. (Figure 33) Elite institutions such as the *Beijing International Art School*, the *Beijing Dance Academy,* and the *Beijing Opera*, as well as China's most famous musical artists had been contracted for the show that displayed political and historical highlights of the city. As members of the international acrobatic team of the *Beijing International Art School*, we four Western students were also selected to play a small part in the large production. Not for our acrobatic skills, however - we were hired due to our foreign appearance.

The four of us, hailing from Australia, the United States, and Germany, were dressed as flight attendants (Figure 34) of world leading airlines. We exited, while waving and smiling, a full-scale airplane that was projected on the stage screen (Ala-Rashi, 2018). The scene depicted the first Western airlines arriving at the *Beijing Capital International Airport.* Our performance, which was accompanied by multiple singers, reflected on the improvement of the relationship and diplomacy between China and the West, emphasizing the recognition from US President Jimmy Carter in 1979, which was a major milestone in the countries' relationship. The dress rehearsal was visited by officials of the Chinese government who had a TV crew in tow. They thanked the performing artists, and expressed that they were looking forward to the show. (Figure 35) The direct involvement of the author in this theatrical display of political prowess, with meticulous attention to detail and final approval from government officials during the dress rehearsals, further revealed the gravity and the influence the government has on performing arts in China.

Fig. 33 Poster of the *Tiananmen* Show 2012.
(Copyrights: Mariam Ala-Rashi)

Fig. 34 Backstage at the Tiananmen Show
2012: Performer of the Beijing Opera
and Mariam Ala-Rashi dressed as Flight
Attendant. (Copyrights: Mariam Ala-Rashi)

Fig. 35 Government officials at the dress rehearsal, 2012. (Copyrights: Private archive Mariam
Ala-Rashi)

The importance of showcasing physical strength as a representation of political power was analyzed in a 2020 article for the *Journal of Experimental Political Science* and examines the beneficial effects that sports events have on public opinion. In their research article *Bread and Circuses: Sports and Public Opinion in China*, the authors Dan Chen, assistant professor in the Department of Political Science at the University of Richmond, and Andrew W. MacDonald, assistant professor of social science at Duke Kunshan University, describe the effects:

> Sports victory constitutes an important part of propaganda in authoritarian states. The heavy state investment in sports industries and sports culture in China illustrates the political importance of sports. However, few studies have systematically examined the exact impact of sports propaganda on public opinion. Using a survey experiment conducted in two Chinese cities, this article finds that broadcast highlighting national sports achievements has significant positive effects on general satisfaction and compliance with the local governments. These results expand on the small, but growing, literature on the effects of sports on political opinions and help detail the specific ways in which sports can affect political attitudes (Chen and MacDonald, 2020).

The article presents the immediate effects of sports events on political opinion. It stands to reason that similar observations can be made when circus performances are utilized as a display of political power, especially given the political apparatus' endorsement of the circus arts. The deployment of the "disciplined body" has proven beneficial to facilitate China's relations and negotiations with neighboring countries and the West. In return, governmental subsidies enabled the revival of the acrobatic culture and heritage by creating a nationwide apparatus of state-run acrobatic institutions with world-class training facilities and employment prospects. The spirit of the past still echoes in today's education system, for example in the video release *China's Patriotic Education* by news channel *SBS News Australia*. In a nationally televised media event in China, the Australian news channel accompanied the students of the *Yue Fei Martial Arts School* in Henan, China. In addition to their training, the martial arts students study patriotism alongside core subjects such as math and science, to propagate China's President Xi Jinping's ideology of nationalism that pursues the "China Dream" of power and prosperity. Professor Feng Chongyi from the *University of Technology Australia* reflects on President Xi Jinping's influence on China's education system: "The Party-state relies exclusively on nationalism as the tool for its legitimacy. From kindergarten up to university, they are indoctrinated with the narrative of the Chinese Party-state nationalism" (SBS Dateline, 2021). The education ministry China further stated, that it will incorporate the "Xi Jinping Thought" into the national curriculum beginning with primary schools so that teachers can "plant the seeds of loving the party, the country and socialism in young hearts" (JapanTimes, 2021). The inheritance of the socialist era is an ongoing process, and socialists' values remain embedded in contemporary China. The influence of the government on educational institutions is not a new concept and has been applied for centuries. In order to "produce" a generation that follows and embodies the ideologies of its government -- and that serves as a high-profile cultural export -- state-run schools in China are administered to supervise and monitor the education of the students. Acrobatic schools offer a particularly suitable environment to create "disciplined bodies" through and extensive training curriculum and supervision that are often supported through government funding.

CHAPTER 5: FOUCAULT AND THE TRAINING METHODS IN CHINESE ACROBATICS

This chapter draws a comparison between the Western system of prisons, military, and legal hierarchies and the *Beijing International Art School* (BJIAS) and its training methods, by considering Michel Foucault's book *Discipline and Punish-The Birth of the Prison* (1975), where the social theorist describes how the human body was utilized by governments. There are a number of similarities between these institutions that use architectural structures, surveillance, selection processes and training methods in order to control society. This study analyses in particular, how the education system in China "produces" disciplined, acrobatic bodies.

The *Beijing International Art School* (BJIAS) is a governmental institution and is not only home to the world-famous *Chinese National Acrobatic Troupe* (CNAT) but also offers full-time education in Chinese acrobatics, Chinese traditional dance, drama and theatre, singing, fine arts (painting), and martial arts, as advertised on its official website:

> Beijing International Art School, formerly Beijing Acrobatic School, is the largest comprehensive art school in China teaching circus arts, martial arts, dances and arts of other categories. Students from all over the world, of all ages, from different cultural backgrounds, choose to study here. Most students have previous training already, and they will graduate

as professional performers and artists. We provide a constant stream of talents. [...] There are about 550 students currently at the school, and about 10% of them are international students. The ages of Chinese students are in the range from 8 to 18, and that of international students are various: teens, 20's, and 30's. Teachers and staff members are about 150. [...] Class Content: The courses of acrobatic major focus on the circus skills of flexibility, tumbling and handstands, based on which students will master the advanced skills of controlling bodies and apparatuses, including aerial tissue, tightrope walking, hoops, cycling, bowl/cup balancing, poles, equilibrium, contortion, pyramids, German wheels, Russian bars, ... all those you can find in a modern circus. Acrobatics teachers and students take no summer break or spring break. Only the Acrobatics Department keeps teaching during the summer. The Acrobatics Department has only a two-week break following the Chinese New Year. A school year spans from September to August. It has two semesters: The Autumn Semester from September to January, and the Spring Semester from March to June, inclusive (Beijing International Art School, 2021).

Covering 66,000 square meters, the campus that is located in the South of China's capital Beijing, and offers performing art facilities including 30 gym rooms. This chapter will explore its structure, living environments, and the training methods through a Foucauldian approach.

Michel Foucault discusses in his book *Discipline and Punish-The Birth of the Prison* the Western system of prisons, the military, police, and legal hierarchies in the discourse of power. In his chapter *Docile Bodies*, he discusses the education of soldiers from the 17th to the 18th century, starting with the recruitment and selection process of the soldier and how the human body was utilized by the government. Although soldiers were selected according to rigid standards of an ideal body type during the 17th century, the selection process during the late 18th century became more subtle but not less strict. Training methods had evolved, and governmental institutions had been established to transform and shape the human body and mind systematically into a desired "construct" which could then be utilized by the state. The education of solders particularly focused on three concepts: the control of time, which describes the very regulated time-schedule; the concept of space, which controls the living environment of the soldiers; and lastly the concept of surveillance, which describes permanent observation of soldiers, including their privacy. This analysis explores the similarities between Foucault's arguments and the military education methods that have been developed in socialist China and are still applied today in acrobatic institutions such as the *China National Acrobatic Troupe* and *Beijing International Art School*.

Foucault observes that in every society, the human body was manipulated and controlled through various power dynamics that forced rules and regulations on it: "What was so new in these projects of docility that interested the eighteenth century so much? It was certainly not the first time that the body had become the object of such imperious and pressing investments; in every society, the body was in the grip of very strict powers, which imposed on it constraints, prohibitions or obligations. However, there were several new things in these techniques" (Foucault, 1975:136). He describes different methods that have been used by governmental or religious institutions throughout the 17th and 18th century to discipline and control the masses. According to Foucault, these governments and religious leaders have been using three methods of controlling and disciplining their subjects:

1. *The Scale of the Control* that is exercising a subtle coercion on the body at the level of the mechanism itself: movements, gestures, attitudes and rapidity.

2. *The Object of the Control* which was no longer the signifying elements of behavior or the language of the body, but the economy, the efficiency of movements, their internal organization with its most important tool: exercise.

3. *The Modality* in which the former techniques are executed: Through uninterrupted, constant coercion and surveillance, the processes of the activity are supervised rather than its result, with exercises according to a codification that partitions as closely as possible time, space, and movement.

Foucault however emphasizes the importance of distinguishing these techniques from slavery, service, vassalage, or asceticism since those were "merely appropriating" the body, forcing it into submission or labor:

> They were different from slavery because they were not based on a relation of appropriation of bodies; indeed, the elegance of the discipline lay in the fact that it could dispense with this costly and violent relation by obtaining effects of utility at least as great. They were different, too, from 'service', which was a constant, total, massive, non-analytical, unlimited relation of domination, established in the form of the individual will of the master, his 'caprice'. They were different from vassalage, which was a highly coded, but distant relation of submission, which bore less on the operations of the body than on the products

of labour and the ritual marks of allegiance. Again, they were different from asceticism and from 'disciplines' of a monastic type, whose function was to obtain renunciations rather than increases of utility and which, although they involved obedience to others, had as their principal aim an increase of the mastery of each individual over his own body (Foucault, 1975:137).

In opposition to slavery, service, vassalage, or asceticism he specifies methods of *Modality, Object of the Control,* and *Scale of the Control,* which allowed command over the operations of the body, by calling them *disciplines.* He further marks the historical moment of the disciplines as an art of the human body:

These methods, which made possible the meticulous control of the operations of the body, which assured the constant subjection of its forces and imposed upon them a relation of docility-utility, might be called 'disciplines'. The historical moment of the disciplines was the moment when an art of the human body was born, which was directed not only at the growth of its skills, nor at the intensification of its subjection, but at the formation of a relation that in the mechanism itself makes it more obedient as it becomes more useful, and conversely. What was then being formed was a policy of coercions that act upon the body, a calculated manipulation of its elements, its gestures, its behaviour. The human body was entering a machinery of power that explores it, breaks it down and rearranges it. A 'political anatomy', which was also a 'mechanics of power', was being born; it defined how one may have a hold over others' bodies, not only so that they may do what one wishes, but so that they may operate as one wishes, with the techniques, the speed and the efficiency that one determines. Thus, discipline produces subjected and practised bodies, 'docile' bodies (Foucault, 1975:137).

The establishment of a "political anatomy" and "mechanics of power" allowed various political institutions to administer and dominate the human body. Foucault's principles of disciplines share remarkable parallels with the training methods and living environs at the *China National Acrobatic Troupe* (CNAT) and the *Beijing International Art School* (BJIAS).

The *China National Acrobatic Troupe* (CNAT) and the *Beijing International Art School* (BJIAS) have won more than 20 gold and silver medals at the most prestigious circus festivals all over the world. Competing regularly at the *Monte Carlo International Circus Festival, Cirque de Demain,* as well as China's own *Wuhan International Circus Festival,* the troupe is synonymous with excellence. As one of the world's most prestigious acrobatic troupes, CNAT only offers membership contracts to the most skillful graduate students of the circus education program at the *Beijing International Art School.* Moreover, the training sessions of the school are visited monthly by leading agents in the circus industry to recruit the best students for their shows directly from the classroom. The majority of BJIAS's teachers are alumnae of the school, and have successful careers with *Cirque du Soleil* and other major, international companies. In order to achieve world-class qualifications and to align with former generations of elite performers, the students have to undergo years of rigorous training.

Similar to a boarding school system, the *Beijing International Art School* is one of the very few acrobatic schools in China which can provide visa

224

sponsorship for foreign students, offering full-time education, as well as room and board. The school is also open for talented domestic children who wish to pursue a career in the arts sector. The socialist tradition of offering an education to poor and orphaned Chinese children continues through today. They are offered an education, a profession, and employment possibilities within the acrobatic troupe (Zhang, 2016:410). Acrobat Jingjing Xue describes in his chapter *The Chosen* why he was selected from the orphanage the Youth Village in Shanghai in the 1950s at the age of nine. He became an orphan at the age of two and the *Youth Village* was already the fifth orphanage he had lived in by the time he turned nine:

> Before 'liberation'- the word we were taught to use for the Communist revolution that had taken control of China seven years earlier, in 1949- acrobats, or 'trick-players,' were from the lowest stratum of society. Only those families who could not make a living would send their children to an acrobatic troupe to learn 'tricks,' in the hope that they would have a trade to support themselves. After liberation, the status of acrobats sank even lower. Finding students became so difficult, the *Shanghai Acrobatic Troupe* had to turn to the orphanages (Jingjing, 2021:3).

Orphans who are recruited by the school to learn an artistic profession are allocated to a guardian who will make decisions on behalf of the student until they reach legal age, which is eighteen in China. Foreign students who are under the age of eighteen and wish to train at the *Beijing International Art School* are asked to bring either a parent or to arrange a legal guardian for the duration of their training. Neither local nor foreign students under the age of eighteen are permitted to leave the campus without a legal guardian or a written letter of permission. Foucault describes this concept of boarding as the most effective way to shape and educate bodies, and as the "protected place of disciplinary monotony" (Foucault, 1975:141). Becoming an acrobatic student, therefore, means to live on campus full-time and to act in accordance with the school's regulations.

To be accepted to the acrobatic program, foreign and local students alike must first pass an audition where strength and flexibility are tested, and the prospective student's physical build is examined. Local students usually start at the age of four and undergo a basic training first, which consists of daily flexibility, strength, handstand, tumbling and dance training, as well as basic object manipulation and wire-walking. The basic training supports the development of absolute body control, allowing the teachers to observe the children's development over the course of four years. Around the age of eight, the children will be assigned to certain departments for specialization according to their talent and body type. Older students (around the age of ten) are sometimes accepted to the program, but must prove their commitment as they endure rigid training during a probation period. Every student who has been accepted to the program has to live on campus in order to fully commit to the education. Many children come from remote parts of China to the capital to start their education and it is therefore not only advised out of convenience reasons, since the daily commute would be exhausting and expensive, but the training process and overall development of the student must be monitored at all times under the Chinese model. The large campus of the acrobatic school and the troupe is situated in an industrial area in the outskirts of Beijing and its architecture offers all amenities, which makes the campus not unlike a small town. A very similar concept can be identified in Foucault's description of governmental institutions.

Here, Foucault unpacks the structure and hidden agenda of Western prisons, factories, and military camps, as well as the intended psychological effect it had on the inhabitants in consequence. The architecture of those "towns within towns" was a powerful tool to control the behavior of prisoners, workers, and soldiers alike and was often structured comparably to an ordinary town with facilities that make it unnecessary for the inhabitants to leave. Worker's accommodation, for example, were built into the factory itself and explicitly compared to the fortress, the monastery, and the walled town, or as Foucault describes it: "The aim is to derive the maximum advantages and to neutralize the inconveniences [...]" (Foucault, 1975:142). Furthermore, the premises were guarded and under surveillance with Foucault identifying this as the "distribution of individuals in space" (Foucault, 1975:141). Essentially identical key features can be observed at the *Beijing International Art School* and its campus structure.

The *Beijing International Art School* encloses a large campus with multiple training buildings, dormitories, a canteen that serves warm meals four times per day, a small supermarket, a theatre, academic buildings with a library, office buildings, a medical office, a physiotherapy practice, a gym, a supervised laundrette, a post office, a sports field and the teacher's quarter. The campus is surrounded by high walls and fences with barbwire on top of them and has only one main gate that is guarded by two security officers. The employees of these facilities are employed by the school, with most of them living on campus as they come from provinces and villages far from the capital. Because of its size, the campus is situated in the industrial area of Beijing and offers many amenities that make it unnecessary to leave the campus. The nearest train station is 20 minutes on foot, and a train ride to the city center will take around 1.5 hours. The design and location of the campus present an undeniable parallel of confinement through spatial borders and control that were applied during the 17th and 18th century by the architecture and use of space of military institutions. It also reveals the surveillance opportunities of such an architecture: 'The whole will be enclosed by an outer wall ten feet high, which will surround the said houses, at a distance of thirty feet from all the sides; this will have the effect of maintaining the troops in order and discipline, so that an officer will be in position to answer for them' (Foucault, 1975:142). The entire campus of the *Beijing International Art School* is equipped with surveillance cameras and with personnel that monitors the inhabitants and visitors of the campus 24/7.

The way the school's architecture influences the daily life of its students allows for extensive surveillance through the continuous monitoring CCTV system. The system is primarily set in place to monitor every movement within the premises and to prevent new show concepts from being stolen -- many foreign students have tried to videotape choreographies with their smartphones without asking for permission first. However, this confined situation also maintains a closed training environment.

In his chapter *Panopticism*, Foucault introduces the *panopticon* as a central architectural figure of total surveillance to enforce the *panoptic* disciplining technique that uses the awareness of the students of being under permanent surveillance to discipline them:

> An annular building; at the centre, a tower; this tower is pierced with wide windows that open onto the inner side of the ring; the peripheric building is divided into cells ,each of which extends the whole width of the building; they have two windows, one on the inside, corresponding to the windows of the tower; the other, on the out- side, allows the light to cross the cell from one

end to the other. All that is needed, then, is to place a supervisor in a central tower and to shut up in each cell a madman, a patient, a condemned man, a worker or a schoolboy. By the effect of backlighting, one can observe from the tower, standing out precisely against the light, the small captive shadows in the cells of the periphery. They are like so many cages, so many small theatres, in which each actor is alone, perfectly individualized and constantly visible (Foucault, 1975:200).

Due to the permanent visibility achieved through 24/7 camera surveillance the students can no longer tell when or when not, they are being observed and therefore behave at all times. Thus, instead of forcefully disciplining the students, the discipline comes from the students themselves which makes the panopticon an effective tool to control large groups of people at the same time. The panopticon therefore becomes a tool of discipline designed to induce "a state of conscious and permanent visibility that assures the automatic functioning of power" (Foucault, 1975:201). To ensure order and discipline and the automatic functioning of power, rigid campus rules are set in place.

The campus and dormitory rules are strict and apply to local and foreign students alike, no matter what age they are. The dormitory rooms are supervised by so-called "life teachers" who occupy a room on each floor next to their student's rooms. The room for the "life teacher" who is in charge of the entire dormitory, is right next to the main entrance of the building. Her bedroom consists of a bed, a bathroom, a desk with screens of the surveillance system, and has a large window towards the corridor of the building, to monitor who leaves and enters the dormitory. This concept is similar to Foucault's surveillance theory, where the perfect disciplinary apparatus makes it possible to constantly observe every inhabitant and visitor of the building.

In this way, the acrobatic school functions as a tool for 24/7 surveillance, "with rooms that were distributed along a corridor like a series of small cells; at regular intervals, an officer's quarters were situated for observation, recording and training" (Foucault, 1975:173). Similar to Foucault's example of the small cells the dormitory rooms in the acrobatic school are distributed along a corridor that can easily be surveilled. The role of the "life teachers" is to be constantly present to guide, and monitor the children with their rooms situated next to the children's rooms on each floor. The position is engaged by women who pose as motherly figures in the lives of the younger students. Their task is similar to that of a mother: to care for and to protect the children, as well as to teach them daily tasks such as how to wash their training clothes, how to clean up their rooms, manners, bodily hygiene, how to eat healthy, and the importance of going to bed early. The rooms of both adult and youth students have no locks and are subject to inspection at any time of the day. The corridors of each floor are under camera surveillance. Students may not own sharp objects such as knives—or even scissors—nor are they permitted electronic devices, as the school deems them a fire hazard. This is not without reason, however, as a dormitory building burned down in the early 2000s due to poor installation of electronic sockets. A group of foreign students who lived in that dormitory used every electric outlet at the same time, which led to a scorching fire. As such, outlets and appliances are warrant to daily inspection.

During the daily inspections, the "life teacher" will remove such objects and the room will be graded for cleanliness. Every day, points for cleanliness are given or deducted—and are published together with the name of the tenant on a screen in the main hall. When leaving the room in the morning to go to the training building, students have to turn a color-coded key on a display inside the office of the life teacher, who then knows if the students have all left their rooms to attend classes. This procedure signals the morning patrol-time and inspection of the rooms. If a key has not been turned in the morning, the life teacher automatically knows that a student is still in the building and did not attend class. The student has then to inform the teachers about the reason for their absence, which will then be recorded in the student's file.

Hot water is only made available between nine and ten o'clock every night so that students are forced to be home on-time in order to take a hot shower. The lights are then turned off by the life-teacher at ten o'clock, and the curfew comes into force with the main entrance being locked until five o'clock in the morning, just before the students prepare for the first training sessions of the day. In his chapter on Panopticism, Foucault describes the general principle of a discipline mechanism similar to the school's curfew, the availability of hot water, and other amenities, to gain power over a group of individuals:

> The panoptic arrangement provides the formula for this generalization. It programs, at the level of an elementary and easily transferable mechanism, the basic functioning of a society penetrated through and through with disciplinary mechanisms. [...] A functional mechanism that must improve the exercise of power by making it lighter, more rapid, more effective, a design of subtle coercion for a society to come; a so-called disciplinary society (Foucault, 1975:209).

The Foucauldian design of the BJIAS's campus—paired with its success as an acrobatic training facility—seem to demonstrate that this all-consuming lifestyle and panoptic surveillance produces skilled acrobats.

To enter the campus, every student receives a rechargeable student ID card that acts as identification, as key and as a bank account, "topped up" through cash deposits. These cards allow students to pay for their meals and to purchase goods at the campus supermarket. Access to the campus is only permitted to cardholders, and IDs must be presented upon arrival at the gate. Visitors to the school are required to make an appointment with the school's administration office and sign a form agreeing to campus regulations. Visitors are allowed to take pictures but have to follow special regulations. Young students are not allowed to be photographed. This isn't only to protect the students' privacy, however. In recent years, many documentaries about Chinese acrobats have been produced, and foreign TV teams preferably videotaped the morning stretching routine, which is hard to endure for very young children who often cry during this training process. It is explicitly outlined in the written agreement that visitors are not allowed to take pictures or videos of crying children, as it would harm the image of the school and let it appear in a negative light, depending on how the images were presented. Most visitors of the school are either elite talent scouts, governmental officials who inspect the school's premises and training program, or TV teams filming documentaries or materials for the Chinese government's propaganda wing. Prestige and image cultivation are sensitive topics for governmental institutions, especially with regular visits of important guests. Students and teachers are obliged to be "presentable" at all times, which includes (among other things), a strict dress code.

During official visits by the Chinese government, or when representing the school off-campus, local and foreign students are obliged to wear either an all-black attire or the school's uniform that was provided to them upon arrival and which consists of long training pants, a t-shirt, and sport jacket with the school's logo. It is prohibited to train barefoot or to wear sandals on campus. Moreover, during the training when executing assisted stretches, or in general, when the touching of a student's body is necessary, the teachers will wear white slip-proof cotton gloves to maintain the professional image.

These strict guidelines help enforce a culture of discipline: the dressing up in uniforms, the constant surveillance, and the surrender of ones' freedom when setting foot on campus, resemble how political puppets are subjected, used, transformed, and improved through empirical and calculated methods related to the army (Foucault, 1975:136). These mechanisms are controlled regularly and visits by governmental officials are scheduled annually to inspect the dormitories and training facilities to make sure that the school meets the requirements and standards of a state-run facility that represents China. By meeting the required standards, the school secures subsidies and maintains its status to provide student visas to foreign students. These official visits also include the audits of training sessions, where state officials inspect the level and progress of their national acrobatic troupe. The school's support through governmental subsidies to uphold its status is therefore entirely dependent on the training success of the acrobatic troupe. In addition to the confined environment, remote location of the school, and the 24/7 surveillance of the students, a sophisticated and strict training schedule is implemented to guarantee the ongoing success of the troupe and to produce the desired aesthetics of a docile body.

The training schedule is a strict model that aims to establish rhythms and a daily routine, to impose particular occupations, and to regulate the cycles of repetitions (Foucault, 1975:149). It is divided into four training sessions throughout the day, with the first class being a general warm-up at 6:30 am in the morning. There, only two teachers are present to supervise and support the students during light stretches and handstand- or tumbling exercises. The breakfast break is from 7:30 am to 8:15 am, when the rest of the faculty arrives. At 8:20 am, students of all acrobatic specialties gather in the tumbling room, aligned according to their body height. The tallest students stand on the right-hand side of the room and the shorter students stand towards the left. They greet the director of the department in this formation every day. The main training session starts at 8:30 am and finishes at 12:30 pm. This block of training time covers the most important and the most difficult exercises and stretches, and enhances the strength, stamina, mental toughness, and endurance of the students. Lunch takes place from 12:30 pm to 2:30 pm, and students are encouraged to nap after lunch in order to regain strength for the rest of the training day. Every attempt is made to ensure the quality of the time used: through constant supervision, the pressure from supervisors, and the elimination of anything that might disturb or distract the schedule. These efforts guarantee that every minute of the training sessions is used by its full potential (Foucault, 1975:150).

The afternoon session begins at 2:30 pm and runs until 5:00 pm. Here, the advanced students practice choreographies together with their coaches while less advanced students either repeat the exercises of the morning session or practice additional disciplines. Dinner is served from 5:00 pm until 6:30 pm. Working members of the *China National Acrobatic Troupe* leave campus around this time for their daily show in the city center. Similar to the early morning session, the final training session of the day from 7:30

pm to 10:00 pm is supervised by just two teachers and is considered an "open" training session. Classes are scheduled from Monday to Saturday, and the body is constantly applied to its exercise. Similar to Foucault's observations of early 19th century education systems, timetables are meticulously planned considering precision and application, and with regularity being the fundamental virtue of "disciplinary time" (Foucault, 1975:151). Furthermore, to maintain a balanced discipline, the school also teaches "standard" subjects such as math, history, reading, and writing on Wednesdays and Saturdays. 90-minute dance classes are also attended in addition to acrobatic training. Foreign students are obliged to take Chinese language classes every Wednesday, while the local students are having their own academic lessons. Punctuality and attendance are recorded and forwarded to governmental officials. Foreign students who fail to attend training sessions or skip Chinese language classes might lose their student visa and have to leave the country. There are no exceptions at BJIAS. Upon entering a contract with the school, every student must comply with the campus regulations and accept the power dynamics that are set in place if they aspire to complete the program.

Overall, this comparison has shown that similar to Foucault's system, BJIAS established a tight relationship between time, space, and surveillance that build on each other; by creating a confined space and by enforcing a strict time schedule on an individual, total control and surveillance are possible. In this construct of discipline, the students are continuously transformed and shaped and as Foucault describes it: "the human body, was entering a machinery of power, that explores it, breaks it down and rearranges it, [...] for one may have a hold over other's bodies, not only so that they may do what one wishes, but so that they may operate as one wishes, with the techniques, the speed and the efficiency that one determines' (Foucault, 1975:138). The striking similarity between the living environment of the students at the *Beijing International Art School* and Foucault's concepts of time, space, and surveillance, display how governments have systematically designed and applied concepts of control for centuries. How the Chinese government administers the educational system discloses the efficiency of a rigorously designed structure of control, and how it is the foundation for a successful training outcome and finally, the "production" of the docile body.

CHAPTER 6: CONTORTION TRAINING

Having explored the environmental structures and hierarchies of the *Beijing International Art School*, this section gives insight into the training methods of the contortion department and the synergy between teacher and students. Building on the extreme aesthetics of contortionism, as analyzed in Chapter Three, this chapter will examine the training techniques of the contortion students.

The performance art-form contortionism is taught in the acrobatics department of the *Beijing International Art School*, and its sole purpose is to prepare students for a professional contortion career from an early age. To guarantee an efficient and successful contortion education, students begin their training at the age of between four and six when the skeletal muscle and connective tissue, such as ligaments and tendons are soft and able to quickly adapt to the training methods. The focus of the training is on strength and flexibility. It consists of different levels of difficulty including handstands, leg flexibility and back bending.

Contortion is divided into three styles:

    1. *Front bending*, performed by so-called front benders, requires the extreme forward flexing of the spine into numerous different positions. (Figure 36)

Fig. 36 *Frontbender*. Front bending acrobat from Cirque du Soleil. Nouvelle Experience Finale 1994, Cirque du Soleil. Photo credit: StuSeeger. Available: at:https://commons.wikimedia.org/wiki/File:An_acrobat_performing_in_the_contortion_act_of_Cirque_du_Soleil%27s_Nouvelle_Exp%C3%A9rience,_1994.jpg

Fig. 37 *Backbender. Contortionist, posed in studio, ca. 1880*. Photo credit: George Eastman House. Uploaded by PD'Tillman. Available: https://commons.wikimedia.org/wiki/File:-Contortionist,_posed_in_studio,_ca._1880.jpg

Fig. 38 *Dislocation of Joints*. Captain Frodo performing his contortionism act. 2006. Photo credit: Allysonk. Available: https://commons.wikimedia.org/wiki/File:Captain_Frodo.jpg

2. *Back bending*, which requires the extreme backwards flexing of the spine into different poses. (Figure 37)

3. *Dislocation of the joints*, where the performer slips certain joints out of their socket to the effect of having "rubber bones." (Figure 38)

Although contortionists will often choose to only perform their preferred style of either front- or back-bending on stage in their career, it is common—and even encouraged—to train both styles of contortion. In order to maintain a healthy body with homogenous body flexibility, they must train both to a high level. Young contortionists usually complete their training at the *Beijing International Art School* after a period of around six to eight years of full-time training, to then perform, for example, in circus shows, varieté theatres, or on TV shows.

Contortion teacher and director of the contortion department, Teng Li, was trained at the *China National Acrobatic Troupe* from a very young age. (Figure 39) In the 1990s, she was selected from BJIAS as a contortionist for *Cirque du Soleil* where she performed for many years. After retiring from the stage, she returned to the *Beijing International Art School* as a contortion coach where she trains local and foreign artists of different age and level. As the head of the contortion department, she selects her own pupils from the pool of candidates. In the beginning of their training, each student is educated in the four central skills: tumbling, flexibility, handstand, and dance. They specialize at a later stage in their training. A study guide about the *National Acrobats*

Fig. 39 Contortion student Lan-Lan, Mariam Ala-Rashi, Teacher Teng Li, contortion student WeiWei (from left to right). (Copyrights: Mariam Ala-Rashi)

of China, written for the University of California Berkeley gives insight into the importance of the four fundamental skills in the early stages of an acrobat's education:

> Students work daily on core skills: the handstand, tumbling, flexibility, and dance. They are also expected to be skilled in juggling. Each student will have a more pronounced talent for one of the four core acrobatic skills. The handstand is considered the essence of Chinese acrobatics. Many signature acrobatic acts include some form of handstand. Master teachers have commented that, "handstand training is to acrobats what studying the human body is to a medical student." An acrobat trains in progressive steps from basic to advanced handstands. Training directly affects three areas of the body — shoulders, lower back, and wrists. A weakness in any one area compromises the acrobat's ability. Beginning students begin by doing handstands against a wall. In three to six months, they build up to a half hour of wall handstands. The three areas of the body become stronger until at last students are able to hold the free handstand (Abrams, L. et al. 2009:4).

A very similar training pattern is applied at BJIAS. Furthermore, the *Beijing International Art School* has published its very own handbook for teachers titled *Zaji Jiaocheng (Acrobatics Curriculum)*, which includes teaching instructions and a curriculum. It is therefore suggested that this is a tried and tested curriculum and applied nationwide. All four skills of handstand, tumbling, flexibility, and dance come into action during a contortion routine (some more than others, depending on the choreography), and therefore have to be mastered to a high level. Every teacher at the *Beijing International Art School* knows how to teach the fundamentals of these four central skills. However, the privilege to study contortion and to learn from the head of the contortion department not only requires a certain body type and grace but also determination and a positive mindset to guarantee a successful training for the duration of at least six years. Students that have been accepted to the program are closely observed in the first two weeks of their training and assigned to a different teacher if their demeanor does not meet the teacher's standards.

In the past, teachers at BJIAS applied an old-fashioned training method during the flexibility training, called "breaking". Here the teacher uses extreme force during the assisted leg stretches (called扳腿 *ben tui*) in order to intentionally tear the leg's ligaments. It has been argued by older teachers (who have experienced those methods themselves when they were students) that once ripped, ligaments and muscles stay soft for the rest of the student's life after they have healed. These questionable methods promise quick success, but have been slowly replaced by more sophisticated and medically-sound methods nationwide. However, it is possible that these methods are still applied today in schools of lower repute. In a biannual external examination, the instructors at BJIAS are tested on how they apply their teaching skills. Teachers such as Teng Li do not "break" the ligaments, as the author could witness during her studies with the teacher, but apply rigorous drills and demand hard work from all of their students. During the assisted stretch segments, she would constantly ask "Is it painful? (痛吗 *Tòng ma*)" so that she could adjust the force with which she would stretch the student. In order to cope with the strict training methods and to guarantee a successful training outcome, the requirements for contortion candidates to be selected are high. Each discipline a student wants to specialize in requires a certain body type.

The ideal contortionist would demonstrate certain signs of a suitable mentality and physique. The candidates who apply for the contortion program present their level of flexibility and other skills, such as dance and tumbling, in short auditions. These additional skills will bolster their candidacy in the selection process. Other non-athletic criteria such as manners, grace. and beauty are essential as well. The preferred body type is slender but short, with a long neck, slim arms, as well as long legs and fingers.

The contortion department is designed to meet the particular requirements of the contortion students and is equipped with a thick carpet, which dampens and supports the contortionist's exercises (Circocan, 2011). One wall consists of large mirrors while the other walls are equipped with thick ballet bars that can withstand huge amounts of force that are applied in stretching drills during training sessions. Based on the school's training schedule, the contortion teachers divide their students' practice according to their individual level, with advanced stretches in the morning and choreographic practice during the afternoon. Less advanced students undergo a customized training session in the afternoon. To give insight into the training process, the synergy between teacher and student, and the effort and attention each movement requires, only the most essential stretches will be introduced here. The curriculum for contortionists of any style consists of hundreds of exercises.

However, the training sequences for contortionists around the world is very similar. Contortionists usually start their day's practice by stretching their legs and hips. Then, they proceed to stretch the upper body, while simultaneously keeping their legs and hips warm and flexible. This is to build up flexibility throughout the whole body and to maintain full flexibility of the spine. The contortion training starts in earnest with practicing oversplits for both box (middle) and front splits by using a bench to place the front foot on. After five repetitions, the teacher will assist the stretch and push the back leg down so that the upper thigh may touch the floor. (Figure 40) This is called *ban tui* 扳腿 (*ban*= to stretch, *tui*= leg). These assisted stretches force the body to move beyond its natural range of motion. Combined with daily repetition, they aim to increase the flexibility towards extreme results. Numerous variations of passive and active leg-stretches follow; amongst them, the wall stretch where the contortionist has to climb behind the ballet bar and, while facing the wall, lifts one leg into a standing split. The contortionist remains in this passive stretch for up to five minutes, following the teacher's instructions. Then, the teacher places yoga blocks under the front heel of the student to deepen the stretch while the student remains in this position for another minute (Figure 41). The teacher will now actively pull the front heel backwards

Fig. 40 Oversplit training on a bench, Mariam (2012). (Copyrights: Mariam Ala-Rashi).

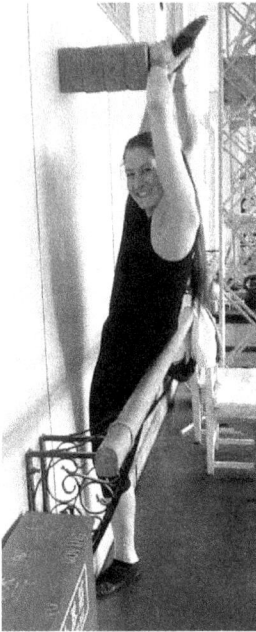

and away from the wall, to achieve maximum flexibility of the leg. (Figure 42) Overall, the legs are stretched for over an hour and then kept flexible and warm for the following hours to proceed with the back-stretches and the contortion routines. The stretching of the spine always follows the leg stretches. It is crucial to warm up the leg muscles and hips first, as their active engagement supports back flexibility in a positive way. Should the contortionist forget to properly warm up their legs and hips first, they would disallow their backbend the range it needs to achieve maximum flexibility. Therefore, a contortionist's training sequential starts "from toe to head".

Spinal stretches are the heart of a contortionist's training. Contortionism is one of the most complex ways to enhance the flexibility of this delicate part of the body, and therefore requires immense physiological knowledge as well as a deep practical understanding. The contortion coach represents a vital role during the training sessions as the synergy between coach and student is dependent on mutual trust and respect. In order to achieve a deep back-stretch that goes beyond the natural movement of the spine and attached muscles, the practitioner must breathe calmly and

244

relax entirely, while trusting that the coach is aware of how far their spine can be stretched without causing any injuries. (Figure 43) Only then is the success of professional contortion training ensured. The training sequences of back-stretches consist of basic exercises that prepare the spine for more complex routines while the difficulty is gradually increased. Once the spine has been warmed up and has achieved its maximum flexibility in every range of motion, the contortionist is ready to practice maneuvers, such as complex handstand variations and choreographies.

Fig. 43 Assisted back stretch, Taiwanese exchange student (left, name unknown) and Teacher Teng Li (right). (Copyrights: Mariam Ala-Rashi).

Although the training sequential for contortion is internationally similar, the daily training load, repetition of exercises and choreographies of BJIAS are still unparalleled to other contortion institutions. This is one reason for its international success. The extreme repetition of exercises and choreographies and the aim for perfection is at the heart of Chinese training methods. Choreographies are always executed as though a live audience is present, so that students embody every detail of the performance, including facial expressions. Tricks, training routines, and choreographies are repeated endlessly until the contortionist's body meets the high standards of the school. A student therefore, may be required to repeat a single trick hundreds of times per day - for as long as six months - until the coach decides that it meets their expectations. In comparison to contortion institutions in other countries, where students train up to "only" four hours per day, a Chinese contortionist practices up to eight hours daily, and sometimes even more. To increase the level of difficulty in performances (and to stand out internationally as a unique and advanced culture of contortionism), Chinese contortion trainers have also mastered the use of props such as glass pyramids and swirling carpets.

Once their trainers have decided they have met certain requirements, young artists are allowed to gain stage experience in performing. They are sometimes broken into a small group of three to five students, but are more

Fig. 44 (left) Jon Mili Guangzhou Acrobatic Troupe, (Chinese name 孙佳音 Sun Jia Yin) from China performing a contortion act while spinning carpets for the 13th Festival Mondial du Cirque de Demain, 1990. Photographer: Gilles-Henri Polge. "Festival Mondial du Cirque de Demain-Paris". Courtesy and Copyrights: Association Française pour le Cirque de Demain. Available at: https://www.cirquededemain.paris/en/medias/galleries/gallery/13

Fig 45 (right) He Jia from China performing a contortion act with bowl balancing for the 12th Festival Mondial du Cirque de Demain, 1989. Photographer: Wanda Zacharias. "Festival Mondial du Cirque de Demain-Paris". Courtesy and Copyrights: Association Française pour le Cirque de Demain. Available at: https://www.cirquededemain.paris/en/medias/galleries/gallery/12

commonly placed into duo acts where a young student is partnered with a more experienced artist. Here the young student starts to learn classic routines (*Rolling with Cups, Rolling with Lights* and so on) that include props in order to increase their fine motor and balancing skills. These contortion routines often include different kinds of props, such as large glass pyramids for the choreography of *Rolling Cups* that are balanced on hands and feet, the forehead and with the mouth (as explored in Chapter Three). The afternoon training is usually reserved for the practice of choreographies that oftentimes include props. Other props are swirling velvet carpets (antipodism props) of around 50 x 50 cm, that are balanced and spun on the finger or toe tip. (Figure 44) Performing with multiple chandeliers and burning candles used for *Rolling Cups and Rolling Lights* performances is another common element in Chinese contortion routines, as well as performing with multiple porcelain bowls that are balanced on the head, hands, and feet. (Figure 45) The latter is a prop that is both used in Chinese and Mongolian contortion performances, and it is currently not evidenced which country invented the act of bowl balancing. It is feasible that the bowls used for a performance are different in each country and that a Mongolian contortion performance with bowls entails an entirely different meaning than a Chinese contortion performance with bowls. The use of props such as the glass chandeliers or spinning carpets however, are unique to traditional Chinese contortion and enhance the level of difficulty in addition to the technical perfection during the contortion act itself. Other requisites that are internationally used are metal canes (see example image 16) with wooden blocks on which contortionists perform complicated handstand routines, or the aforementioned Marinelli bend (Figure 46) which involves a mouth-piece attached to a raised platform for balancing with the performer's bodyweight supported only by their jaw.

Fig. 46 Mongolian Contortionist Agiimaa Jargalsaikhan practicing the Marinelli Bend, called zubnik (зубник) in Mongolia (2014). Mongolia. Photograph courtesy of Agiimaa Jargalsaikhan.

When preparing for a performance, all choreography is repeated numerous times, with full energy and controlled exertion, as though it were being performed for a live audience. The students have to smile and "stay in character" for the entire duration of the performance. Each movement and detail need to be flawlessly executed while the teacher gives verbal corrections from the bench. The expectations of the students are high and performing under the school's name ultimately means to represent the entire nation, its countrymen, and its government. Typical mistakes such as not smiling, not holding poses for the required duration, not being perfectly synchronized with the other performers, or simply not keeping the toes pointed, will be punished. Some teachers use psychological methods and shout at the students or insult them, and some punish through endless repetitions of the movements the student fails at. In the same sense as skills and choreographies are passed on from one generation to the next, so are the training methods. Having experienced the same strict training as children themselves, the teachers evaluate what can be expected from the students and when to punish them. The atmosphere during performance practice is tense and focused; students and teachers interact in a professional manner and do not exchange much small talk. However, after a successful training day, some teachers hand out fruits or candy to reward the young students.

Jingjing Xue describes in his chapters *Endure!* and *All Bitterness will turn to Sweetness* the hardships of the training, his relationship with his teachers and how the training was ultimately designed to prepare the students to perform internationally. As the winter months were particularly cold in Shanghai and the large training rooms were not properly heated, Jingjing Xue remembers his first winter at the acrobatic troupe in 1956 and a conversation with his teacher Wong:

> "The winter freezes lazy people. [...] As long as you exercise you will not feel the cold. For us, in this trade, we exercise during the hottest days of summer, and the coldest days of winter, so that our bodies will become strong and fit for all weather conditions. No matter which part of the world you find yourself performing in, you can survive and perform well." Wong made it clear that he was talking about not only the acrobatic trade, but also a correct attitude to life. Day after day, the drills drove each of us to the extremes of endurance. We became numb to the muscle-wrenching and skin-ripping exercises. It was cruel beyond belief, but it did its job. As we passed the initial training stage, I discovered the huge potential in the simple fact of endurance (Jingjing, 2021: 32).

The training conditions in Shanghai and Beijing are very similar and not much has changed regarding these training environments, as the author could experience first-hand during her training at BJIAS from 2011 to 2015. The training rooms are large and very cold in winter and extremely hot in summer. It is a shared experience that the teachers had to go through themselves when they were students and it is still part of the training environment today. By design, these conditions are set in place to create resilient acrobats that are ready to perform internationally and upon retiring from the stage, pass on their skills and experience to the next generation.

Heralded as the cornerstone of both the CNAT and BJIAS's success, these training methods launch young contortionists into international careers with every graduating class.

They characterize one of the internationally most sophisticated training programs that secures the training success of the next generation of Chinese acrobats. Equipped with the knowledge of centuries old training traditions, future acrobats will continue to set new benchmarks and represent China on the international stage through technical perfection, extreme discipline, and strong aesthetics.

CONCLUSION

For centuries, the art of Chinese contortionism has traversed through countless transformations. Rooted in performing arts that depict labor, religious sacrifice, and other aspects of daily life, Chinese contortion has been passed on from one generation to the next to serve various functions: from street entertainment in feudal society in ancient China, to court performance, as part of international exchange in the era of the Silk Road, as political tool in socialist and post socialist China and onto the stage of 21st century *Cirque du Soleil*.

The analysis of desired aesthetics and rigid training methods in China through a Foucauldian lens revealed how the human body was utilized by governments. Drawing on multiple similarities between the Western system of prisons, military, and legal hierarchies, this study identified how the education system in China "produces" disciplined, acrobatic bodies and revealed aspects of body control for political gain.

Yet, Chinese contortionism is not defined by how it adapts within constantly shifting dynamics in culture, society and politics. Rather, it is defined by its perseverance as traditional practice that still conveys its ancient legacy that stems from Chinese philosophy.

Depicting circular movements and constantly revolving circular backbends, Chinese contortion embodies the philosophy of the circle as symbol for moral integrity, perfection, and proficiency that are considered one of life's highest goals in Chinese society. This motif is at the heart of many Chinese performing arts, and contortion in particular, and is conveyed physically and conceptually with the aim to set new benchmarks on the international stage through technical perfection and extreme discipline. Although practices of body flexibility in other cultures, as seen in Egyptian acrobatic dance and Tlatilco figurines in Mexico, have vanished, Chinese contortionism is a tradition that continues today. It is evolving and transforming through the ages and reflects its ever-changing environments of politics, society, culture and even technology, as it experiences growing popularity on social media, while still conveying the core values of ancient Chinese philosophy embedded in the fabric of artistic practice.

Although this monograph is only the starting point for further research of this complex art-form, it outlines the value of contortionism yesterday and today. Further investigation however, is necessary to cover deeper aspects of this art form in different contexts. By exploring the historical development of Chinese acrobatic theatre, which (although recognized as unique art form) contortionism was a part of; this research aimed to explore a comprehensible link regarding the development of Chinese traditional contortionism that we see today. The analysis of the desired aesthetics in today's contortion practices in China, that have gradually developed over the past centuries, together with the author's observations as contortion practitioner in China, suggest a linear evolution aimed towards the refinement of extreme abilities and world-class status in the performance industry.

Future research could, therefore, aim to investigate numerous questions: How is the iconography of Chinese traditional contortionism embodied? What is the spiritual context of Chinese contortionism? How can Western schools consider some of the traditional training methods and cultural aspects of Chinese contortionism? What is the historical connection between Chinese and Mongolian contortionism and the possible hybridity of contortionism in Inner Mongolia? How is local culture in various areas in China reflected in Chinese contortionism? What are the gender roles in Chinese contortionism and what are the values of female, male, and non-binary contortionists in Chinese society?

An interesting aspect of future research could be how body flexibility and contortion were deployed in ancient Chinese ritualistic and ceremonial practices. How was the early version of Chinese contortion "Body Art beyond the Limits" rooted in culture and society and how did it develop? There is also abundant room for further progress in determining how contortion developed and transformed through the ages: From representation of daily life aspects to court entertainment to spiritual practice and so on. Are there similar ways to determine how Chinese contortion skills progressed throughout the dynasties as it can be observed in the practice of acrobatic dance in Egypt in the Old, Middle and New Kingdoms?

Aiming to contribute to this growing area of research, it is imperative to position the art of contortionism in scholarly literature as an aspect of valuable Chinese heritage. Not only to open up this valuable field for future discussion and research but also to contribute to a better understanding of this art form for current and future contortion practitioners. It is also the author's hope that such academic inquiry helps elevate the status of the Circus Arts on the whole, as a rich collection of diverse art-forms with unique histories and cultural values.

LIST OF ILLUSTRATIONS

My sincere gratitude goes to all the individuals who gave their permission to use their illustrations/photographs.

1. Performer: Mariam Ala-Rashi. *Ballet*. Germany (2011). Photographer: Hamid Sheikh

2. Performer: Mariam Ala-Rashi. *American Tribal Fusion*, Germany (2010). Photographer: Rainer Westerwinter.

3. Performer: Mariam Ala-Rashi. *Belly Dance* (2012). Copyrights: Cicilia, Cat Dance Beijing.

4. Dance Performance Mariam Ala-Rashi at *Orientale* Germany (2010). Photographer: André Elbing.

5. Performer: Mariam Ala-Rashi. Beijing (2014). Photographer: Andreu Pardales.

6. Performer: Mariam Ala-Rashi. *Oriental Fusion*. Germany (2011). Copyrights: Arnd Wende.

7. BH4 Beni Hasan, Lightroom-1040087: Female acrobats and girls playing with the ball – 15th Tomb of Beni Hasan. Photo credit: kairoinfo4u, 2009. Available at: https://www.flickr.com/photos/manna4u/4127122259/

8. RoHa 2292. Karnak Egypt, Red Chapel of female pharaoh Hatshepsut, Exterior wall. Link: Photo credit: kairoinfo4u, 2007 (Flickr). Available at: https://www.flickr.com/photos/

manna4u/444059506/in/photolist-FeVqo-FeXvb-FeX6Q-
FeVdh-FeVLS-FeWxL-FeWKq-cvEWy-FeXZn-4pnuB7-
4pirRz-83QSp4-4pis2P-8ZyjZV-7k19qc-7k5Tnq-cvEZe-
4tZKUF-4tZKZg-7k1dcR-6CbcYi-7jZywM-cvEUv-cvERd-
7k1gUt-7jZCeP-7k4K5f-7k1Ndx-cvETd-5Qjb21-7pUcTG-
7k6b74-7k5PTu-7jZYbD-7k1ApM-7k1kwv-7jZMJP-7k1wSB-
cvEYo-7k1EbV-sL1i4H-YsSJhw-2cYYBjH-SeF9Rj-23Ljh7c-
YsTbhN-YsS3Ls-5Lqeo8-YsTgWJ-YsTiQy

9. *Feast of Opet Panel*, Luxor Temple constructed approximately 1400 BCE. The Festival of Opet depicted on the western wall of the court. Photo credit: Ovedc. Link: https://commons.wikimedia. org/wiki/File:By_ovedc_-_Luxor_Temple_-_56.jpg

10. Ostracon (limestone) from Deir el-Medina: Dancer/Acrobat in Backbend. Found at the Worker's Village Deir el-Medina near Luxor (1292 and 1076 BCE). *Tänzerin auf einem altägyptischen Ostrakon, gefunden in Theben, heute im Turiner Museo Egizio*; Malerei auf Kalkstein, 10,5x16,8cm, 19. Dynastie, um 1300 v. Chr. Photo credit: Public Domain/Author unknown. Available at: https:// commons.wikimedia.org/wiki/File:Female_topless_egyption_ dancer_on_ancient_ostrakon.jpg

11. Tlatilco Figurine. Ceramic art recovered from Tlatilco, pre-Columbian village in the Valley of Mexico, commonly known as the "Acrobat", circa 1300 - 800 BCE. Photo credit: El Comandante. Available at: https://en.wikipedia.org/wiki/ File:Acr%C3%B3bata_de_Tlatilco.JPG

12. (Front view) Portion of a Pilaster with an Acrobat. MET Museum. French; Pilaster; Sculpture-Architectural Date: circa 1150 –70,

Medium: Limestone. Geography: Made in Lyonnais, France. Credit Line: The Cloisters Collection, 1947. Photo credit: Public Domain/Met Museum. Available at: https://commons. wikimedia.org/wiki/File:Portion_of_a_Pilaster_with_an_ Acrobat_MET_cdi47-101-25.jpg

13. (Side View) Portion of a Pilaster with an Acrobat. MET Museum. French; Pilaster; Sculpture-Architectural Date: circa 1150 –70 Medium: Limestone. Geography: Made in Lyonnais, France. Credit Line: The Cloisters Collection, 1947. Photo credit: Public Domain/Met Museum. Available at: https://commons. wikimedia.org/wiki/File:Portion_of_a_Pilaster_with_an_ Acrobat_MET_cdi47-101-25s4.jpg

14. Female acrobat shooting an arrow with a bow in her feet; Gnathia style pelikai; 4th century B.C. Antikensammlung Berlin. Photo credit: Marcus Cyron. Available at: https://en.wikipedia.org/ wiki/File:Antikensammlung_Berlin_525.JPG

15. Hydria Acrobat Vase. British Museum, Townley Collection, Upper floor, room 73: The Greeks and Italy. A female acrobat next to a potter's turntable. Detail from a Campanian red-figure hydria, ca. 340-330 BC. Photo credit: Jastrow. Available at: https:// en.wikipedia.org/wiki/File:Hydria_acrobat_BM_VaseF232.jpg

16. Photo credit: Mongolian Contortion Center SF, Serchmaa Byamba. Contortionist: Khulan Myagmarsuren. Photographer: Robin Gee.

17. Yoga Pose *Ghanda Bherundasana* by Indian yoga practitioner ManinderYoga (Photo credit: With friendly permission from ManinderYoga, 2017)

18. Contortion Pose *Chest-Stand* by Mongolian contortionist Urnaa Uranbileg. (Photo credit: With friendly permission from Uranbileg, 2017)

19. Clay figurines on a tray: Music, dancing and acrobatic figurines from the Western Han Dynasty, unearthed from a Han tomb, Jinan, Shandong Province. Photo credit: Yargai Galtat.

20. Clay Figurine from figurine tray *Contortionist*: Music, dancing and acrobatic figurines from the Western Han Dynasty, unearthed from a Han tomb, Jinan, Shandong Province. Photo credit: Yargai Galtat.

21. Stone relief with "Hundred Entertainments" depicting a juggler (right), a dancer Qipanwu - Seven Plates Dance (center) and an artist performing a contortion-like trick while balancing on stacked benches (right). Relief from Szechuan, China. Han or Qing dynasty. Photograph: Courtesy of Prof. Arthur Lewbel.

22. *Figurines of Entertainers.* Han Dynasty (206 BCE–220 CE). Front and center, acrobat in contortion-like posture. Henan Provincial Museum, Zhengzhou Ceramic tomb figurines of jugglers, dancers, acrobats, and musicians provided entertainment for the afterlife, and allow today's viewer to imagine scenes of everyday enjoyment in the world of the Han. Photo credit: G41rn8. Available at: https://commons.wikimedia.org/wiki/File:China_2006_8-70.jpg

23. *Han Pottery Acrobats.* Han Dynasty (206 BCE–220 CE). Left and front: Acrobat executing a handstand while bending the legs forward. Han Gallery, Henan Provincial Museum, Zhengzhou. Photo

credit: Gary Todd. Available at: https://commons.wikimedia.org/wiki/File:Han_Pottery_Acrobats_(10340375955).jpg

24. Stone Brick displaying Acrobats. Second from left: Acrobat in contortion-like posture balancing on stacked tables/benches. Eastern Han Stone Tomb Brick 21. Nanyang Museum of Han Dynasty Stone Carving, Henan Province, China. Photo credit: Gary Todd. Available at: https://commons.wikimedia.org/wiki/File:Eastern_Han_Stone_Tomb_Brick_21.jpg

25. Body Flexibility on Pole. *Acrobats. Northern Wei. Datong City Museum.* Image description: File: Datong 247. In this lively painted-pottery composition, two children spin and balance on a pole that is supported by a strongman on his forehead. To the left, another member of the troupe bangs a pair of cymbals. Such performances are documented as early as the Eastern Han Dynasty, for example in tomb bricks from Henan. Photo credit: G41rn8. Available at: https://commons.wikimedia.org/wiki/File:Datong_247.jpg

26. The rare relief from the Han Dynasty *State of Etiquette* made of 14 pottery portrait-tiles depicts various acrobatic disciplines and is currently exhibited in the Quzhou Museum (2021). Photo credit: Thom Wall.

27. Illustration of Chinese Characters: Illustration of Chinese Charactres for Rou Shu. Photo credit: Mariam Ala-Rashi.

28. Troupe de Fujian, China, performing the contortion act "Rolling Cups" for the 16th Festival Mondial du Cirque de Demain, 1993. Photographer: Bertrand Guay. "Festival Mondial du Cirque de Demain-Paris". Courtesy and Copyrights: Association

Française pour le Cirque de Demain. Available at: https://www.cirquededemain.paris/en/medias/galleries/gallery/16

29. Dai Wenxia from China performing the contortion act "Rolling Cups" for the 5th Festival Mondial du Cirque de Demain, 1981. Photographer: Paul de Cordon. "Festival Mondial du Cirque de Demain-Paris". Courtesy and Copyrights: Association Française pour le Cirque de Demain. Available at: https://www.cirquededemain.paris/en/medias/galleries/gallery/5

30. Shanghai Acrobat performing "Rolling Cups" Contortion Act. *Contortionist Shanghai Acrobatic Troupe.* Available at: https://commons.wikimedia.org/wiki/File:ContorsionistShanghai.jpg

31. Glass props for mouth (*left*), hand and feet (*center and right*). Photo credit: archive Mariam Ala-Rashi.

32. Temple of Heaven. Title: *Teil des Himmelstempels.* Built in 1420 by Emperor Yongle. Available at: https://commons.wikimedia.org/wiki/File:Teil_des_Himmelstempels.jpg?uselang=de

33. Poster of the *Tiananmen* Show 2012. (Copyrights: Mariam Ala-Rashi)

34. Backstage at the *Tiananmen* Show 2012: Performer of the *Beijing Opera* and Mariam Ala-Rashi dressed as Flight Attendant. (Copyrights: Mariam Ala-Rashi)

35. Government officials at the dress rehearsal, 2012. (Copyrights: Private archive Mariam Ala-Rashi)

36. *Frontbender:* Front bending acrobat from Cirque du Soleil. *Nouvelle Experience Finale 1994, Cirque du Soleil.* Photo credit: StuSeeger. Available: at:https://commons.wikimedia.org/wiki/File:An_acrobat_performing_in_the_contortion_act_of_

Cirque_du_Soleil%27s_Nouvelle_Exp%C3%A9rience,_1994. jpg

37. *Backbender. Contortionist, posed in studio, ca. 1880.* Photo credit: George Eastman House. Uploaded by PDTillman. Available: https://commons.wikimedia.org/wiki/File:Contortionist,_posed_in_studio,_ca._1880.jpg

38. *Dislocation of Joints.* Captain Frodo performing his contortionism act. 2006. Photo credit: Allysonk. Available: https://commons.wikimedia.org/wiki/File:Captain_Frodo.jpg

39. Contortion student LanLan, Mariam Ala-Rashi, Teacher Teng Li, contortion student WeiWei *(from left to right).* (Copyrights: Mariam Ala-Rashi)

40. Oversplit training on a bench, Mariam (2012). (Copyrights: Mariam Ala-Rashi).

41. Oversplit training on the wall with yoga blocks, Mariam Ala-Rashi (2012). (Copyrights: Mariam Ala-Rashi).

42. Assisted stretch, wall split. Mariam *(left)* and teacher Teng Li *(center)*, 2012 (Copyrights: Mariam Ala-Rashi).

43. Assisted back stretch, Taiwanese exchange student *(left,* name unknown) and Teacher Teng Li *(right).* (Copyrights: Mariam Ala-Rashi).

44. Jon Mili Guangzhou Acrobatic Troupe, (Chinese name 孙佳音 Sun Jia Yin)

from China performing a contortion act while spinning carpets for the 13th Festival Mondial du Cirque de Demain, 1990. Photographer: Gilles-Henri Polge. "Festival Mondial du Cirque de Demain-Paris". Courtesy and Copyrights: Association Française pour le

Cirque de Demain. Available at: https://www.cirquededemain.paris/en/medias/galleries/gallery/13

45. He Jia from China performing a contortion act with bowl balancing for the 12th Festival Mondial du Cirque de Demain, 1989. Photographer: Wanda Zacharias. "Festival Mondial du Cirque de Demain-Paris". Courtesy and Copyrights: Association Française pour le Cirque de Demain. Available at: https://www.cirquededemain.paris/en/medias/galleries/gallery/12

46. Mongolian Contortionist Agiimaa Jargalsaikhan practicing the Marinelli Bend, called zubnik (зубник) in Mongolia (2014). Mongolia. Photograph courtesy of Agiimaa Jargalsaikhan.

47. (Illustration) WeiWei 魏炜, Chinese contortionist and alumni of the Beijing International Art School. Photograph courtesy of WeiWei 魏炜.

48. (Illustration) Pyramid of Contortionists displayed in the city center of Beijing, 2012. Copyrights: Mariam Ala-Rashi.

BIBLIOGRAPHY

Abrams L.; Anderson R.; Anthony N.; Huey W. (2009) "National Acrobats of China." Study Guide for the University of Berkeley, USA and their School Time Series.

Ala-Rashi, M. 2021. *Mongolian Contortion-An Ethnographic Inquiry*. Philadelphia, United States: Modern Vaudeville Press.

Alter, M. 1952. *Science of Flexibility*. Champaign, United States: Human Kinetics

Ban Wang, 2010. *Words and Their Stories: Essays on the Language of the Chinese Revolution (Handbook of Oriental Studies: Section 4, China, Band 27)*. Leiden, Netherlands: Brill Academic Pub.

Barakat Gallery. 2021. *Tlatilco Sculpture of an Acrobat*. [online] Available at: https://store.barakatgallery.com/product/tlatilco-sculpture-of-an-acrobat/ [Accessed: 23. August 2021]

Basavaraddi, I. 2015. *Yoga: Its Origin, History and Development*. [online] Available at: http://www.mea.gov.in/in-focus-article.htm?25096/Yoga+Its+Origin+History+and+Development [Accessed: 19. December 2021]

Beijing International Art School. *Welcome*. [online] Available at: https://www.beijing-art.com/home.php [Accessed: 05. May 2021]

Brunner-Traut, E. 1958. *Der Tanz im Alten Ägypten. Nach bildlichen und inschriftlichen Zeugnissen.* Hamburg: Verlag J.J. Augustin.

Carter, J. 2021. *Power of Symbolism: The Swim that changed Chinese History.* [online] Available at: https://supchina.com/2021/07/14/power-of-symbolism-the-swim-that-changed-chinese-history/ [Accessed: 14. July 2021]

Chuluunbaatar, Enkhbold. "Mongolian Circus Industry in the Post-Transitional Economy." *International Journal of Cultural and Creative Industries.* Volume 1, 2 (2014): 68-74.

Chen and MacDonald. Bread and Circuses: Sports and Public Opinion in China. *Journal of Experimental Political Science*, Volume 7, Issue 1, Spring 2020, pp. 41 - 55 DOI: https://doi.org/10.1017/XPS.2019.15

Circus Dictionary, 2018. (A)*Contortion.* [online] Available at: http://thecircusdictionary.com/moves/?category=contortion [Accessed: 06. July 2018]

Circus Dictionary, 2018. (B) *Bendy Handstand Z.* [online] Available at: http://thecircusdictionary.com/moves/1006/bendy-handstand-z/ [Accessed: 06. July 2018]

Circopedia, 2018. *Beijing Acrobatic Troupe.* [online] Available at: http://www.circopedia.org/Beijing_Acrobatic_Troupe [Accessed: 04.July 2018]

Dange, Sadashiv A. "*SEX IN STONE AND THE VEDIC MITHUNA.*" Annals of the Bhandarkar Oriental Research Institute: 58/59

(1977): 543-60. Accessed August 24, 2021. http://www.jstor.
org/stable/41691726.

Fu Q., 1985. *Chinese Acrobatics through the Ages*. Beijing, China: Foreign
Language Press.

Fu Q. and Li X. 2003. *A Primer of Chinese Acrobatics*. Beijing, China:
Foreign Languages Press.

Google Trends A, 2021. *Contortion Definition*. [online] Available at:
https://trends.google.com/trends/explore?q=contortion%20
definition&date=2008-04-04%202021-05-04 [Accessed: 06.
May 2021]

Google Trends B, 2021. *Contortion & Contortion Poses
(comparison)*. [online] Available at: https://trends.
google.com/trends/explore?cat=3&date=today%20
5-y&geo=US&q=contortion,contortion%20poses [Accessed:
25. September 2021]

Grimes, M. 2015. *Solid Potato Salad-Why there's no reason a scene in a Movie
has to have anything to do with the Movie itself.* [online] Available
at: https://thedailygrime.wordpress.com/2015/07/30/
solid-potato-salad-why-theres-no-reason-a-scene-in-a-movie-
has-to-have-anything-to-do-with-the-movie-itself/ [Accessed:
13. June 2018]

Havva, M. 2007. *Orientalischer Tanz-Folklore und Hoftänze*. Illertissen:
Oriental Dance Art

Hernandez, F. 2021. *Examining Tlatilco Figurines*. [online] Available at: https://unframed.lacma.org/2020/11/02/examining-tlatilco-figurines [Accessed: 23. August 2021]

Hopkins Medicine. 2021. *9 Benefits of Yoga*. [online] Available at: https://www.hopkinsmedicine.org/health/wellness-and-prevention/9-benefits-of-yoga [Accessed: 19. December 2021]

Houston, R. 2018. The Growth of Literacy in Western Europe from 1500 to 1800. [online] Available at: https://brewminate.com/the-growth-of-literacy-in-western-europe-from-1500-to-1800/ [Accessed: 24. August 2021]

JapanTimes. 2021. *China's Kids get schooled in Xi Jinping Thought*. [online] Available at: https://www.japantimes.co.jp/news/2021/09/01/asia-pacific/xi-jinping-china-schools/ [Accessed: 06. September 2021]

Jingjing, X. 2021. *Shanghai Acrobat. A True Story of Courage and Perserverance from Revolutionary China*. New York: Apollo Publishers.

Jinan City Museum, 2020. *Introduction Video of the Western Han Dynasty Dance and Acrobatic Ensemble*. [online] Available at: https://www.bilibili.com/video/av200935105/ [Accessed: 24. June 2021]

Kolb, A. 2017. *Dance and Politics in China. Interculturalism, Hybridity, and the ArtsCross Project*. In: Kowal, R. *The Oxford Handbook of Dance and Politics*. New York: Oxford University Press. Pages: 347-370

Marinelli bend. 2020. *Wang Xiaoqian's triple Marinelli bend at Chinese Henan TV channel*. [online] Available at: https://www.youtube.

com/watch?v=mrc103vjWeA&ab_channel=Marinellibend [Accessed: 25. August 2021]

NHS. 2021. *A Guide to Yoga.* [online] Available at: https://www.nhs.uk/ live-well/exercise/guide-to-yoga/ [Accessed: 19. December 2021]

Oxford English Dictionary, 2018. (A) *Contortion.* [online] Available at: http://www.oed.com/view/ Entry/40295?redirectedFrom=contortion& [Accessed: 13. June 2018]

Oxford English Dictionary, 2018. (B) *Contortionist.* [online] Available at: http://www.oed.com/view/Entry/40297 [Accessed: 13. June 2018]

Oxford English Dictionary, 2018. (C) *Contortionism.* [online] Available at: http://www.oed.com/view/Entry/40296? [Accessed: 13. June 2018]

Parezo, N. and Fowler, D. 2007. *Anthropology goes to the Fair. The 1904 Louisiana Purchase Exposition. Critical Studies in the History of Anthropology.* Lincoln: University of Nebraska Press.

Radchenko, S. The Sino–Russian relationship in the mirror of the Cold War. China Int Strategy Rev. 1, 269–282 (2019). https://doi.org/10.1007/s42533-019-00030-x

Rao, R. 2018. Erotic Sentiment in Indian Temple Sculptures. [online] Available at: http://indiafacts.org/erotic-sentiment-in-indian-temple-sculptures/ [Accessed: 24. August 2021]

SBS Dateline. 2021. *China's Patriotic Education.* [online] Available at: https://www.youtube.com/watch?v=P6V-Mh9Vffk&ab_channel=SBSDateline [Accessed: 02. September 2021]

Spencer, P. (2003). Dance in Ancient Egypt. Near Eastern Archaeology, 66(3), 111-121. doi:10.2307/3210914

Stewart, T. (Trav S.D.). (2005). *No Applause Just throw Money, or, The Book that made Vaudeville famous: A high-class, refined Entertainment.* New York: Farrar, Straus and Giroux. Kindle Edition.

Suzanne, 2014. *Who were the amazing Ross Sisters?* [online] Available at: https://www.ripleys.com/weird-news/who-were-the-amazing-ross-sisters/ [Accessed: 13. June 2018]

The Soraya, 2012. *The National Circus of The People's Republic of China presents Cirque Chinois.* [online] Available at: https://www.thesoraya.org/assets/Uploads/education/archive/pdf/CirqueChinois-CueSheetrev.pdf [Accessed: 28. July 2018]

UNESCO. 2021. *Temple of Heaven: An Imperial Sacrificial Altar in Beijing – UNESCO World Heritage Centre.* [online] Available at: https://whc.unesco.org/en/list/881/ [Accessed: 02. September 2021]

V&A. 2021. *V&A – The Story of Circus.* [online] Available at: https://www.vam.ac.uk/articles/the-story-of-circus#slideshow=58613815&slide=20 [Accessed: 05. May 2021]

Vaishnav, M. 2019. *Sex, Love, and Relationships: My Journey of 40 Years.* [online] Available at: https://www.ncbi.nlm.nih.gov/pmc/articles/PMC6862977/ [Accessed: 19, December 2021]

Wapbaike. 2018. *Rou Shu.* [online] Available at: https://wapbaike.baidu. com/item/柔术/1696?fr=aladdin [Accessed: 07. July 2018]

Yudong Observation, 2020. *The rare Han Dynasty "State of Etiquette" Pottery Portrait Tiles with Acrobatic Pattern at the Quzhou Museum.* [online] Available at: http://www.manyanu.com/new/ fac29469fa904263b36a5e09240f332e

Yuni, 2016. *History of Contortion.* [online] Available at: https://yuni. deviantart.com/journal/History-of-Contortion-611109596 [Accessed: 12. June 2018]

Zhang, T. 2016. *Bending the Body for China: The uses of acrobatics in Sino-US diplomacy during the Cold War.* In: Tait, P. *The Routledge Circus Studies Reader.* New York: Routledge. Pages: 405-429

Zhang, T. *From China to the Big Top: Chinese Acrobats and the Politics of Aesthetic Labor, 1950–2010.* In: International Labor and Working-Class History, No. 89, Spring 2016, pp. 40–63

Zlata, 2018. *The Worlds most flexible Woman.* [online] Available at: http:// zlata.de/index.php [Accessed: 12. June 2018]

Zuchowska, M. 2014. *Dancers' Representations and the Function of Dance in Han Dynasty (202 bc – 220 AD) Chinese Society.* In: Soar, K. *Archaeological Approaches to Dance Performance.* Oxford: Archaeopress. Pages: 67-73

Pictures

Galtat, Y. 2019. Book Cover. Tokyo

Maninderyoga. 2017. *My lovely memories.* [online] Available at: https://www.instagram.com/p/BResOSFDBPp/ [Accessed: 04. July 2018]

Powers, A. 2018. *Pinterest. Zi Jin Guan.* [online] Available at: https://www.pinterest.co.uk/pin/60094976252120637/ [Accessed: 04. July 2018]

Sciencesource. 2021. *Acrobat 1200-600 BC.* [online] Available at: https://www.sciencesource.com/archive/Image/Acrobat--1200-600-BC-SS2771430.html [Accessed: 05. May 2021]

The Met. 2021. *Portion of a Pilaster with an Acrobat.* [online] Available at: https://www.metmuseum.org/art/collection/search/471266 [Accessed: 05. May 2021]

Uranbileg. 2017. *Body Shape Series.* [online] Available at: https://www.instagram.com/p/BRqLZCwlkWT/ [Accessed: 04. July 2018]

Videos

Ala-Rashi, M. 2018. *Tiananmen – Where the Five-Star red Flag is raised (Dress Reherasal).* [online] Available at: https://vimeo.com/286246885 [Accessed: 22. August 2018]

Cb3815, 2007. *Rolling Cups.* [online] Available at: https://www.youtube.com/

watch?v=q3UK3g48hLg&index=12&list=PLp4SJN2XP_
zLTnI1V_hUqWdhKUVmGr4Hx [Accessed: 08. August 2018]

Circocan, 2011. *Training Room at Beijing Acrobatic School.* [online] Available
at: https://www.youtube.com/watch?v=EeQIB3R4tVI
[Accessed: 24. June 2018]

Real Stories, 2015. *Caning Children to become Gymnasts-Real Stories.*
[online] Available at: https://www.youtube.com/
watch?v=hPkNwyLhAIU [Accessed: 22. August 2018]

SschevyBB, 2012. *Little gymnast-Is this abuse- Communist China showing
ownership over Kids rights to be a kid.* [online] Available at: https://
www.youtube.com/watch?v=D4athsHqH_w [Accessed: 22.
August 2018]

The Kakubei Jishi

The Rise, Fall, and Restoration of a Japanese Folk Performing Art

Mariam Ala-Rashi

THE KAKUBEI JISHI

The Rise, Fall, and Restoration of a Japanese Folk Performing Art

HISTORY OF KAKUBEI JISHI

EARLY 18TH CENTURY (1700-1750) TSUKIGATA

Establishment of the Kakubei Jishi lion dance. A folk performing art that originates in the Tsukigata Village.

1755-1886 EDO CITY

The lion dance is in high demand. Numbers of Kakubei Jishi Troupes increase rapidly during the Edo period (1603-1867). Child performers are exploited for the sake of extreme body flexibility. Stylization of the original art form takes place.

MEIJI PERIOD (1868 - 1912)

Economic and social modernization. Between 1900 and 1911 compulsory education is declared and numerous prohibitions put into place that protect children from exploitation. Kakubei Jishi performances decrease and the ones watching them pity the children.

PREVENTION OF CRUELTY TO CHILDREN ACT 1933

When the law prohibiting cruelty to children is passed in 1933, the Kakubei Jishi have already disappeared.

1936 & 1959 REVIVAL AND CULTURAL HERITAGE

The *Kakubei Jishi* Preservation Society is established in 1936 with research being implemented to recover knowledge about the history of the Kakubei Jishi. In collaboration with local schools a new lion dance troupe is founded in 1959 in Tsukigata. The wellbeing of the child performers is of utmost importance. Folk acrobatics are showcased and extreme body flexibility is discontinued.

2013 TSUKIGATA

The Kakubei Jishi lion dance is acknowledged for its historical and cultural significance and granted the status of Niigata City's *Intangible Folk Cultural Property* on April 15, 2013.

275

ABSTRACT

This research study proposes an introduction to the folk performing art Kakubei Jishi by examining its history and functions. The art of Kakubei Jishi—a lion dance that is exclusive to the Niigata prefecture and that originated in the Tsukigata Village—is an acrobatic dance that is showcased by child performers wearing wooden lion masks on top of their heads. This monograph further explores the downfall of the art form during the Meiji era and its revival in the 20th century, starting with the analysis of the origin stories of the Kakubei Jishi and the developments of street performances during the Edo period (1603-1867). Through qualitative research methods, it investigates the popularity of street performances during the Edo period which introduce extreme body flexibility and lead to the transformation and stylization of the folk-art form. The increasing popularity of the lion dance led to the exploitation of the child performers who endured abuse and neglect at the hands of their troupe leaders. With the modernization of society and the establishment of labour and child protection laws during the Meiji restoration (1868-1912), Kakubei Jishi performances declined and eventually vanished. However, with the establishment of the Kakubei Jishi Preservation Society of the Tsukigata Village in 1936, research was implemented to recover knowledge about the history and developments of the Kakubei Jishi, and the lion dance was restored as cultural heritage. By examining the genesis and history of the Kakubei Jishi, this monograph explores parallels between the stylized version of the lion dance from the Edo period that utilized extreme body flexibility and the revived folk performing art that we know today. It details the development of aesthetics and how religious symbolism is incorporated in Kakubei Jishi performances and how training is executed in the 21st century. As of June

2022, only seven children are left to continue the tradition of Kakubei Jishi performances. As more and more young families move away from the village and into bigger cities, the future of the Kakubei Jishi is uncertain. It is currently expected that only four performers will continue their training for the 2023 performance: the bare minimum needed for a performance. This monograph examines these challenges the Kakubei Jishi lion dance community is confronted with today in the face of decreasing birth rates, a drastic decline in the Japanese population, and urban migration. It proposes solutions such as extending recruitment efforts to include performers from neighboring villages for the safeguarding of this art form and cultural heritage, to ensure its continuation for future generations.

Keywords: Body Flexibility, Lion Dance, Kakubei Jishi, Folk Arts, Tradition, Genesis, History, Aesthetics, Development, Cultural Heritage, Safeguarding.

Für Papa
*16.03.1945
†23.06.2022

ACKNOWLEDGEMENTS

I want to take a moment to express my deepest gratitude to Mayor Masaki Ikarashi of the Tsukigata Village, whose unwavering support and invaluable insights have been a guiding light throughout this entire research journey. His vision for the development of the Kakubei Jishi tradition has inspired and motivated us all. I would also like to give a heartfelt thanks to Tomomi Homma, whose dedication and attention to detail have been crucial to the success of this project. Her tireless efforts have not gone unnoticed, and I am forever grateful for her contributions. I cannot express enough my appreciation for Wataru Toishi, whose expert guidance and advice have helped shape the direction of this research. His wealth of knowledge and experience regarding the history and development of the Kakubei Jishi have been indispensable. I am also indebted to Tuchida sensei for her thoughtful feedback and encouragement. Her insights have been vital in shaping the final outcome of this study. Finally, I would like to extend my sincere thanks to the community of the Tsukigata Village, and particularly the lion dancers and their parents, for their support and participation in this study. Their involvement has been invaluable, and without their contributions, this research would not have been possible.

CONTENT WARNING

This publication includes images of the swastika, a symbol present in many world religions. Though its design is related to the Nazi 'Hakenkreuz,' it is a distinct marker that does not refer to the right-wing ideology. In Hinduism, Buddhism and Jainism, this ancient symbol means protection, good fortune and well-being. It is one of the oldest written symbols and can be found in various cultures with varying renditions. In Japan, the swastika can be found in Japanese temple iconography and every-day items such as pottery, fabrics and family crests. The Kakubei Jishi lion dancers wear the swastika symbol for their own protection and safe travels.

INTRODUCTION

This monograph examines the performance art-form Kakubei Jishi and the practice of body flexibility in Japan, looking specifically at its theories and functions as well as discussions across social, historical, political and performance studies. Kakaubei Jishi is a folk performing art that integrates aspects of spirituality, agriculture, nature, and mythology unique to the Niigata region. The art-form's popularity increased drastically during the Edo period, which subsequently led to its stylization and commodification as a spectacle. This monograph will examine the historical progression of the traditional art-form as it diverged from its origins and describes how efforts were taken towards restoring its authenticity. Kakubei Jishi employs bodily flexibility as a technique to convey movements in an unembellished and genuine manner. Present-day Kakubei Jishi performances are truer to their origins with a focus on cultural components that hold importance to the area and showcase the region's identity.

The art of Kakubei Jishi, a lion dance that is exclusive to the Niigata prefecture and that originated in the Tsukigata Village, is an acrobatic dance that is showcased by child performers wearing wooden lion masks on top of their heads. I investigate the history and developments of the Kakubei Jishi performances that originated in the Edo period (1603-1867), the ban of child labor and the establishment of compulsory education during the Meiji era (1668-1912), and the revival of Kakubei Jishi performances as cultural heritage of the Tsukigata Village in 1959, supported by the Kakubei Jishi Preservation Society that was founded in 1936. This monograph analyzes traditional training and performance methods and considers developments within this art-form through an anthropological lens. Through ethnographic research, this project considers traditions and symbolism and provides insights into training methods, aesthetics, costuming and spiritual elements by making use of primary research methods. Observations, interviews, and informal conversations with the residents of the Tsukigata Village, the Kakubei Jishi performers and their family members, their teacher, as well as other members of the performing group are considered in this research study. Lastly, the monograph evaluates the decline of the art-form caused by Japan's low immigration and birthrates that were additionally exacerbated by the Coronavirus pandemic.

In January 2020, only a few weeks before the outbreak of the Coronavirus pandemic hit Japan, I found myself sitting in the waiting area of Studio Nugara, the first contortion school in Japan. I was about to interview Ayumi "Moco" Osanai, founder of contortion studio Nugara in Tokyo, for my three-part series Mapping Contortion in Japan for the online magazine Circus Talk. My research has brought me to Japan, to tie in with my earlier projects that investigated the practice of contortion and body flexibility in East Asia, in particular China and Mongolia, where I had resided in previous years to study contortion. Moco and I discussed the history of contortion and body flexibility in Japan, as well as the confluence of acrobatic styles that were introduced to or originated in Japan over the past centuries. That conversation laid important groundwork for that article, but I found myself thinking back to one small remark she made about the Kakubei Jishi. Sometime later, I decided to pursue a more extensive investigation – this is the fruit of that labor.

Kakubei Jishi (Japanese: 角兵衛獅子), also known as Tsukigata Lion, Echigo Jishi, Kambara Lion, or Echigo Lion, is a folk performing art that originated in the Tsukigata Village of the Niigata Prefecture and was developed during the Edo period (1603-1867). Throughout this monograph when referring to this art-form, the spelling "Kakubei Jishi" and "lion dance/lion dancers" will be utilized. The term Kakubei Jishi refers to the art-form and to those performing it. Kakubei Jishi is an acrobatic dance that is showcased by children aged 5 to 15 who perform acrobatic tricks such as tumbling, handstands, and body flexibility poses that any Westerner would identify as contortion poses. It is important to note that the art of Kakubei Jishi is not affiliated with the circus industry. It is perceived by locals of the Tsukigata Village as an acrobatic dance and folk performing art, and the performers are referred to as artists and actors. The elements of body flexibility as part of their performance, however, are a crucial aspect when looking at the overall history and development of body flexibility, acrobatics and contortion in East Asia and Japan in particular (Circus Talk, 2020). Wooden lion masks are worn on top of the children's heads, and their traditional Japanese costumes are made of shirts with wide sleeves and pants. The Kakubei Jishi perform to live music and are accompanied by three musicians: two drummers, one of whom gives verbal commands to announce new poses throughout the performance, and one flute player. This lineup of three musicians never changes except when there is a shortage of musicians. Kakubei Jishi performances are held twice every year in June and September during the Tsukigata Festival either in the Tsukigata Rural Environment Improvement Center (Japanese: 月潟農村環境改善センター) or on the grounds of the local Hakusan Shrine (Japanese: 白山神社). Due to the global Covid-19 pandemic, the festivals in 2020 and 2021 were cancelled. However, with the development of new vaccines, the countrywide inoculation of the Japanese population, and the implementation of appropriate safety measures such as social distancing and PCR testing, the festival in 2022 was able to be held for the first time in two years.

During these two years, when the world was in lockdown, I was able to establish contact with Tomomi Homma, advisor of the Town Development Minami-Ward of the Niigata Prefecture which oversees the activities of the Kakubei Jishi, to gather in-depth information about the history of the Tsukigata lion dancers. The online interview with Tomomi Homma resulted in the final part of my series Mapping Contortion in Japan. Part Three: Cultural Heritage for Circus Talk and served as a precursor to this monograph. In March 2022, after the countrywide state of emergency has widely been lifted, I was invited by Tomomi Homma to visit Tsukigata to conduct further research. During my field trip, I was able to meet village locals and learn about the community, the history of the village and its cultural heritage. I met the mayor of the Minami Ward of the Niigata Prefecture, Masaki Ikarashi, a strong supporter of the continuation of the Kakubei Jishi performances. The exchange of information and numerous online meetings with Tomomi Homma and mayor Masaki Ikarashi between 2020 and 2022, laid the groundwork for my visits of the Tsukigata Village. One of the most important events of this research was the 2022 Tsukigata festival that was held on June 26, where I had the opportunity to watch the live performance on the temple grounds of the local shrine and to meet the performers, as well as their parents and teachers, to conduct further interviews.

During these conversations, I learned that some of the children will soon graduate from junior high school and stop performing in order to focus on their education. As of June 2022, there are a total of seven children that have signed up to continue the tradition of Kakubei Jishi performances. Due to the drastic decline of Japan's population and the migration of young families away from villages and into bigger cities such as Tokyo and Osaka, the future of the Kakubei Jishi looks grim. Local officials expect that only four performers will continue their training for a 2023 performance - the bare minimum needed for a performance. Mayor Masaki Ikarashi expressed fears that the 2023 performance will be the last, as the population is decreasing and more children are moving to bigger cities for higher education. It can take three years to train a new child acrobat to a level suitable for performance. That, combined with a declining population, makes things complicated – especially because only children of the Tsukigata Village are allowed to become Kakubei Jishi performers.

The rationale for this monograph is, therefore, threefold:

First and foremost, to examine a threatened art-form by addressing the decrease of performers due to a drastic decline in the country's population.

Secondly, to provide an analysis about its multiple traits and functions throughout the ages: how and why this art-form was originally developed as well as how it transformed during the Edo period (1603-1867), was banned during the Meiji Restoration, and became a cultural heritage in the 20th century. This examination considers its function, history, and development through the ages. It details historic and contemporary aspects of the Kakubei Jishi training and the perception of body flexibility in Tsukigata. It further explores the development of aesthetics and the spiritual elements that can be observed in performances. Additionally, economic and community aspects around this art-form are analyzed as well as future developments.

Thirdly, this monograph aims to outline ways that this cultural heritage might be safeguarded. As Kakubei Jishi is uniquely threatened by the effects of a declining population, this monograph explores the question: what could possibly be done to restore it?

In the course of this research about the lion dance, I conducted short-term field work in Tsukigata, Japan (as far as Covid restrictions permitted) using ethnographic data collection methods such as observation, informal conversation, and formal interviews and surveys. During Japan's state of emergency and the height of the pandemic, I used the time leading up to my visit of the Niigata Prefecture by reviewing relevant literature, encyclopedias of Kakubei Jishi history and folk arts. This included images, photographs, archival documents and brochures. The Minami-Ward administration provided me with literature of historic and public records, online resources and press releases, as well as restoration reports from the city's archive. Some copies included textual materials form as far back as the Edo period (1603-1867).

Relevant literature considered for this research are Local Performing Arts-Kakubei Lion (1997) by Chuzo Kondo, Song of the Kakubei Lion (2019) by Taro Genma, Street Performers and Society in Urban Japan, 1600-1900. The Beggar's Gift (2016) by Gerald Groemer, Children standing on their Heads- Read about the Acrobatics of Kakubei Shishi (2001) by Iwao Akune, the 2012-2014 Report Kakubei Lion Tradition Support Project by the Minami-Ward Distinctive Ward Development Project based on joint research efforts of the Executive Committee for Kakubei Jishi Traditional Activities (角兵衛獅子保存会 founded in 2011) and the Kakubei Jishi Preservation Society (角兵衛獅子保存会 founded in 1936). To provide a clear overview of the art-form Kakubei Jishi and its development, this monograph, therefore, discusses the following segments: the history and genesis of Kakubei Jishi, the development of techniques and styles, the training methods in Tsukigata, the development of aesthetics, spiritual elements and symbolism and. Finally, it offers a proposal that ensures a future for the Kakubei Jishi.

CHAPTER 1: THE GENESIS AND DEVELOPMENT OF THE KAKUBEI JISHI IN JAPAN.

Available information about the Kakubei Jishi varies wildly. Records about the history and development of this folk performance art often contradict one another and the following overview is based on what literature and qualitative studies are available. Given the nature of these sources, the information contained therein needs to be interpreted with discretion. Historical texts, oral history, and mythology as well as modern surveys present a range of different theories of how the Kakubei Jishi came into existence. Therefore, epistemological ambiguity prevails with regards to the veracity of the different theories under consideration. All of the theories, however, ultimately fall into two camps: "The Manhunt Theory" (Theory One) and "The Annual Floods Theory" (Theory Two). The available evidence suggests that Kakubei Jishi may have emerged from one of two potential sources, either as a means of seeking out a murderer (Theory One) or as a response to pressing needs for survival (Theory Two). This paper, therefore, examines the history of the Kakubei Jishi in relation to these two main theories and analyzes the function of the lion dance within the context of each theory.

When hearing the words lion dance, many immediately think of China and Japan's New Year performances of large, colorful lions with elongated, snake or dragon-like bodies (Figure 1) carried by multiple dancers who are dancing on temple grounds or in shopping malls. The lion first became

Figure 1: Shishimai-Lion Dance Hong Kong.

a popular mythical creature in China and its popularity spread to Korea and Japan with the transmission of Buddhism around the 6th century CE. The performance art-form Shishimai, as it is called in Japanese, involves numerous dancers hidden under a large, colorful lion costume. The dancers jump and spin in circles, accompanied by traditional music which brings good fortune for the new year while driving away evil spirits. Shishimai is a popular dance form with currently around 845 lion dance groups operating in Japan. Even as the Kakubei Jishi (Figure 2) is often performed on temple grounds together with other entertainment acts such as the Shishimai, and as both share the lion head and the belief that it repels evil as a prominent trait, these are two distinctly different art-forms and should not be mistaken for one another. The Shishimai lion dance was introduced to Japan already around the eighth century whereas the

Kakubei Jishi are believed to have emerged in the Niigata prefecture during the Edo period (1603-1867). The Edo period (1603-1867) can be regarded as the height of the Kakubei Jishi's popularity as numerous groups were dispatched from the Niigata prefecture to perform all over Japan.

To establish an understanding of the origins and the development of the Kakubei Jishi, it is imperative to outline the overall environment in which the art-form originated. Both theories are tied to the geographical setting of the Tsukigata Village and its economy, with agriculture and craftmanship being two of its main pillars. This monograph will next review important elements of the village culture such as traditions, craftmanship, agriculture, climate, location, and population of the village to provide a better foundation of the aesthetics and choreography of the Kakubei Jishi that are later explored.

Figure 2: Kakubei Jishi. Copyrights: 南区産業振興課 商工観光推進室 (Commerce, Industry and Tourism Promotion Office, Industry Promotion Division, Minami-ku)

Tsukigata - Cradle of the Kakubei Jishi

Tsukigata, a small village in the Niigata Prefecture, belongs to the ward Minami-ku and is situated in the Northeast of Japan. In 2022, the village had a reported population of 916. In the outline of the brochure for the Municipal Administration of the Niigata Prefecture, the area is described as followed:

Minami-ku (Minami Ward) covers an area comprising of one former city and two former villages- Shirone City, Ajikata Village and Tsukigata Village- located almost at the center of the Niigata Plain. It is green farmland, the Shinano River on its east side and the Nakanokuchi River running through the ward (Niigata City, 2022: A).

The area is characterized by agriculture as well as manufacturing, with focus on traditional crafts including butsudan (family Buddhist altars) (Figure 3) and sickles (Figure 4), which are promoted as traditional local brands. The Shinano River rises in the Japanese Alps in Honshu and flows through the Nagano and Niigata Prefectures before it enters the Sea of Japan. It is the longest and widest river in Japan. The old town area of the Tsukigata Village is located on the left bank of the Nakanokuchi River that connects with the Shinano River (Figure 5) and when crossing the Tsukigata Bridge (Figure 6), one will find an abundance of rice fields, local manufactures, and fruit plantations (Figure 7, 8, 9, 10, 11). The Niigata Plain, also known as the Kambara Plain or Echigo Plain, is a plain that extends from central to northern Niigata Prefecture (Figure 12). The plain takes up some 2,000 km2--close to the footprint of Tokyo--and is the largest plain on the Sea of Japan side of Honshu. Since ancient times, Niigata has been famous for its rich production of vegetables and fruits.

Figure 3: Butsudan Shrine. Copyrights: No machine-readable author provided. Gakuro assumed (based on copyright claims)., CC BY-SA 3.0. Available at: https://upload.wikimedia.org/wikipedia/commons/a/aa/Butsudan_at_ShinDo_Buddhist_Temple.jpg

Figure 4: Sickles manufactured in Tsukigata. Copyrights: Mariam Ala-Rashi, 2022.

Figure 5: Nakanokuchi River entering Shinano River. Copyrights: 新潟市, CC BY 2.1 JP. Available at: https://upload.wikimedia.org/wikipedia/commons/c/ca/NiigataCityOpenData_kuusatsu001.jpg

Figure 6: Tsukigata Bridge. Copyrights: Mariam Ala-Rashi, 2022.

Figure 7: Rice Fields Tsukigata. Copyrights: Mariam Ala-Rashi, 2022.

Figure 8: Greenhouse Tsukigata.
Copyrights: Mariam Ala-Rashi, 2022.

Figure 9: Fruit Plantation Tsukigata.
Copyrights: Mariam Ala-Rashi, 2022.

Figure 10: Local Manufacture Tsukigata.
Copyrights: Mariam Ala-Rashi, 2022.

Figure 11: Bonsai Tree Nursery Tsukigata.
Copyrights: Mariam Ala-Rashi, 2022.

Figure 13: (above) Fruit Plantation (Grapes)
Tsukigata. Copyrights: Masaki Ikarashi, Mayor
of Minami Ward, 2022.

Figure 14: (right) Fruit Plantation (Peaches)
Tsukigata. *ibid.*

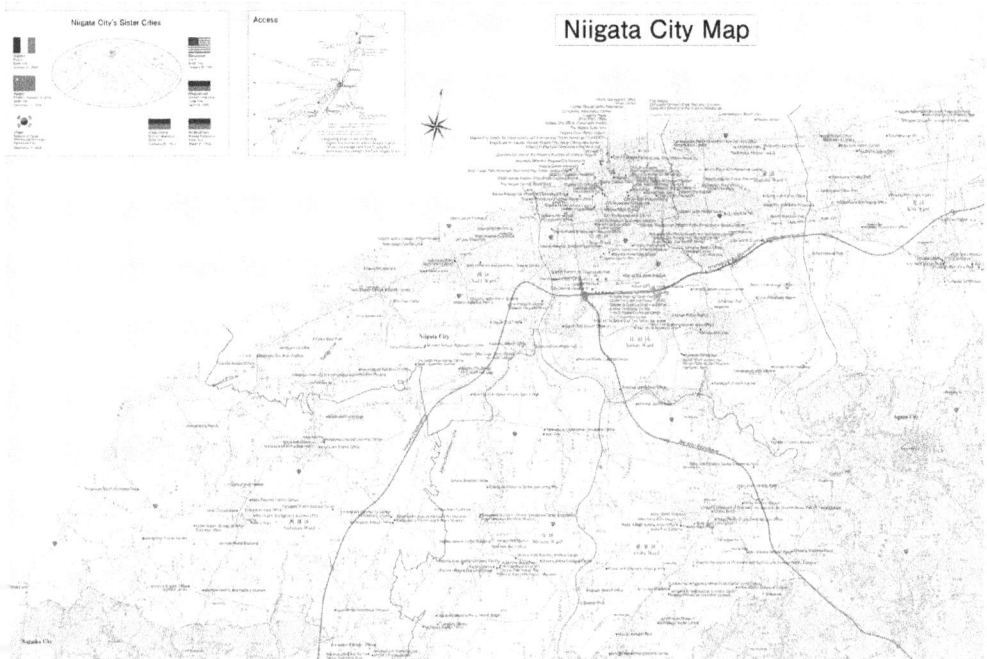

Figure 12: Niigata Map. Copyrights: Niigata City, 2022. (A) Outline of Minami-ku.
Available at: https://www.city.niigata.lg.jp/minami/

Rice, sake (an alcoholic beverage made of fermented rice), peaches, and pears are particularly popular (Figure 13, 14, 15, 16, 17). Produce and products from this area can be found all across Japan.

Statistical data presented by the Municipal Administration of Niigata City provides crucial information about Niigata's history, economy, and trends in population and households with the following key events that took place since earliest documentation of the area was recognized:

Present-day Minami-ku once belonged to the ancient province of Echigo and recordings of first settlements on the Niitsu Hills of the Niigata Prefecture date back to 18,000 BCE. In 4000 BCE settlements on the sand dune areas of the Echigo plains were recorded and between the 17th and 18th century new rice paddies were developed, implementing growth

Figure 15: Fruit Plantation and Flower
Fields Tsukigata. *ibid.*

Figure 16: Local Fruit Market Tsukigata
(A). *ibid.*

Figure 17: Local Fruit Market Tsukigata
(B). *ibid.*

Figure 18: Drainage and Water Control
Systems Tsukigata (A). Copyrights:

Figure 19: Drainage and Water Control
Systems Tsukigata (B). Copyrights:
Mariam Ala-Rashi, 2022.

Figure 20: Drainage and Water Control
Systems Tsukigata (C). *ibid.*

Figure 21: Mountain Range Niigata. *ibid.*

of the agricultural economy. The year 1922 marked the completion of the Okozu-bunsui diversion aqueduct (as structure built to convey water) to reduce risk of flooding and in 1948 large-scale drainage pump stations were installed to drain muddy rice paddies. In 2010 the APEC (Asia Pacific Economic Cooperation) Meeting was held to discuss food security and in 2015 Niigata City was designated the Culture City of East Asia (Niigata City, 2022: B).

When visiting the Niigata Prefecture, especially when walking through the fields of the Tsukigata Village, one notices large grain elevators to store the annual rice harvest, as well as the drainage and water control systems that span throughout the entire region to support the farmland (Figure 18, 19, 20). The vast expanse of rice fields is encircled by a vast mountain range. Niigata Prefecture is famous for its 613 named mountains, with Mt. Mikunisakai being the highest peak of the region. This makes the Niigata Prefecture not only famous

Figure 22: Manhole Cover with Kakubei Jishi and Local Fruit Trees, Tsukigata. *ibid.*

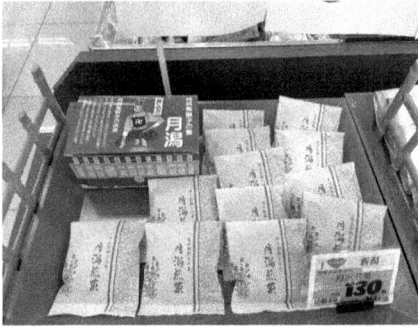
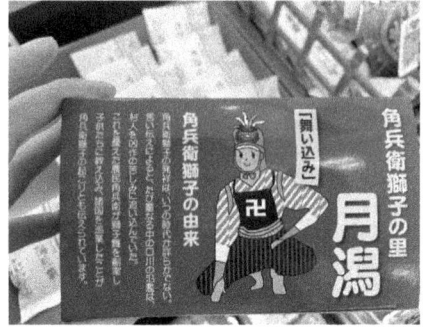

Figures 23 & 24: Food Packaging with Kakubei Jishi, Tsukigata. *ibid.*

Figure 25: Grain Elevator with Kakubei Jishi, Tsukigata. *ibid.*

for its landscapes and agricultural bounties but also a popular tourist destination. It has one of Japan's heaviest snowfalls with snows that often reach an adult's waist (around 120 cm) during the winter season, making it one of the most frequented ski destinations in Japan (Figure 21). Cultural attractions, festivals, and traditions only add to the charm of the region, with every city and village presenting and representing their own cultural heritage and traditions.

Figure 26: Multipurpose Hall, Tsukigata. *ibid.*

For Tsukigata Village, this is even visible in some of the smallest and most unsuspecting objects one could discover in a city or village landscape. Manhole covers in Tsukigata, for example, bear the colorful image of Kakubei Jishi dancers (Figure 22), and images

Figure 27: Tsukigata Local Products Reference Room 郷土物産資料室 [角兵衛獅子].
ibid.

of lion dancers are displayed on cookie and dried fruits packaging (Figure 23, 24). The most prominent structure that carries Kakubei Jishi imagery, however, is the grain elevator that is located at one of the main roads of the Tsukigata Village to store the local rice harvest (Figure 25). The road leads up to the Tsukigata Rural Environment Improvement Center which consists of a large multipurpose hall with a stage and a projector screen (Figure 26), two training rooms, conference rooms and the Tsukigata Local Products Reference Room (Japanese: 郷土物産資料室 [角兵衛獅子]). The Tsukigata Local Products Reference Room was established to provide information about the Kakubei Jishi where visitors can watch videos, see costumes up close, and find explanations about the history of this art-form and the historical materials on display (Figure 27).

At the entrance of the center, five life-sized bronze statues are installed representing the most prominent poses of a Kakubei Jishi performance, allowing visitors to study the movements up close (Figure 28, 29, 30, 31, 32, 33, 34, 35, 36). The grain elevator, therefore, bearing the image of four lion dancers, not only serves as a signpost to the Kakubei Jishi reference

獅子の子落しの形

302

Figures 28-36: Kakubei Jishi Bronze Statues.
Copyrights: Mariam Ala-Rashi, 2022.

Figure 37: Guest House Goo Goo, Tsukigata. *ibid.*

Figure 38: Main Road, Tsukigata. *ibid.*

Figure 39: Traditional Buildings, Tsukigata. *ibid.*

Figure 40: Sasagawa Residence, Tsukigata. Copyrights: 新潟市, CC BY 2.1 JP. Available at: https://commons.wikimedia.org/wiki/File:NiigataCityOpenData_kyusasagawake02.jpg

room and as storage for the annual rice harvest, but it also demonstrates the strong link between agriculture, nature, climate, and cultural heritage that are so closely intertwined in this region.

The townscape of Tsukigata very much reflects the relationship between its population and the environment, with the architecture being predominantly two-story buildings with narrow streets and only a few bigger roads that lead directly to the farmland and neighboring villages (Figure 37, 38, 39). With Japan being an earthquake-prone country, the

Figure 41: Main Gate - Sasagawa Residence, Tsukigata. Copyrights: 新潟市, CC BY 2.1 JP. Available at: https://commons.wikimedia.org/wiki/File:NiigataCityOpenData_kyusasagawake01.jpg

Figure 42: Garden - Sasagawa Residence, Tsukigata. Copyrights: yamakidoms, CC BY-SA 2.0. Available at: https://commons.wikimedia.org/wiki/File:%E6%97%A7%E7%AC%B9%E5%B7%9D%E5%AE%B6%E4%BD%8F%E5%AE%85_(2728026495).jpg

architectural structures throughout the village are primarily traditional Japanese wood houses as they are (to some extent) resistant against seismic activities. Woodworking in Japan is a respected craft, and Tsukigata is home to some fine examples of wooden architecture. The Sasagawa residence (Figure 40, 41, 42), for example is one of the oldest wooden structures and was built during the Tensho period (1573-1591). The Sasagawa family was in charge of over eight villages in the area, exercised police and judicial authority, and contributed to flood control and the development of new rice paddies in the area, which were prone to flooding (Niigata City, 2022: C). Being an agricultural area, one must walk only a few minutes from the village center before arriving at the Nakanokuchi River that connects the village with the farmland via the Nakanokuchi bridge. The road between bridge and rice paddies is lined with small manufacturers that specialize in traditional crafts by producing sickles and family Buddhist altars. However, the Nakanokuchi bridge does not only connect one part of the village with another, it also plays an important role in the annual Shirone Giant Kite Battle (Figure 43, 44). As outlined in the brochure

Figure 43: Shirone Giant Kite Battle Tsukigata (A). Copyrights: Masaki Ikarashi, Mayor of Minami Ward, 2022.

Figure 44: Shirone Giant Kite Battle Tsukigata (B). *ibid.*

of the Municipal Administration of the Niigata Prefecture, the Tsukigata village is host to a number of cultural events and landmarks:

In Minami-ku, old, traditional events are kept alive, including the Shirone Oodako Gassen (Shirone Giant Kite Battle) with its 300-year history, and the Tsukigata Kakubeijishi (acrobatic dance by children wearing lion heads). Visiting the former residence of the Sasagawa Family, village headmen in the Edo period, one can feel the richness of the Kanbara farming breadbasket and something of what it was like to be a farm village in those days (Niigata City, 2022: A).

Cultural heritage and crafts are another main pillar in Tsukigata's economy. With a tightknit community, many of the traditional crafts and performing arts are preserved and passed on through generations. The 300 years old tradition of the Shirone Giant Kite Battle, as described by the Niigata Prefecture Tourism Association:

> [...] is an event where two teams on either side of the river raising their kites and then deliberately entangling them. Once the kite falls in the river the two teams then engage in a tug-of-war until one team's kite rope snaps. It is an impressive sight to see 300 5m x 7m kites take to the skies in battle. Once the kites plunge into the river the tug-of-war begins in earnest [...] (Enjoy Niigata: 2022).

Figure 45: Lion Mask for Kakubei Jishi Performance しし頭. Copyrights: Mariam Ala-Rashi, 2022.

During her field trip to Tsukigata in March, the author had the opportunity to join local artists by drawing on traditional handmade Japanese washi paper, made of local plant fibers. The kites are made entirely by hand – from the paper to the string. The frame is made of bamboo, and the ropes are handmade from Japanese hemp. Local craftsmen spend 100 days to twist the rope that has a length of 130meters and weight of 40kg. These are serious crafts that take serious time and effort to make – the price for one of these long ropes is around $15,000USD. As a final step, traditional

Figure 46 (below): Hakusan Shrine with two Lion Statues as Guardians, Tsukigata. Copyrights: Mariam Ala-Rashi, 2022.

Figure 47 (right): Lion Statue, Hakusan Shrine, Tsukigata. *ibid.*

Figure 48 (above left): Lion Statue in Front of the Stage for the annual Kakubei Jishi Performance, Hakusan Shrine, Tsukigata Festival. *ibid.*

Figure 49 (above right): Torii (Gate) of the Hakusan Shrine with handcrafted straw decorations for the Tsukigata Festival. *ibid.*

designs are hand-painted onto washi paper – one of them depicting a Kakubei Jishi performer. Young and old come together every year, to build the kites from scratch and to fight together in the annual giant kite battle.

The same efforts go into the preparations for the Kakubei Jishi performances, from the design and crafting of the costumes, the restoration of original musical instruments and sheets of music, to the carving of the wooden lion heads (Japanese: lion head しし頭). The lion heads are easily the most prominent feature of the entire costume and are handmade by local carvers and lacquerers (Figure 45). Lions bear significant spiritual meaning in the Buddhist religion. They are believed to repel evil and are at the centerpiece of the Kakubei Jishi performance. These wooden lion heads are passed on through generations of lion dancers and are used for performances on shrine and temple grounds. The Hakusan shrine, where the annual Tsukigata Festival is held, is guarded by two large lion statues (Figure 46, 47, 48, 49). What might look like a children's performance from the outside actually encompasses a complex representation of history, geographical impact, nature/climate, culture, spirituality, community, craftsmanship, and agricultural economy.

Etymology

As previously established, Kakubei Jishi (Japanese: 角兵衛獅子) has numerous alternative spellings depending on which origin theory is being discussed: Kakubeijishi, Kakubei Shishi or Kakubee Jishi, also known as Tsukigata Lion, Echigo Jishi, Kambara Lion or Echigo Lion. The alternative versions, Tsukigata Lion, Echigo Jishi, Kambara Lion and Echigo Lion all refer to one and the same region, Tsukigata, the origin of the art-form. The area in which the Tsukigata Village is located has been referred to as Niigata Plain, Kambara Plain, or Echigo Plain. The various forms of spelling Kakubei Jishi, Kakubeijishi, Kakubei Shishi or Kakubee Jishi can be related to different vernaculars, as well as misspellings. However, all these names refer to one and the same region and one and the same art-form. There are many different myths and stories about why the Kakubei Jishi lion dance was created. Many folktales exist that describe the various origins of the Kakubei Jishi. Understanding the etymology aids in comprehending the various theories about the art-form's origins.

Dr. Gerald Groemer, professor of ethnomusicology and Western musicology at University of Yamanashi, describes how the word shishi was used to describe Japanese lion dance in his book Street Performers and Society in Urban Japan, 1600-1900. The Beggar's Gift: "Masked dancers arriving singly, in pairs, or in small groups often impersonated a fabulous beast of Chinese provenance known as shishi – conveniently, though not quite accurately, translated as lion" (Groemer, 2016: 162).

In Japanese, Kakubei Jishi 角兵衛獅子 is translated to Kakubei: 角兵衛 + shishi / jishi: 獅子, with Kakubei (or Kakubee) referring to the name of the presumed founder of the respective lion dance, and shishi or jishi meaning "lion" in Japanese. In Japanese, there are two ways to use the word lion; Raion is the common Japanese word for lion, whereas shishi, as described by Dr. Groemer, was derived from the Chinese language.

The Japanese alphabet consists of three scripts: Hiragana, katakana and kanji. Hiragana and katakana are phonetic alphabets, using syllables, whereas kanji consists of Chinese characters. Kanji has a few thousand characters. Hiragana and katakana have 46. Together with romaji, the romanization of the Japanese language that was first developed in 1549 and derived from Portuguese orthography, there are four writing systems in place. Katakana is used for foreign words (such as lion = raion = ラ イオン), whereas hiragana is used for words of Japanese origin. Kanji consists of logographic characters, which represent pictures or symbols.

The spelling in Japanese for "lion" is as followed:

Romaji: Ra-i-o-n
Katakana: ライオン
Hiragana: らいおん

For "shishi" the spelling is as followed:

Romaji: shi-shi
Katakana: シシ
Hiragana: しし
Kanji: 獅子

The search for the origin of the word Kakubei or Kakubee, begins at the same time as the investigation of the art-form Kakubei Jishi. There are multiple theories on how the lion dance in Tsukigata developed. Dr. Groemer remarks in Kakubee-jishi (Echigo-jishi):

The meaning of "Kakubee" had already puzzled Edo-period scholars. According to one theory, the Hikawa shrine in Musashi province owned a wooden shishi mask with the chrysanthemum insignia of the Tokugawa clan emblazoned on its horns. The inscription of this prop read, "Wrought by Kakubee, known as the 'first under heaven.'" On this account Kakubee was a distinguished carver of wooden shishi heads. Others argued that the dance was first produced by an Echigo farmer named Kakubee. In 1781 a Tsukigata village headman recording the lore of local performers reports that a man from Mito (Ibaraki prefecture) bearing the name Kakubee had invented the dance. Another theory, no better substantiated than the others, identified "Kakubee" as simply a mispronunciation of "Kanbara" (Groemer, 2016: 170-171).

The lore about the origin of the Kakubei Jishi, as described here, asserts that the word Kakubei either refers to a person and family name or that it was derived from the area Kambara. The interviews conducted for this research with the villagers from Tsukigata between 2020 and 2022 point in the same direction. However, the mythology about the reasoning for the establishment of the Kakubei Jishi is quite varied. Numerous folktales exist about the origins of the Kakubei Jishi. This paper, therefore, introduces and examines two major theories, that were time and again repeated during the interviews as well as in relevant literature.

Joint research efforts of the Executive Committee for Kakubei Jishi Traditional Activities (founded in 2011) and the Kakubei Jishi Preservation Society (founded in 1936), accumulated and restored knowledge about the history of the Kakubei Jishi. Consisting of community volunteers, craftsmen, musicians, and researchers from major Japanese universities such as Tokyo University of the Arts, the Musicology Department of Joetsu University of Education, the Kunitachi College of Music and the Council for the Protection of Cultural Properties Niigata City, the oral history and mythology about the Tsukigata lion dance was recovered from historical records and the few surviving documents from the Edo period. The restoration of musical instruments, the retracing of costume designs, and the production of sheet music from old performance recordings was undertaken. The results of these efforts were published in the 2012-2014 report Kakubei Lion Tradition Support Project with a foreword from Chuzo Kondo, former chairman of the Council for the Protection of Cultural Properties Niigata City who is as well author of the book Local Performing Arts-Kakubei Lion (1997). Both theories presented here about the origins of the Kakubei Jishi, were published in above mentioned research studies. They were as well described during interviews with residents of the Tsukigata village, city officials of the Minami Ward and members of the lion dance group, as possible origins of the folk performing art. Both theories are as well established in the relevant literature being utilized for this study.

Theory One: Inventing an Art-form to track down a Criminal.

The first theory follows a former resident of Mito of the Hitachi Province by the name of Kakubei who had moved to Tsukigata where he made a living as a local farmer together with his family. According to the local legend, he got into an altercation with a stranger and was killed. However, during the fight, he had bitten off his opponent's toe. The killer escaped unidentified, and Kakubei's two sons, Kakunai and Kakusuke, came up with a plan to find the man who killed their father by searching for someone with a missing toe. They invented the Kakubei Jishi practice that included a lot of handstand routines which would allow them to observe the feet of their audiences undetected. As a performance troupe, they traveled around the country to search for the murderer. With a song that was sung during the performance, the sons invited people in the audience to join the practice so they could look at people's toes without drawing any suspicion, in the hope of finding their father's murderer.

In the song, the two brothers invite audience members to join them in performing handstands and, thus, exposing their feet. Chuzo Kondo, former chairman of the Council for the Protection of Cultural Properties Niigata City, director of the Niigata Folklore Association and author of the book Local Performing Arts-Kakubei Lion conducted extensive research about the Kakubei Jishi art-form. In chapter two, Origins of the Name, the folklore reveals the lyrics of the song: "Put your feet up and watch out for the person who has no toes" (Kondo, 1997: 22) (Alternative translation: "Do a handstand and watch out for the person/man who has no toes." [author's translation]). With this command, audience members were instructed to attempt a handstand, revealing their feet. Whether or not the murderer was ever captured, however, remains a mystery.

According to this first theory, it appears that the Kakubei Jishi performances were invented for the sole purpose to capture a criminal and to seek revenge on the killer of farmer Kakubei, rather than to offer entertainment to the public. The elements of body flexibility and handstand tricks were therefore a necessity, to make the search for the murderer an easy task.

However, the research of the Executive Committee for Kakubei Jishi Traditional Activities and the Kakubei Jishi Preservation Society presents a second theory, to which academics give equal credibility as the first. Both have been published to offer a historic account for the Kakubei Jishi performance. Illustrating this, on June 26, 2022, before the lion dancers entered the stage of the annual Tsukigata Festival, both folktales were read aloud to the audience to provide a historic backdrop to the performance. They are based on the findings of the Kakubei Jishi Preservation Society and printed in the Niigata City Designated Intangible Folk Cultural Property brochure that is distributed during the festival, allowing the audience to enjoy both possible histories.

Theory Two: Annual Floods and Agricultural Downtime during Winter.

In this theory, it is reported that annual floods frequently destroyed the harvest of local farmers of the Tsukigata Village which caused great economical damage and left many families starving. The Kakubei Jishi lion dance was developed as a means of augmenting the economic resources of the village via public street performances. In the 2012-2014 Report Kakubei Lion Tradition Support Project, Mihoko Nogawa, Professor at the Tokyo University of the Arts, states the results of her research in her chapter Reconstruction of the History of the Kakubei Jishi:

> The folk performing art of Tsukigata, Minami Ward, Niigata City "Kakubei Jishi", was originally a street performance. Several children wearing lion heads, performed acrobatics to the beat of the master's drums and flutes and toured various places [...]. According to folklore, Kakubei Jishi was developed when a farmer by the name of "Kakubei" invented a lion dance and traveled around the country to save the people of the Tsukigata Village from starvation because regular floods were destroying the harvest (Nogawa, 2014: 4, translated from Japanese to English by the author).

Chuzo Kondo, Member of the Niigata City Council for the Protection of Cultural Properties and executive director of the Niigata Folklore Association, provides additional details in his chapter Origins of the Name, that are based on the research findings of the Kakubei Jishi Preservation Society:

> The area around the Shinano River used to be a swamp. Year after year, the periodic flooding of the river drove the villagers into the throes of starvation. Concerned about the survival of the villagers, farmer Kakubei invented the Kakubei Jishi, taught it to the villagers and traveled around the country (Kondo, 1997: 22) (Translated from Japanese to English by the author).

The close proximity of the village to the Nakanokuchi River and Shinano River, together with historic records of periodic floods, make this a feasible theory. According to oral tradition, another rationale for the creation of the Kakubei Jishi as an additional source of income was the agricultural downtime in winter. As previously established, the Niigata Prefecture is well-known for its harsh winters and waist-high snow. Additionally, historic records show evidence of the Sasagawa family contributing to flood control and the development of new rice paddies in the area, which was prone to flooding (Niigata City, 2022: C).

Although this version of Theory Two is the most well-known throughout Japan when discussing the origins of the Tsukigata lion dance, there is a slightly different version of theory two, told by Chuzo Kondo's grandfather, which should not be withheld here:

> Kakubei, a native of Hitachi, came to Tsukigata and made a living by teaching children in the village. After deliberating on how to support the poor peasants at the time, he gathered the children of the village and trained them in the art in order to send them to tour the country and earn money. My grandfather often told me that this was the origin of the lion (Kondo, 1997: 23) (Translated from Japanese to English by the author).

Both versions of the second theory share the same rationale for the invention of the Kakubei Jishi, as a way to support the Tsukigata Village with additional income through street performances. Its function here being primarily for entertainment and financial reasons. What all theories have in common, though, is that the children would return home every summer. Since the Edo period, the festival has taken place on

June 25th or 26th, allowing children to celebrate the art-form and their accomplishments with their families.

Unfortunately, there is limited material evidence to back up any of the claims set forth by these theories such as historical records that testify to the facts of the "origin story." These shortcomings are also recorded by the researchers who investigated this art-form. Mihoko Nogawa states: "The roots and history of Kakubei-jishi have already been investigated in previous studies, and there are various speculations [as to whether or not these folktales are true]" (Nogawa, 2014: 4, translated from Japanese to English by author). Chuzo Kondo states in his research study after listing numerous theories including Theory One and Two "Of the various theories listed above, it is a difficult question to decide, which one is the most appropriate" (Kondo, 1997: 24, translated from Japanese to English by author).

Some variations of the origin tale describe the inventor Kakubei not as farmer but either as samurai, ronin (a samurai without a master), or, as Dr. Groemer states in one of his theories, "a distinguished carver of wooden shishi heads" (Groemer, 2016: 170). It is also important to mention that, according to the Kakubei Jishi Preservation Society, an exact date as to when the art-form was invented is unknown. Both Chuzo Kondo and the Kakubei Jishi Preservation Society lament that over the years many documents have been lost or destroyed either by fire, floods, or other natural disasters.

Most of these researchers ultimately conclude, however, that the lion dance was presumably invented around the middle of the Edo period (1603-1867). For example, texts of the Kakubei Jishi Preservation Society that are published in the chapter Origin of Kakubei Lion of the Niigata

City Designated Intangible Folk Cultural Property brochure state, that the earliest available record of the Kakubei Jishi dates back to around 1756 when the art-form was first mentioned in a book titled Echigo Nayose by author Maruyama Genjun (1682-1758). A second source titled Echigo Yashi dates back to 1815.

According to the findings of the Kakubei Jishi Preservation Society, the most reliable source were the people of Mito (Hitachi), the birthplace of farmer Kakubei. It is stated that the majority of the residents believe in Theory One, where farmer Kakubei had been murdered (Niigata City Designated Intangible Folk Cultural Property, n.d.). Dr. Groemer writes about speculations regarding the true origin story of the Kakubei Jishi:

> Whatever the truth may have been, during the early eighteenth century enterprising farmers from Tsukigata, or the nearby villages of Koyoshi and Kotaka, had evidently either been trained to dance by the mysterious Kakubee or had modified a local shishi dance. One variant of the dance common in rural Echigo featured a trinity of holy beasts romping about in an unbridled frenzy. With a little ingenuity these movements could be adapted to allow individuals, pairs of performers, or modest parties to take to the road and earn a living. According to an account from 1890, based mostly on writings from 1756, life in Tsukigata was so hard that a farmer named Kakubee, who some said had learned to dance in Kyoto, had taught spry youngsters a shishi dance and dispatched them to "beg" (kanjin) (Groemer, 2016: 170).

Together with the findings of the Kakubei Jishi Preservation Society and Dr. Groemer's observations, it seems evident that the art-form was established some time before 1756 and had reached popularity already by 1756. Further, the information provided by Dr. Groemer gives insight into the poor economy of the Tsukigata Village at the time and indicates the direction in which this art form will evolve in its future stages. Specifically, it suggests that the growing popularity of lion dancers would result in the establishment of numerous additional Kakubei Jishi troupes engaged in the same craft. One sentiment towards the Kakubei Jishi from the general public towards the end of the Edo period becomes clear both in interviews with the local community of the Tsukigata Village in 2022 and also in Dr. Groemer's findings: The environment the child performers of these troupes found themselves in was incredibly grim. As stated by Dr. Groemer: "[...] harsh treatment of youngsters was so common that until recently naughty Niigata children were told, "If you don't behave, we'll give you away to a 'lion-dance' troupe" (Groemer, 2016: 175).

All in all, this section aimed to illuminate the genesis and function of Kakubei Jishi performances and proposed two different theories advanced by local practitioners and historical experts. Kakubei Jishi seems to have come from one of two different origins – either about finding a murderer (and possibly exacting revenge!) or from the necessities of survival. As noted in the first theory, the Tsukigata village is remote, and the resources to solve crimes centuries ago were limited. The second theory asserts that Kakubei Jishi was born out of necessity to guarantee the survival of the Tsukigata Village that was prone to flooding and harsh winters. The flooding of the Tsukigata Village has been recorded in historic documents of the Niigata City Archive. The geographic situation also points towards harsh winters and agricultural downtimes that could leave a small village during the Edo period potentially fighting for survival. However, as interviews with the local community show, a large group of residents of Tsukigata (and Mito, as outlined by the Kakubei Jishi Preservation Society) believe in theory one as the true origin story -- the murder of farmer Kakubei. A serious weakness with the latter argument, however, is that there is no definite evidence. Understanding the limits of material evidence when studying these developments and theories, it is evident that the final form of Kakubei Jishi as we know it today was rooted in Edo period folk dance and folk acrobatics with elements of body flexibility. However, born out of necessity, this folk performing art quickly developed into a popular spectacle and street performance that would entertain the masses.

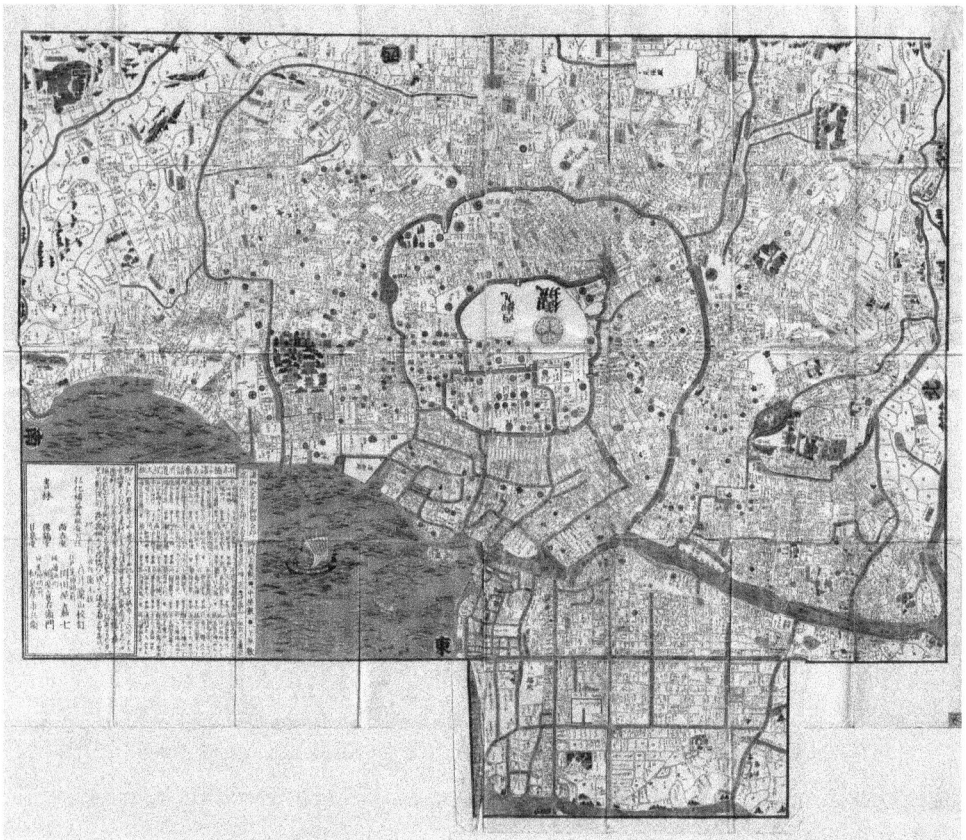

Figure 50: Map of Edo around 1840's. Copyrights: Scanned University of Texas Libraries, Public domain, via Wikimedia Commons. Available at: https://commons.wikimedia.org/wiki/File:Edo_1844-1848_Map.jpg

THE DARK HISTORY OF THE KAKUBEI JISHI: CHILD EXPLOITATION AND THE POPULARITY OF STREET PERFORMANCES DURING THE EDO PERIOD.

The contemporary iteration of Kakubei Jishi bears little resemblance to its historical antecedent. To elucidate the historical provenance of Kakubei Jishi, it is necessary to provide a succinct overview of Japan's history. Edo, the former name of Tokyo, became the capital of Japan in 1603 and the residence of the Tokugawa shogunate which was the military government of Japan. Edo quickly grew to become one of the largest cities in the world (Figure 50) and was renamed as Tokyo after the Meiji Restoration, the reestablishment of imperial rule in 1868.

Edo was a rapidly expanding city and with the growth of its population came the need for entertainment. By the end of the 1500s, the remote fishing village Edo in Eastern Japan was positioned as the political hub for the entire country, and in the following years, its population increased rapidly. Thousands of families of the burgeoning upper class settled in Edo, "supported by a roughly equal population of merchants and artisans producing and providing everything from infant wear to tombstones" (Groemer, 2016: 1). Edo soon became the religious hub of Japan as well, with "some 26,000 Buddhist monks and possibly a quarter that number of nuns, several thousand Shinto clerics, countless ritualists and 'mountain ascetics,' an endless stream of tourists and litigants moving in and out, and more beggars and outlaws than anybody cared to tally. This huge agglomeration of humankind exhibited a seemingly unquenchable thirst for music, dance, and verbal or theatrical entertainment" (Groemer, 2016: 1).

In the beginning, most forms of arts and entertainment were brought in from Kyoto and Osaka that are 450km North-East of Tokyo and the artistic and cultural hubs of the Edo period. However, as the city expanded and the thirst for entertainment grew, artists from all corners of Japan flocked to the capital. This entailed a range of performance ensembles of diverse artistic backgrounds who catered to the demand of the Edo population, including lion dance troupes that offered their services as street performers:

> By 1755 seven or eight ensembles, drawn from a total of fifty-one performers in Tsukigata Village, were forging their way to the capital to take advantage of the demand for auspicious street performances. In 1781/2 the headman of Tsukigata village reported that no fewer than seventy-five local families, most of them embracing more than one performer, were touring the length and breadth of the land. Troupes of agile players trekked to what is today Nagano and Gunma prefectures, advanced down the Tōkai highway to Kyoto and Osaka, and then headed southward as far as Nagasaki some 600 kilometers away. Others set off for the north, sometimes extending their forays to the remote regions of Tsugaru and Nanbu (Aomori prefecture) (Groemer, 2016: 170).

Figure 51: Kakubei Jishi in Edo. 江戸勝景 (Picturesque Scenery of Edo). Copyrights: Utagawa Hiroshige, Public domain, via Wikimedia Commons. Available at: https://commons.wikimedia.org/wiki/File:NDL-DC_1301981-Utagawa_Hiroshige-%E6%B1%9F%E6%88%B8%E5%8B%9D%E6%99%AF-crd.jpg

This account, given by the headman of the Tsukigata Village in the early 1780s, documents the rapid increase of Kakubei Jishi performers that travelled to the capital to join its nascent entertainment industry (Figure 51). Not only were these lion dancers headed to the capital but they also found themselves swept to all corners of Japan. Exact numbers of dancers, however, were not placed on record at the time:

> Kakubee-jishi [performers] needed little documentation to pass through barriers, for their unique appearance was immediately recognized by guards. Many performers visited Edo during the sixth month [June] and returned in late autumn. As the fortunes of kakubee-jishi rose, however, over half the players did not bother to revisit their home villages during the course of a year, though not a few city inhabitants thought year-round performances odd. By the last decades of the era, a head, eight

"elders" (oyakata), and no doubt the child performers they exploited were residing at Yanagi-chō in the Koishikawa area of Edo (Groemer, 2016: 170)

Residents of villages and towns beyond Tsukigata were inspired by the popularity of Kakubei Jishi performances – and the economic mobility it offered its players – and soon decided to join the trade. The lion dancers were all children, supervised (and exploited) by elders (oyakata). They were so popular that the theme of Kakubei Jishi was often adapted and performed independently by other art-forms such as Kabuki. The oyakata were in charge of the group and often the lead drummer and vocalist. According to the 2012-2014 report of the Kakubei Lion Tradition Support Project, the Kakubei Jishi dance was "loved by many" (Figure 52) during the Edo period and was "widely used in people's lives." The Kakubei Jishi were so popular that it led to the establishment of various disciplines within the performing arts that also incorporated themes and tricks used in the now-famous lion dance. Kabuki

Figure 52: Popularity of the Kakubei Jishi in Edo. Copyrights: Kobayashi Kiyochika; Kobayashi Kiyochika died 1915; Kobayashi Tetsujiro, Public domain, via Wikimedia Commons. Available at: https://commons.wikimedia.org/wiki/File:Straatartiest_uit_Edo-Rijksmuseum_RP-P-1989-220.jpeg

performers, for example, began wearing small lion masks and had a little drum strapped around their stomach during their performances [to imitate a Kakubei Jishi dancer] (2012-2014 Kakubei Lion Tradition Support Project, 2014: 5). Even amateurs picked up the theme of the Kakubei Jishi which led to many imitations: "... nonprofessionals also capitalized on the popularity of the art becomes evident from a prohibition issued in 1797 noting that city adults and youths were using a tangerine box for a shishi mask, wrapping themselves in straw, and dancing into the homes of the citizenry" (Groemer, 2016: 174).

The public's love for this new dance, alongside the rapid growth of new cities and a growing want for entertainment, led to further development of the techniques and tricks used by performers. Reviewing these historical records from the Edo period, one begins to wonder – where did these child performers come from? What did their lives look like? Were they all handed over by their families to join the life of a street performer? Education was not compulsory during the Edo period, and children often helped their parents with farm work. Were these children provided with education, food, shelter, and safety? How did their working hours and "payment" look like? As further research has revealed, children who joined a Kakubei Jishi ensemble didn't experience an easy life. They were exploited by their superiors to make as much profit on the streets as possible. Given the fact that there were numerous Kakubei Jishi troupes roaming the streets, competition must have been fierce. The average Kakubei Jishi troupe would employ up to four lion dancers and around three musicians as oyakata of the group. The children began their training at age 3 and started performing at age 7. By age 8, they were considered professionals.

Girls retired at age 14 or thereabouts; boys could usually hold out for an additional year. Youngsters from unrelated families were sometimes contracted for a stint of three or five years. Some people reported that the young acrobats were given vinegar to drink in order to "soften their bones" (Groemer, 2016: 174-175).

Photographs from Edo period performances of Kakubei Jishi children often show their high level of flexibility, similar to that of modern-day contortionists. In interviews with residents of the Tsukigata village, many people remarked on how children were specifically sought after as lion dancers due to their flexibility. Historical drawings that list the various poses of the lion dancers are evidence for the extreme flexibility these children cultivated throughout their training and performance careers (Figure 53). Today, children perform voluntarily, and poses are altered or chosen from a catalogue of poses to fit the child's natural flexibility. However, during the heyday of the Edo period, training was rigid, and the performers' wellbeing was not much of a consideration. If the dancers were not able to perform the desired tricks that their superiors (oyakata)

Figure 53: 逆立ちする子供たち - コ ピー Children Standing on Their Heads. Copyrights: 図.阿久根巌、「 おもちゃ絵 四種」『逆立ちする 子供たち―角兵衛獅子の軽業を見 る、聞く、読む』(小学館、2001 年4月1日)p.5〜8. Provided and permission to use granted by Masaki Ikarashi, Mayor of Minami Ward.

326

had chosen for them, they would be beaten: "That the portion of youngsters could be cruel indeed is suggested by a newspaper report of 1885 recounting that the leader of a Mikawa-based kakubee-jishi troupe performing in Tokyo had beat to death a poor 13-year-old boy for his inveterate clumsiness" (Groemer, 2016: 175). Moreover, the rapidly growing number of Kakubei Jishi troupes is evidence that the financial gain for the leaders of the troupes must have been substantial. As Dr. Groemer points out, "the cost of raising a youngster for three or four years was recouped in half a year," and many children were recruited from other prefectures. Tsukigata Village, with its small population had long lost its agency over the art-form. With the increase in troupes came the increase of competition. Not just between Kakubei Jishi troupes but also other performance art-forms that roamed the streets. Appealing to folk-religious sentiments appeared to be profitable:

Alert non-outcaste sacred performers also recognized that divine presentations were more likely to command admiration than profane ones. Among arts replete with encouraging folk-religious, Shinto, and yin-yang overtones, three stood out in Edo: the combination of invocations, songs, and badinage known as manzai; and the two subgenres of "lion dances," daikagura and kakubee-jishi. (Groemer, 2016: 152-153).

Japanese Shinto rituals that include ceremonial, sacred dances, and music are known as kagura (神楽.) Daikagura (also shishimai) and Kakubei Jishi belong to the lion dance troupes. Both shishimai and Kakubei Jishi wear shishi masks and often perform at the same venues and temple grounds. Shishi are believed to repel evil and prevent misfortune and large lion figures made of stone are often placed on sacred grounds as shrine and temple guardians. During the Edo period, both shishimai and Kakubei Jishi would go from house to house to offer their "exorcism" services.

Shishimai leading city parades were believed to fight off evil spirits across an entire city or town. The Kakubei Jishi were often employed by private households to protect them from malevolent entities and bestow blessings upon the occupants and their home. These "exorcism" services that were offered by both the Kakubei Jishi and the shishimai for a few coins were believed to exorcise bad spirits and purify homes, drive out evil, and repel famine and disease. Oftentimes, the shishi dance troupes got into quarrels over territory and legitimacy with the law as they lacked proper documentation. Kakubei Jishi and other street performers were often in dispute with authorities due to lack of proper permits to offer their services.

Yet kakubee-jishi were poorly placed to defend themselves, for they could not summon a Buddhist temple, Shinto shrine, family of courtiers, or approved occupational association to their defense. They could only rely on the weight of archaic religious connotations, forged documents, shaky precedent, and a hazy tradition (Groemer, 2016:172).

In the final quarter of the Edo period, the market was reaching a point of saturation, leading to competition that could sometimes become hostile, and all kinds of claims were made and fabricated by troupes in order to secure the next performance. Performance companies multiplied to benefit from the economic growth, and by the end of the Edo period, the city was brimming with performers.

However, with the dawn of the Meiji Restoration (1868), major political changes brought about an economic and social modernization. The Meiji Restoration marked the end of the military government of the Tokugawa shogunate and, ultimately, the end of the Edo period. The control of the country was placed under imperial rule with Emperor Mutsuhito, and the

Meiji Restoration led to an era of economic, political, and social change - the modernization and Westernization of Japan. Motomori Eriko of the Meiji Gakuin University Sociology department examines in her article The Disappearance of the Kakubei-Jishi Child Performers: Rethinking the Construction of Modern Childhood the slow demise of the lion dance street performances:

In the late 1890s, when modern childhood began to prevail, society began to view kakubei-jishi as objects of pity. Social philanthropists considered their existence to be a "social problem" and coined the term "cruelty to children" in response. Middle class families, however, only used these pitiful children as examples to inspire their own children to be thankful for their circumstances, behave better, and study harder. Meanwhile, the acrobats began to disappear, not because they were protected but because the job was regarded with disdain and became obsolete.

The wave of modernization and Westernization in Japan had a significant impact on the social outlook towards children, which permeated the educational sector and contributed to the gradual advancement in child protection measures. This transformation ultimately played a role in the decline of Kakubei Jishi street performances.

Between 1900 and 1911, compulsory education for minors was declared, and numerous prohibitions were put into place that protected children from exploitation. Kakubei Jishi performances decreased. and the audiences watching them pitied the children:

The "Kodomo no Shinbun" a newspaper reporting about issues regarding education and childcare seemed to reflect the situation of the times, with the free and compulsory elementary schooling clearly announced in 1900, and the six-year compulsory education system established in 1907:

"As we move toward an era in which elementary school enrollment (at least numerically) exceeds 95%, it is an era in which the collective representation of "children" has been established (albeit in varying forms of notation and expression). At the same time, it is a period in which various systems for the inclusion of children who had fallen through the cracks is being put in place…"

In 1900, the Reform Act was enacted, which stipulated the treatment of children who would now be subject to child welfare and juvenile justice, and in 1911, the Factory Act was enacted, which included provisions forbidding child labor. The "Kodomo no Shinbun" would have been a platform for children who were already enclosed by the modern family and the modern schooling system. The column describes the Kakubei lion to its readers as follows:

"You may have seen the Kakubei Lion, a small lion head, playing the drum and blowing the flute, with two or three lions standing in front of him. When I was at the shrine yesterday, I saw a group of thirteen playing drums and two eight- or nine-year-olds walking along with them. They are truly pitiful, and unlike you, they are not allowed to be around their fathers, mothers, brothers, and sisters, to be sent to school, or to play with their friends." (Motomori, 2019: 13-14) (Translated from Japanese to English by author).

These observations not only give insight into the changing perception of the wider public when watching Kakubei Jishi performers in the streets or on temple grounds but also their miserable circumstances. They were not with their families but had been "given away" (or perhaps more accurately, sold) to troupe elders, or simply kidnapped and trafficked. Furthermore, according to Wataru Toishi, lead drummer of the Kakubei Jishi in Tsukigata since 2012, a majority of the Kakubei Jishi children were orphans, making their status even lower than the already-low position of children during the Edo period. Furthermore, Wataru Toishi states that when leaders of the lion dance troupes died during the Edo period, they would leave instructions that their documentation and records of the troupe were to be burned in order to destroy evidence of how they mistreated child acrobats. The children were denied an education as well as a "modern" (innocent) childhood, and they had to work for their daily bread and accommodation.

Education became compulsory and accessible to children of all societal backgrounds. In their article Meiji Development: Modernization of Education-Educational Reform, Drs. Camille Romano and Shrusti Goswami from the Rutgers State University of New Jersey outline the restructuring of the education sector under the Meiji government:

> Modernization of the education system was one of the main goals of the new Meiji government. After the Meiji Restoration, class restrictions vanished and allowed education to be open to all people. Gakusei, the First National Plan for Education, formalized the future of education in Japan and focused on modeling Japanese education after Western education systems (Romano & Goswami, 2022).

Although this also included the implementation of curricula and mandatory attendance, the outlook of society on child performers did not change until much later as the Prevention of Cruelty to Children Act wasn't made into law in Japan until 1933:

> The Prevention of Cruelty to Children Act was finally enacted in 1933 but did not clearly prohibit child acrobats and trafficking, which left some children working in newer businesses such as Western-style circuses. Ironically, during the 1920-30s, kakubei-jishi began to be praised as a vanishing local performing art, and appeared in novels and films as popular, romanticized representations of a pitiful but innocent childhood——even though many real children at the time were being excluded from such a "childlike" [sic] childhood (Motomori, 2019).

Though the law banning cruelty to children was passed in 1933, the cultural shift did not happen overnight, and, counting from the establishment of the Meiji era in 1868, it took 65 years to finalize the Prevention of Cruelty to Children Act in 1933. During the transition period when opinions of the wider public seemed divided, some were referring to Kakubei Jishi as an art-form that is cultural heritage of Echigo and some were condemning it as child abuse (Motomori, 2019: 10-11, translated from Japanese to English by author). Indeed, changing the perception of the public regarding child performers would take time. Many would still enjoy the Kakubei Jishi performances and look at the young acrobats -- sometimes as young as three years old -- with delight, thinking they were "cute" instead of recognizing their miserable living conditions.

Furthermore, the change of the collective perception was aggravated as certain groups, such as children from rural villages, were targets of discrimination and looked down upon in Japanese society. This outlook of society on people who were deemed "less than human" took root already in medieval ages. In his chapter The Medieval Legacy from his article The Creation of the Edo Outcaste Order, Dr. Groemer describes how certain groups of a society were dehumanized and discriminated against based on their societal status, occupation, or appearance, with street performers being part of that target group:

> The complications of terminology for naming, describing, and stigmatizing medieval people who thrived on the fringes of "majority society" reflect the complexity of social practice. One appellation often recorded in contemporaneous documents is hinin (literally "nonhuman"), originally a Buddhist ex- pression. Hinin included a large and varied assortment of humanity. Some hinin, probably a small minority, were convicted criminals; others were physically disabled, blind, or suffering from leprosy, and abandoned by their families: yet others were penurious vagrants, street performers, holy practitioners or ascetics, and certain types of artisans. [...] Although medieval hinin sometimes skinned and disposed of carcasses, buried the dead, or offered performances of popular arts, begging was perhaps the most common hinin occupation and poverty the most common hinin trait (Groemer, 2001: 265-266)

This centuries-old attitude made it challenging to change a society that regularly labeled specific groups as hinin. As the Kakubei Jishi were street performers who begged for money and went from door to door to offer their services, they were an easy target for this derision.

Motomori further describes how the decline of the Kakubei Jishi was recorded in major newspapers. Even Asahi Shimbun, Japan's second-largest newspaper, reported about the abuse of the child performers with one article from 1912 describing a girl trying to escape the troupe to find her biological parents. In the article she reported that she had been "bought" by the master of the troupe and that she was seeking protection as he was beating her regularly. Another article from a few years earlier in 1908 describes a girl who fell ill. As she was "handed over" to the leader of the troupe, she reportedly said she "couldn't bear the hunger anymore." Themes of child abuse, kidnapping, and child trafficking are found in many news articles from the early 1900s when talking about Kakubei Jishi. Some articles described how the children were forced to drink vinegar in the morning and evening (a nonsensical practice that is known now to add no value to an artist's body flexibility) to learn the tricks of the Kakubei lion which "left their bones damaged and the children as people of no value" (Motomori, 2019: 15, translated from Japanese to English by author). The trafficking of children was an established method used in the geisha system, a system that developed around the 17th century, and it is assumed that similar methods were utilized to "adopt" children for the purposes of a street performance troupe. Caroline Norma, senior research fellow in the School of Global, Urban and Social Studies at RMIT University writes in her article A Past Re-imagined for the Geisha: Saviour of the 1950's Japanese Sex Industry about the methods of child trafficking in the geisha system:

> Girls are trafficked (jinshin baibai) into geisha houses, Kanzaki wrote in 1955, through geisha house managers buying the right to 'adopt' them through payments to parents or brokers. [...] The trafficking of girls into geisha houses, where they lived under the control of a 'proprietor' (ookami), was a longstanding

practice of the geisha system, which used adoption contracts to disguise its trafficking of girls through debt bondage (Norma, 2008: 39).

By 1911, reports in newspapers increased that condemned the cruel leaders of the lion dance troupes and their abuse. With the expansion of the Factory Law, child labor was prohibited, which included "Children employed in the touring Industry". In 1911, Kurahashi Sozo, an early childhood educator, published an essay in the Asahi Shimbun criticizing the street performances stating that "…it is a disgrace to the civilization of the country that young children are used as street performers for children's entertainers in light entertainment […]," and he appealed for "the need for relief" as "the cry of the children who earn" must be heard (Motomori, 2019: 16, translated from Japanese to English by author). As the outcry of the public against the criminal activities of the Kakubei Jishi leaders became louder, new laws were set in place. In his article Labor Legislation in Japan Mitsutoshi Azuma, professor of civil and labor law, elucidates the early stages of the establishment of the Factory Act of 1911, implementing legal provisions for the protection of employees and the working class:

> With the advent of the Factory system as the basis of production, the Meiji Government became aware of the possibility that the reckless and exhausting employment of labor might prove to be a heavy drain on the entire labor force, which was in the long run the mainstay of the factory system, and set to work to institute some legal provisions for the protection of labor. The first tentative draft of the Act of 1887 had to be re-written several times; a number of difficulties caused by the obstinate opposition of the capitalists had to be overcome and after a fight lasting many years, the Factory Act of 1911 was enacted, though

not finally put into effect till 1916. The salient points of the Act were as follows (1) Protection of female and young workers in factories. (a) Limitation of hours of work (to 12 hours) and prohibition of mid-night work. (b) Prohibition of employment in dangerous or deleterious works. (2) Aids to relieve sufferers from accidents. It was made mandatory for the employers to pay compensation for workers killed or injured in factory disasters, or taken ill by occupational diseases. (3) Factory Supervision. To ensure the intended protection of workers as mentioned, a specialized supervisory agency known as factory controllers was set up, charged with detecting violations of the Act, which were liable to penalty (Azuma, 1951: 183).

The Factory Act, thus, not only protected employees but also children from exploitation, as the new law also prohibited child labor. In addition to the establishment of new labor laws, mass media began critiquing the Japanese population for accepting child abuse as many continued attending and watching Kakubei Jishi performances. However, slowly the collective perception of the child being someone who needed to be protected and cared for became more prevalent in the following years.

By the end of the Meiji period (1868 - 1912), most Kakubei Jishi troupes had vanished. Only a few remained in Tokyo and Tsukigata. With the new concepts of the modern family, a carefree and innocent childhood, and a mandatory school system, the underage lion dancers were considered poor and pitiful as they did not fit into the modern societal structures anymore. They became a cautionary tale of a grim childhood. The mass media were quick to denounce the Kakubei Jishi's birthplace, Tsukigata, as the basis for their evil (Motomori, 2019: 18, translated from Japanese to English by author). Even when the few remaining Kakubei Jishi performers of the Meiji period (1868-1912) danced at the annual festival, it was clear by spectators' looks that they were not welcome in Tsukigata anymore. Onlookers frowned as they watched, keeping their distance as though the children carried some unknown disease (Motomori, 2019: 18, translated from Japanese to English by author). The author Kotaro Sugimura visited Tsukigata in 1911 and stated in his article The Problem of Adult Education in Niigata Prefecture: "[...] If you ask where the Echigo lion is today, it will not be in Tsukigata, Echigo Prefecture, but in Tokyo, Musashi Prefecture." He concluded, "In the end, there were no Echigo lions in Tsukigata" (Motomori, 2019: 11, translated from Japanese to English by author).

In the years that followed, the Tsukigata festival customs continued, however, entertainment was hired from elsewhere. The original tradition of the Kakubei Jishi was completely lost:

> The environment surrounding Kakubei Jishi changed rapidly during the period from the Meiji to the Taisho eras [(1912–1926]. Criticism of teaching arts to children and traveling as migrant workers increased day by day, and it became difficult to pass on the tradition that originated in Tsukigata. There were some masters who moved to Tokyo to continue their activities in order to maintain income, but when the Child Abuse Prevention Law was promulgated in 1933 (Showa 8), it [the art-form] completely disappeared (2012-2014 Kakubei Lion Tradition Support Project, 2014: 5, translated by author).

By the time the First World War (WWI) broke out (1914-1918), newspapers had stopped reporting about street performers. Though there was certainly a global crisis that needed documenting, this caused a major gap in literature regarding the Tsukigata lion dance.

One could argue that the "original" folk art was lost long before it came to its demise by the end of the Meiji period (1868-1912). The growing popularity of street performances across the nation meant that the Kakubei Jishi no longer only belonged to the Tsukigata village. As the First World War (1914-1918) dawned, the lion dance had completely vanished. In 1947, the Child Welfare Act was written into law, cementing Japan's position on child exploitation, including regulations for the entertainment industry prohibiting child exploitation. It was, therefore, prohibited to: "(ii) Cause a child to act as a beggar, exploiting a child by forcing it to beg; (iii) Cause a child under 15 years of age to perform acrobatics or stunt horse riding for the purpose of public entertainment" (Japanese Law Translation, 2007). Japan would eventually sign these laws into reality, cementing their position on child welfare once and for all.

THE DARK HISTORY OF THE
Kakubei Jishi

Child Exploitation and the Popularity of Street Performances during the Edo Period.

1755
The first Kakubei Jishi troupes are leaving Tsukigata to find work as street performers in Edo, the capitol of Japan.

1781-1867
Tsukigata Village officials document the rapid increase of Kakubei Jishi performers that travel to the capitol to join the entertainment industry. Inspired by the popularity of the Kakubei Jishi performances, residents of villages and towns beyond Tsukigata join the trade and Kakubei Jishi troupes flock to all corners of Japan. The lion dancers, all children, supervised by elders, are exploited for their abilities to bend their bodies in extreme ways.

1868
The Meiji restoration in 1868 marks the end of the Edo period and enacts the economic and social modernization of Japan.

1890
In the late 1890s when modern childhood begins to prevail, society begins to view Kakubei Jishi as objects of pity. Social philanthropists consider their existence to be a "social problem" and coin the term "cruelty to children" in response.

1900-1907
In 1900, the Reform Act is enacted, which stipulates the treatment of children who would now be subject to child welfare and juvenile justice. Compulsory elementary schooling is announced in 1900 and by 1907 the six-year compulsory education system is established.

1900-1911
Between 1900 and 1911 compulsory education is declared and numerous prohibitions put into place that protect children from exploitation. Kakubei Jishi performances decrease. In 1911 the *Factory Act* is established, which includes provisions forbidding child labor and "Children employed in the touring Industry". Kakubei Jishi Troupes continue to decrease drastically.

1914-1918
WORLD WAR 1
Newspapers focus on the global crisis and stop reporting about street performers which causes a major gap in literature regarding the Tsukigata lion dance.

1933
Finalization of the *Prevention of Cruelty to Children Act* in 1933. Kakubei Jishi troupes have vanished.

1947
In 1947, the *Child Welfare Act* is written into law, cementing Japan's position on child exploitation, including regulations for the entertainment industry. From now on it is prohibited to: "(ii) Cause a child to act as a beggar, exploiting a child by forcing it to beg; (iii) Cause a child under 15 years of age to perform acrobatics or stunt horse riding for the purpose of public entertainment" (Japanese Law Translation, 2007).

RECLAIMING OF A FOLK ART AND CULTURAL HERITAGE

It took many years for the Tsukigata Village to reclaim agency over the folk art that had fallen from grace. In 1933, Kamezo Okuyama, who contributed to the construction of the Niigata Electric Railway (1933) and who appears to have had political ties with the village, regretted the disappearance of the original folk performing art Kakubei Jishi. Together with mayor Ryotaro Aoyagi and local musicians, who would later become part of the new lion dance troupe, he began designing plans of reviving the art-form:

> The musicians were Shinsaku Kobayashi (vocals and drum), Toranosuke Watanabe (small drum) and Toyonobu Domi (flute). Together, they began to incorporate forms from the lion dance of the past. However, local residents of the village were critical of the revival of the Kakubei Jishi and it took another three years of convincing, before the lion dance was accepted again. The first performance took place at the local Hakusan shrine in 1936 and commemorated as well the establishment of the Kakubei Jishi Preservation Society. In 1959, mayor Ryotaro Aoyagi decided that the art-form Kakubei Jishi should be handed down from one generation to the next. That year, thirteen local boys and girls participated in the dance practice with the support of their parents. This was the beginning of the tradition that the Kakubei Jishi are handed down by schoolchildren. The reputation of the folk performing art

slowly improved and the lion dancers began performing at prestigious competition venues. On May 23, 1972, the Kakubei Jishi performed for their Majesties the Emperor and Empress at the National Tree Planting Festival in Tainai-daira, Kurokawa-mura, Kitakanbara-gun for about 20 minutes. On April 15, 2013, the history and cultural value of the Kakubei Jishi was recognized and designated as Intangible Folk Cultural Property of Niigata City (Niigata City Designated Intangible Folk Cultural Property. (n.d.), Brochure).

With the establishment of the Kakubei Jishi Preservation Society in 1936, research was implemented to recover knowledge about the history and developments of the Kakubei Jishi for the Origin Story of Kakubeijishi, which would later become a chapter of the brochure Niigata City Designated Intangible Folk Cultural Property. In the following years and together with volunteers of the village community, historians, researchers from major universities, musicians and craftsmen, the restoration of the lost folk performing art was well under way. The revitalization of the Kakubei Jishi was transformed into a collaborative effort that involved the local community, including families who took great pride in it. Youngsters were allowed to join as lion dancers with the consent of their parents, and new training programs were implemented to guarantee a constructive and enjoyable experience for them while performing as Kakubei Jishi. Multiple research and documentation projects were initiated to recover and publish data about the Kakubei Jishi with the first one being the Kakubei Jishi Preservation Society in 1936 that published the brochure Niigata City Designated Intangible Folk Cultural Property (publication date unknown). The first performance troupe in nearly 20 years went on stage at the local shrine in 1936. In 1997 Chuo Kondo, published his research in the book Local Performing Arts-Kakubei Lion. The research efforts were further continued and expanded by the Executive Committee for Kakubei Jishi Traditional Activities from 2012 and resulted in the publication of the 2012-2014 Report Kakubei Lion Tradition Support Project (published in 2014).

With the revival of the Kakubei Jishi lion dance in 1936, regulations were implemented that would guarantee a safe environment for the new child performers as well as measures preventing the folk art-form from being taught outside of the village. From here on, only children of the Tsukigata Village would be permitted to debut as the next generation of lion dancers. Unfortunately, it would turn out that this restriction would ultimately pose a new threat to the art-form in the 21st century. However, for the moment it meant the safeguarding of an art-form and cultural heritage of the Tsukigata village as well as a means to revive tourism. The revival of the lion dance also came with new training structures for the children, as the old Kakubei Jishi poses and tricks had been revisited and revised.

To summarize: Our knowledge of the Kakubei Jishi centers around the Tsukigata Village, the birthplace of the acrobatic dance Kakubei Jishi, which was prone to floods and harsh winters during the Edo period (1603-1867) as it is located in close proximity to some of Japan's largest rivers and vast mountain ranges in the Niigata Prefecture. The village's main income is through agriculture and manufacturing of various goods such as Buddhist altars and tools and small equipment. The origin story of the Kakubei Jishi is, in part, influenced by the geographic locality of the village and it entails two main theories that have been introduced in this research study. The first theory considers the Kakubei Jishi to be developed out of necessity as to find a criminal that had murdered the farmer Kakubei, the name giver of the art-form. Kakubei's two sons then developed the acrobatic lion dance as a means to hunt down the criminal.

The first theory, therefore, implies that the lion dance was originally invented out of necessity rather than entertainment reasons. The second theory introduces the Kakubei Jishi as a folk performing art that was developed as a means to generate more income during the agricultural downtime in winter and when regular floods of the rivers had destroyed the village's harvest. Invented by a farmer named Kakubei, the children of the village were trained in performing arts and to display their skills of body flexibility on the streets and temple grounds. Today, it is difficult to tell with certainty which, if either, of these two theories is the actual story of origin.

During the Edo period, however, the need for entertainment increased dramatically. Street performances, including the lion dance of the Tsukigata Village, became extremely popular. As the number of Kakubei Jishi troupes multiplied, Kakubei Jishi troupes no longer originated from the Tsukigata Village. With it, however, came the need for more child performers as the lion dance of Tsukigata incorporated a high level of body flexibility that was easily achieved by children. This development ultimately led to the exploitation of children that were forced into child labor as street performers. Even children as young as three years old were exploited for their ability to bend into desired acrobatic poses. During the Edo period, leaders of the Kakubei Jishi troupes would achieve substantial financial gain while the children they employed lived in misery. The Edo period, therefore, marked a time when children were perceived as commodities rather than human beings. Only with the Meiji Restoration in 1868 came a modernization of society, labor laws, child protection, and the introduction of compulsory education. The new education system was accessible to children from all backgrounds and attendance became mandatory. The Meiji Restoration established a change in society's perception of children as human beings. With the increase of newspaper articles that condemned the criminal and abusive methods of Kakubei Jishi troupe leaders, the mass media achieved a shift in society's perception of street performances. In the early 20th century then, the last Kakubei Jishi troupes vanished as the ban of child labor was announced.

By the time WWI broke out, the lion dancers had become a memory of the past, and for nearly two decades the Kakubei Jishi had completely vanished. Saddened by the development of the once beloved folk art of the Tsukigata Village, leaders of the Tsukigata Village assembled to establish a research society with the purpose of reclaiming the Kakubei lions as cultural heritage. By reclaiming agency over their traditional lion dance and through years of research undertaken by faculty members of major universities in Japan, the lion dance was eventually recognized as cultural heritage in 2013. Designated as "Intangible Folk Cultural Property of Niigata City," the origin story of the Kakubei Jishi was restored in joined efforts by the Executive Committee for Kakubei Jishi Traditional Activities and the Kakubei Jishi Preservation Society and published in local reports of the Kakubei Lion Tradition Support Project by the Minami Ward Distinctive Development Project. The revival of the Kakubei Jishi became a community project in which local families, musicians, and craftsmen took pride. With permission of their parents, children could sign up to become lion dancers and with new training structures should ensure that children would have a positive experience while performing as Kakubei Jishi.

CHAPTER 2: TRAINING

Understanding that these child acrobats were often beaten, forced to drink caustic vinegar, starved, and forced into performing extreme flexibility, this section focuses on the later incarnation of the lion dance. Training techniques in the 20th and 21st centuries differ greatly, with young acrobats introduced to the art-form in a gentler, more humane way after the lion dance had been restored as cultural heritage of the Tsukigata Village. This section gives insight into the selection process, the training methods and training duration, the environment and the synergy between teacher and students. Today, performing as a Kakubei Jishi lion dancer is a volunteer activity to maintain cultural heritage. This chapter will highlight the selection process for volunteer dancers, training methods, and practices, the environments where training and performances take place, and the relationship between teacher and students. The decision to re-discover the Kakubei Jishi dance was not a small one, and the road to its re-legitimization was a long one.

The Executive Committee for Kakubei Jishi Traditional Activities talks about their early difficulties in a 2014 report:

> The environment surrounding Kakubei Jishi changed rapidly during the period from the Meiji [1868-1912] to the Taisho eras [1912-1926]. Criticism of teaching arts to children increased day by day, and it became difficult to pass on even the tradition that was based in Tsukigata. However, when the "Child Abuse Prevention Law" was promulgated in 1933 (Showa 8), it came

to an end. In 1936 (Showa 11) Led by Ryotaro Aoyagi, Kakubei Jishi was revived with the cooperation of Shinsaku Kobayashi, Toranosuke Watanabe, Toyonobu Michimi, and Motoe Tsuchida. The Kakubei Jishi Preservation Society was formed to protect the tradition of Kakubei Jishi as a local performing art. At first, local geisha were in charge of the lion dance, but since 1959, with the cooperation of local elementary schools and the community, it has become possible for children to learn and pass on the tradition. Toranosuke Watanabe, who was the sole successor of the musical accompaniment, passed away in 1979. From then on, the lion performance was handed down using tape recordings of the musical accompaniment. Ms. Kayoko, the daughter of Motoe Tsuchida, had inherited the guidance of the children, and the tradition of Kakubei Jishi was preserved as a performing art that is loved by the local people. In April 2013 (Heisei 25) the Kakubei Jishi became a designated intangible folk cultural property of Niigata City. The restoration of the musical accompaniment was carried out as part of the Minami-ku, Niigata City's "Unique Ward Development Project," which started in 2012. For the first time in 36 years, the original appearance of Kakubei Shishi accompanied by a live music, was revived and performed (2012-2014 Kakubei Lion Tradition Support Project, 2014: 5-6)

The Executive Committee for Kakubei Jishi Traditional Activities and early research efforts of the Kakubei Jishi Preservation Society had accumulated and restored information about training techniques, tricks and poses as well as costume designs and music that were performed by the Kakubei Jishi of the past.

Notably, one of the resources for these researchers were local geishas. Before the Kakubei Jishi was recovered by the Kakubei Jishi Preservation Society, the owners of a teahouse in Tsukigata had tried to maintain Kakubei Jishi as a local art-form, insisting that their geishas learn aspects of it and incorporate it into their own performance program. As a consequence, numerous acrobatic tricks were preserved and could be transmitted to the newly established Kakubei Jishi troupe. The acrobatic tricks were now to be performed by schoolchildren of the 20th and 21st century. With their parent's permission, children could now volunteer to become Kakubei Jishi performers with the aim to display their skills and body flexibility at the annual Tsukigata Festival held in June. The children meet once a week on Saturdays for general practice and a full day of work before performances. The children are often accompanied by their parents, some of whom being former Kakubei Jishi performers themselves and who now help with performance preparations, applying make-up and sewing costumes.

Two facilities in Tsukigata serve as training space for the lion dancers. The main training space is the Tsukigata Rural Environment Improvement Center (郷土物産資料室 [角兵衛獅子]) which consists of a large multipurpose hall that abuts the Tsukigata Local Products Reference Room where Kakubei Jishi memorabilia is on display. The second training space is a ceremonial building where the performers get ready on the day of the annual Tsukigata Festival (Figure 54, 55, 56). The multipurpose hall is large enough to fit an entire sports pitch. Located on one end of the hall is a large stage for live performances, complete with a projector screen for movies and presentations. Two doors on the left and right of the stage give access to a backstage area where performers can change their costumes. The hall serves as a training room for the lion dancers and offers enough space for partner work. In the weeks leading up to the Tsukigata Festival,

Figure 54 (top left): Ceremonial Building used on the day of the Tsukigata Festival for performance preparation (A). Copyrights: Mariam Ala-Rashi, 2022.

Figure 55 (top right): Second Floor of the Ceremonial Building that is used on the day of the Tsukigata Festival for performance preparation (B). *ibid.*

Figure 56 (bottom): Kakubei Jishi masks and veils in the Ceremonial Building. *ibid.*

students practice their performance on the stage. The students wear regular training attire such as shorts and T-shirts (Figure 57). Depending on the trick that is being practiced, students wear socks or slippers, or they train barefoot. The students also wear parts of the costume that are actively used during the performance, such as the lion mask, a red veil, and, for certain tricks, a hand towel that is wrapped around the head for

Figure 57: Kakubei Jishi Training. Copyrights: Provided and permission to use granted by Masaki Ikarashi, Mayor of Minami Ward.

protection. These props are not only decorative items but are also used to convey significance and context to the various movements and tricks.

The training sessions are guided by two female trainers of the community, who were both once Kakubei Jishi performers themselves and who have since retired from the stage. Only children between the age of 5 to 15 will perform as Kakubei Jishi. After the age of 15, the children will retire from the troupe in order to focus on their school education and to prepare for university entry exams. The school system in Japan is similar to that in the United States. Compulsory education in Japan lasts from the 1st grade of elementary school to the 3rd year of junior high, or nine years of compulsory education in total (Plaza Homes, 2022). At the age of 15 or 16, students enter high school, graduating at 17 or 18 to enter higher education. The years in high school are designated to intensive studies in preparation for university entrance exams, which does not leave much time to pursue club activities or hobbies. For the continuation of the Kakubei Jishi company, however, this means that a new lion dancer must join the troupe whenever a performer enters high school in order to maintain the minimum number of participants among their ranks. A troupe requires four participants at the bare minimum, a small number, but not always a possible one.

Becoming a Kakubei Jishi performer is on volunteer basis, which means that every child that is born in Tsukigata and that is interested in becoming a lion dancer, can sign up. Tuchida, one of the current Kakubei Jishi teachers, states that there are no particular criteria or physical abilities (such as extreme flexibility) required to become a lion dancer. Tuchida sensei (sensei = teacher: 土田先生) has more than 30 years of experience as a Kakubei Jishi trainer, and her family members belonged to the Kakubei Jishi Preservation Society. She places the performance art-form Kakubei Jishi in the category of acrobatics (karuwasa = 軽業). She states that the only requirement for a child who wishes to join the troupe is to have attended the Tsukigata Elementary School and Tsukigata Junior High School. Both girls and boys are equally welcome to perform, and there are no specific tricks or movements that are reserved for one gender or the other. Each performer may execute the entire breadth of the lion dance repertoire.

The performers, sometimes accompanied by their parents, meet once a week every Saturday evening at 07:30 PM for their training session with Tuchida sensei and another teacher. The training session lasts about two hours. The training is structured into four sections, beginning with a warm-up followed by basic practice of movements. After that, the students focus specifically on individual tricks, followed by general performance and choreography practice. During the training, the three musicians are present and practice with the lion dancers together: Two drummers, one of which gives verbal commands to announce new poses throughout the performance, and one flute player.

Historic and modern versions of Kakubei Jishi performances consist of acrobatic tricks such as tumbling, handstands, and body flexibility, sometimes with a close resemblance to contortion poses. As explored earlier, children during the Edo period were often forced into extreme poses of body flexibility (Figure 58, 59). However, today, this is not the

Figure 58: Extreme Flexibility of Kakubei Jishi Performers during the Edo Period. *ibid.*

Figure 59: Kakubei Jishi Child Performers during the early Meiji Period. *ibid.*

大道芸の角兵衛獅子。新潟県西蒲原郡月潟村は洪水が多く、水田が不作がちで、口べらしと日銭を得るために出稼ぎ巡業に少年たちが出た。明治20年代

case anymore. In fact, there is no specific flexibility training included in the training sessions. Children perform and showcase their natural abilities and flexibility. If one of the Kakubei Jishi poses cannot be achieved by the child performer, the pose will be altered to fit the child's natural flexibility. This means that if the child's back flexibility is not as advanced, tricks such as backbends (bending the back) and the bridge (bending backwards into a position where feet and hands are touching the floor and the back is arched with the stomach facing the ceiling), will simply be reversed into a front bend or the trick will be performed by a child that has a more advanced flexibility. According to Tuchida sensei, there is also no requirement for the children to practice flexibility at home.

During the training session, teachers give instructions and support children throughout the practice of the tricks. Particularly challenging tricks that include partner work are practiced with the teacher's assistance. The other students have to either wait for their turn on the side of the training room or they focus on easier tricks that can be done without supervision in the meantime.

For the performance and choreography training, the students wear their lion masks with veils, and the teachers will kneel in the corners of the stage out of the way, so that they can assist during the performance. To convey different images and meanings of the various movements that are presented, the veil of the lion mask is constantly adjusted and used as a prop. Other parts of the costume, like cotton belts and wide sleeves, are also incorporated into the performance, and the teachers remain kneeling on stage to help with smaller costume adjustments during the performance. The teacher represents a vital role during both the training sessions and the live performance itself, as the synergy between trainer and student is dependent on mutual trust and respect. The trainers, having been Kakubei

Jishi performers themselves in the past, know the choreography and sequences in the routine that need special attention. Should a performer require help during the performance, the teacher can immediately assist to guarantee a smooth continuation of the show. Another vital role during the training and performance are the musicians. Drummer Wataru Toishi, who is also the vocalist, gives commands throughout the performance. The commands include the name of the movement that is about to be presented, as well as a short explanation of it. The audience can, therefore, easily follow and understand the context of the movement. While the drummer announces the next movement, the lion dancers either remain on stage in a kneeling position, or the time is used for a new group of performers to enter the stage as various movements require different numbers of participants on stage. After the announcement of the lead drummer, the music begins, and the performance continues.

Wataru Toishi says that the music that was played during the Edo period was lost, as sheets of music were not written back then by the street performers. This could be due to economic reasons as paper could not be afforded, or because the musicians simply memorized their music. Another reason for a lack of documentation could be, as mentioned earlier, that when leaders of the lion dance troupes died during the Edo period, their possessions and records of the troupe were instructed to be burned to destroy evidence of how they mistreated child acrobats. Oftentimes techniques and performance details were simply passed down to next generations as oral history and never properly written down. It is assumed that, for either artistic or pragmatic reasons, every troupe had made up their own music and that it was inspired by the local music style of the respective area where the troupe was residing at the time . As mentioned earlier, the Kakubei Lion Tradition Support Project had the benefit of a member who was the sole successor of live musical accompaniment for Kakubei Jishi, as he had performed in the pre-war era. When Toranosuke Watanabe passed away in 1979, the Kakubei Jishi Preservation Society was able to secure his music recordings and develop the material that is still used in Tsukigata to this day. Wataru Toishi, who is the current lead drummer, uses the music recorded by Toranosuke Watanabe. However, he takes artistic liberties when it comes to the tempo of the music. According to Wataru Toishi, the tempo depends on his enthusiasm and mood during the performance as well as the overall atmosphere and reaction from the audience. The tempo is oftentimes improvisational, and the relationship between the lion dancers and the musicians has to be well attuned in order for the performance to run smoothly. The musicians are, therefore, present for rehearsals as well as regular training days in order to cultivate this relationship (Figure 60, 61, 62). The duration of an entire performance, as it is showcased during the Tsukigata Festival, is about 45 minutes with a selected number of poses demonstrated.

For direct comparison between Edo period tricks and contemporary performances: When juxtaposing modern poses with images from Edo period Kakubei Jishi performances, it becomes clear that Edo period performance artists put special emphasis extreme body

Figure 60: Kakubei Jishi with Drummer and Flute Player. *ibid.*

Figures 61 & 62: Drums and Flutes used to accompany Kakubei Jishi Performances. *ibid.*

flexibility. Some of those movements and tricks are in close resemblance with typical contortion poses that one could see in a modern circus setting (Figure 63, 64). One pose, for example, that can be identified in Edo period images of the Kakubei Jishi is the chest-stand. The chest-stand is a trick where the performer bends backwards as far as possible, often from a standing position, in order to bring the chest to rest on the floor and to look at the audience through the feet, which are either still touching the floor or are placed under the artist's chin (Figure 65). These postures are excluded from contemporary performances.

The Tsukigata Local Products Reference Room, which holds the Kakubei Jishi archive, displays three distinct paintings with numerous Kakubei Jishi tricks including some of their historic names and explanations. The three paintings are a reference to the street performances, the costuming and breadth of the lion dance repertoire during the Edo period including tricks with extreme flexibility (Figure 66, 67, 68) (see also image 53). The brochure of the Kakubei Jishi Preservation Society that is available to

Figure 63 & 64: Drawings of Edo Period
Kakubei Jishi Performances. *ibid.*

visitors, however, only displays a list of 18 selected movements and poses which do not include chest-stands or similarly extreme poses of body flexibility. Back flexibility such as the bridge and a handstand version where the feet are brought forward to be close to the head, however, are still incorporated in the current list of tricks. It is evident that the Kakubei Jishi and the preservation societies of today aim to represent a healthy training and entertainment program that considers the artist's natural flexibility without force. A performer can showcase a chest-stand if their natural flexibility allows it, however, if a performer is not able to execute a backbend, the movement will be changed to a frontbend. The training of a Kakubei Jishi performer does not include active or passive stretches that can be found, for example, in Chinese and Mongolian contortion training. According to Tuchida-sensei, the 18 poses selected by the Kakubei Jishi Preservation Society during the revival phase after the Meiji Restoration are those printed in the brochure that is still available at the Tsukigata Festival today. These poses have not been changed in the 30 years since Tsuchida sensei became teacher except for

だるま
さかしゅ
きせ〵の
かくさ
ち

the mentioned adjustments from backbend to frontbend to accommodate the student's natural flexibility.

Multiple reasons lead to the assumption that the Kakubei Jishi Preservation Society's premise was to return to the roots of the lion dance and revive the folk performing art before it was stylized into an art-form of extreme flexibility during the Edo period. The reasons for this can be attributed to several factors. Firstly, the dark history of the lion dance during the Edo period that deterred its practice. Secondly, the critique from society that arose during the Meiji Restoration era and contributed to its decline. Lastly, the aim of the Tsukigata Village to distance itself from the association with criminal Kakubei Jishi leaders, which further discouraged the practice of the lion dance. Based on the reports from the Edo period, a stylization and transformation of what was once a folk performing art had taken place to attract a wider audience and to compete with other street performers. This means that the traditional artistic elements of a folk art-form are deliberately altered to fit a particular commercial purpose. Although extreme body flexibility, including tricks like chest-stands, was a staple of Kakubei Jishi performances of the Edo period, these tricks are nowhere to be found in today's performances.

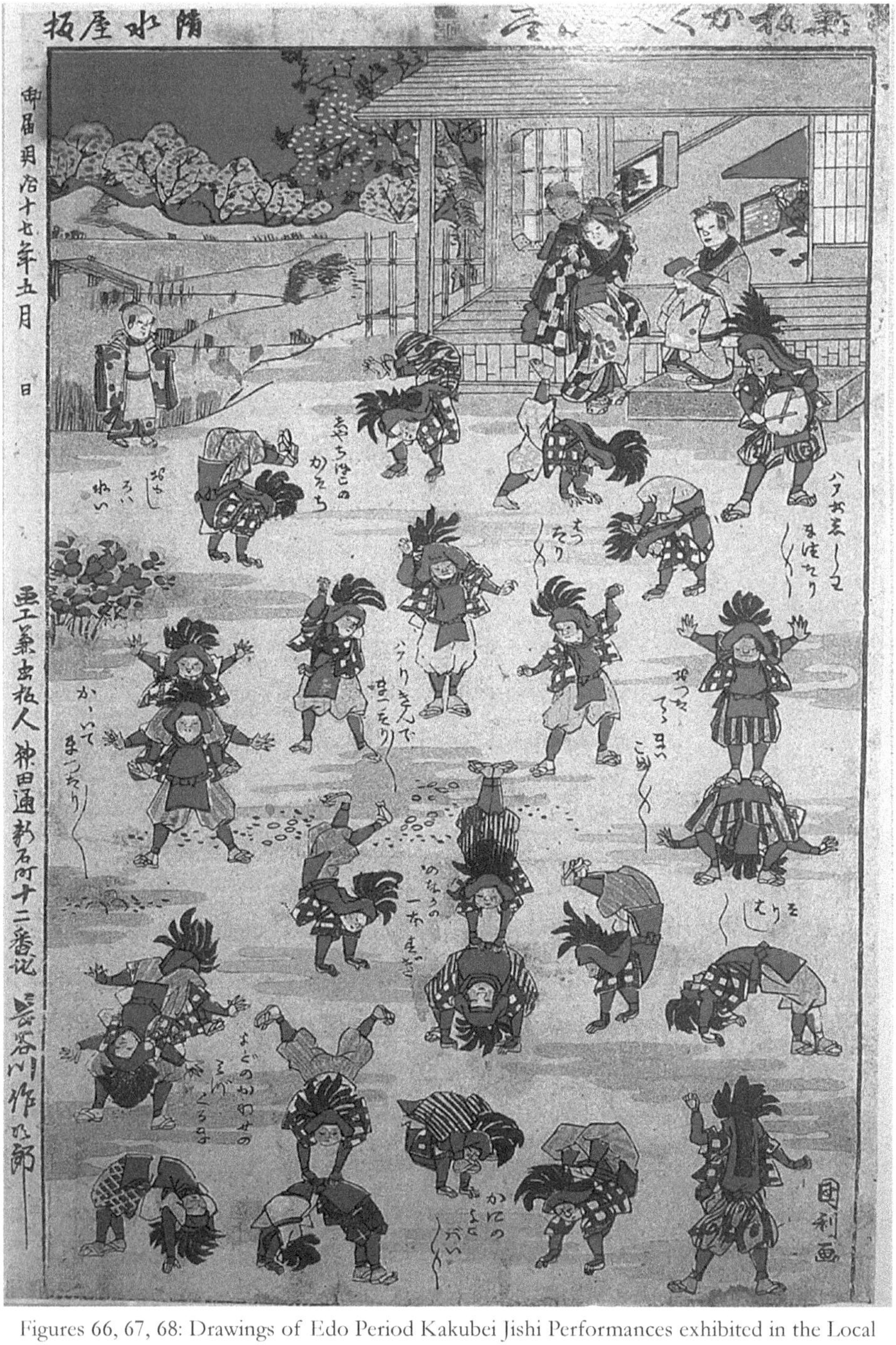

Figures 66, 67, 68: Drawings of Edo Period Kakubei Jishi Performances exhibited in the Local Produce Reference Room, Tsukigata. *ibid.*

360

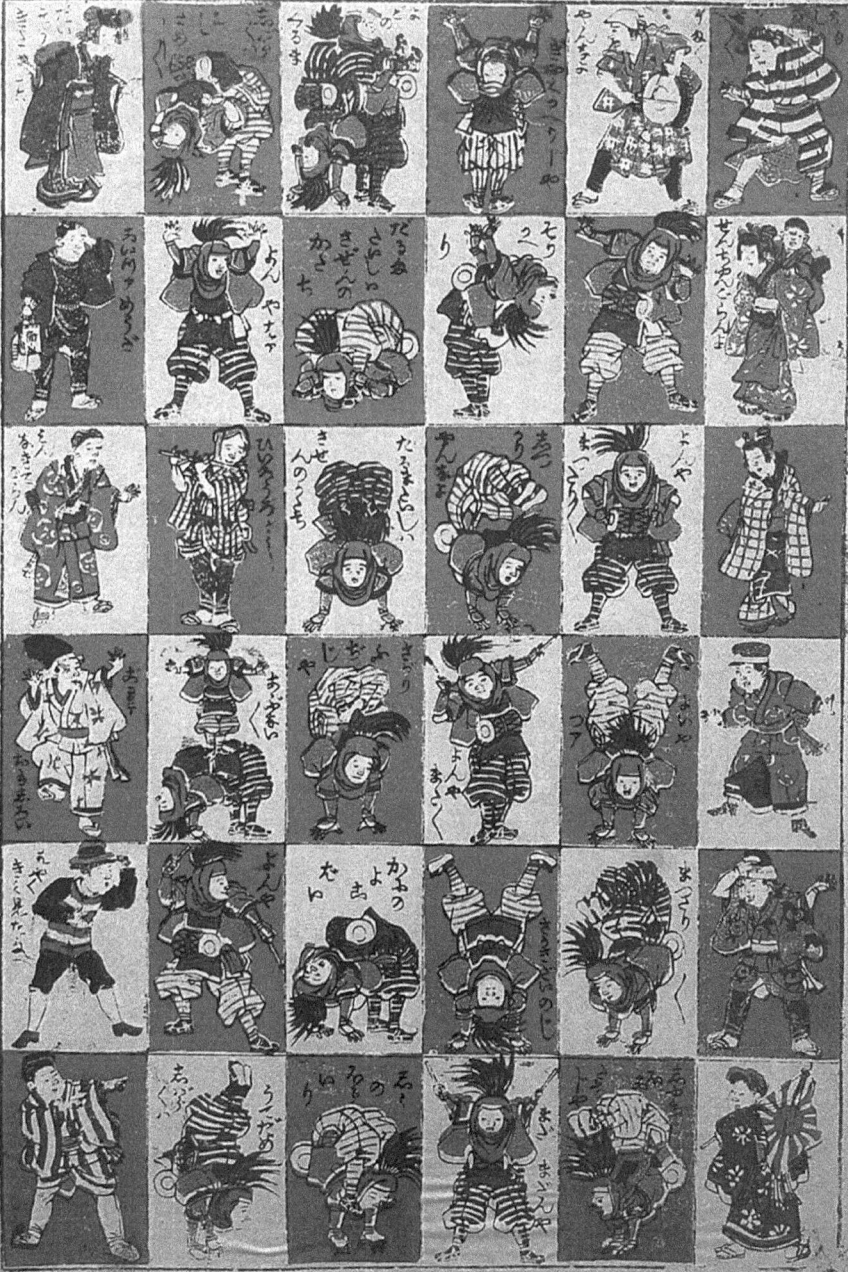

This unique Japanese art-form is not alone, however, when it comes to changes in centuries-old performance art. For comparison, Chinese and Mongolian contortion as they are known today from a circus setting, are both stylized forms of body flexibility that stemmed from folk acrobatics and folk dances and were adapted by the entertainment industry to be transformed into a circus discipline. Similarly, Kakubei Jishi is a form of folk acrobatics and street performance that underwent rigid stylization during the Edo period to meet the demands of a competitive entertainment market at the time and to remain competitive against other street performing arts. It seems that after the establishment of the Kakubei Jishi Preservation Society, the lion dance had been reversed to its assumed authentic form. In the performing arts world, it is a natural development that each generation of performers alters, modernizes, reshapes, revisits and further develops their art-form; it appears that the Kakubei Jishi Preservation society took a "back to the roots" approach. This development appears to serve multiple purposes: To distance the art-form from its dark past, to assure that the child performers experience a healthy training outcome that supports their natural body flexibility, and to revive the folk performing art as close to its original form as possible, with the aim to improve tourism in the region by showcasing a traditional art-form as accurately as possible. All this said, it's impossible to know how accurate this painstaking recreation has been, given the scarcity of historic records – what little primary documentation may have existed has mostly been lost or destroyed. Further research to compare archival imagery from the Edo period and lion dance performances today would doubtlessly prove fruitful, but such research is beyond the scope of this monograph.

Now that the training aspects of Kakaubei Jishi has been discussed, this monograph will focus on the choreography, performance, and costuming. The following section examines the creative process, aesthetic choices, evidence of spiritual use, hidden meanings, and symbolism present in a traditional Kakubei Jishi performance.

CHAPTER 3: SIGNIFICANCE OF MOVEMENTS AND DEVELOPMENT OF AESTHETICS

Kakubei Jishi, the lion dance of the Tsukigata Village, is a folk performing art that consists of purposefully selected sequences that incorporate body flexibility. In this section, it is analyzed by examining its aesthetics and identifying its traditional and cultural values that give it distinct characteristics. As previously discussed, the Kakubei Jishi lion dance evolved from folk acrobatics during the Edo period. As it gained popularity, the repertoire of tricks and poses expanded. This led to the introduction of extreme flexibility that is similar to that of a modern circus contortionist. The Niigata City administration states that from the middle of the Edo period (around 1755) more than 200 acrobatic tricks including handstands, bridges, and somersaults were incorporated as the art-form became popular all over the country. There are clear links between folk acrobatics, traditions, and spiritual practices within Kakubei Jishi, which illuminate the aesthetic development of its performance from the Edo period through the 21st century. A large part of its appeal was the incorporation of national customs into its techniques such as the shape of the golden shachihoko of the Nagoya Castle and the Oi River crossing (Niigata City Newsletter, 2020). Elements from religious practices found in Buddhism and Shintoism were also incorporated.

Symbolic movements are the heart of the Kakubei Jishi, as its original purpose is not to display extreme body flexibility in a stylized sense for the sake of spectacle (as it was the case during the Edo period). Each movement of this art-form has a particular meaning and conveys it by utilizing folk acrobatics and body flexibility. According to Wataru Toishi, a significantly larger number of movements and acrobatic tricks were developed and performed during the Edo period. However, recordings of these were lost to time. Wataru Toishi further asserts that it is not clear how movements were developed during the Edo period, but it is assumed that performances and movements were inspired by the landmarks, natural phenomena, and sights that the performers were exposed to when on tour. Street performances and street artists were low in status. For that reason, images and recordings of movements were not produced in the same way that high arts, such as Noh and Kyogen, were documented. Noh and Kyogen are traditional Japanese performing arts that date back to the 14th century. Noh is a stylized form of drama using masks, while Kyogen is a form of comedic theatre. According to the Japan Arts Council, a public agency dedicated to preserving and promoting traditional performing arts, particular art-forms were supported by the Shogunate (the military government of Japan during the Edo period):

> In the Edo period (17th to 19th centuries), the Tokugawa shogunate went further with the policy of the Toyotomi family of preserving Noh, and established Sarugaku [various performing arts that came to Japan from the Chinese continent] as the official ceremonial entertainment for the shogunate. In addition to the four Yamato troupes, a new school was added to the list of Noh performers. Feudal domains in the regions in turn invited actors to perform for them exclusively, and Noh and Kyogen developed into performing arts of the samurai class

[one of the highest-ranking social castes of the Edo period]. The troupes were given a stable status and economic foundation. Meanwhile, the troupes were demanded to improve their techniques and pass on the tradition to their successors (Invitation to Nohgaku, 2018).

Noh and Kyogen (Figure 69), among other performing arts, were performed for and appreciated by members of "high society" (court nobles and samurai), and these artists were supported financially by these onlookers, who provided school grounds to train the next generation of performers. A curriculum was introduced, ensuring students would develop their techniques to a professional level. However, this patronage was only extended to artistic disciplines that had support of the upper classes. Performers who worked on the street were left to their own devices to develop their techniques, tricks, and routines.

Figure 69: Noh Theatre. Copyrights: Ichigen, CC BY-SA 4.0. Available at: https://commons.wikimedia.org/wiki/File:170421_sumidagawa_001a.jpg

Today, there are 18 movements that Chuzo Kondo lists in his book Local Performing Arts-Kakubei Lion. These movements have been previously selected by the preservation society for the continuation of the Kakubei Jishi art-form. The list includes some transition poses that are presented by each performer before and after each trick. Every movement represents either natural phenomena, spiritual, and mythical connotations or depictions of agricultural elements.

List of Movements performed in the 20th and 21st Century

The following list comprises the 18 movements that are showcased by Kakubei Jishi performers during the Tsukigata Festival each year in June. The order in which the movements have been presented in recent years has changed when compared to the list in Kondo's 1997 book. This might be due to practical reasons, such as costume changes, or simply because the number of participants for the Kakubei Jishi performances varies year to year. It is, therefore, assumed, that the order in which movements are presented is fairly flexible. This does not count, however, for movements 13-18 which represent the climax of the show and which are always presented in the same order. The Niigata City Minami Ward Tourism Association (新潟市南区観光協会) shared the educational video Kakubei Lion (角兵衛獅子), that focuses only on the the 18 main movements instead of the entire performance (Video: 新潟市南区観光協会, 2018). The video's purpose appears to be to facilitate the study and analysis of the 18 movements by Kakubei Jishi apprentices and scholars. The full performance has a duration of around 45 minutes.

The list of movements includes the traditional names of each pose and an explanation of the movement's symbolic meaning. The context of each movement is also announced by the lead drummer during the performance before each pose is executed. Between the main poses, the lion dancers execute cartwheels and use their veils as a prop to depict various shapes before entering their next pose. The red veil is also utilized during changes of positions on stage as each main pose requires a different number of dancers. Here, the lions walk in a circle, veil down in front of their face with each hand holding one corner of the veil, while some dancers either leave the circle to go off stage or other dancers join the circle, depending on how many lions are needed for the next movement. For each of the 18 main poses, the lion dancers will position themselves on a particular spot on the stage, so that the execution of the trick is symmetrical and aligned with the other performers. It also guarantees that each performer has enough space on stage to move. Depending on the number of participating lion dancers each year, however, their positions on stage might change, to maintain a symmetrical image. For example, if 8 performers would display the Kani no yokobai かにの横ばい (The Walk of a Crab), then four lions would stand on the right and four on the left as it is pleasing to the eye for the audience.

Movement Number 1: Maikomi 舞い込み (Entrance of the Lion Dancers)

Upon entering the stage -- as well as before each movement in the entire performance -- the maikomi is executed (Figure 70, 71, 72, 73). The maikomi is a combination of movements that utilize the red veil to showcase various shapes that have different meanings with the veil as well as one distinct movement that is meant to repel evil. This particular movement consists of a hand clap and leg movement done in perfect unison. It is executed before every main pose and is meant to block evil spirits. The dancers enter

Figures 70, 71, 72, 73 (above, opposite page): Maikomi Movement. Copyrights: 南区産業振興課 商工観光推進室 (Commerce, Industry and Tourism Promotion Office, Industry Promotion Division, Minami-ku)

越後月潟　角兵衛獅子

the stage one after another to stand in one line, bow towards the audience and then take their place on stage. The drummer introduces the lion as a brave and fierce animal that can exorcise demons. The lion dancers will kneel next to each other in one straight line, facing the audience. While the drummer announces the movement to the audience, the lion dancers remain in a kneeling position on stage. The right knee remains on the floor while the other is slightly lifted up. Immediately after entering the stage for the first time, the hands rest on the upper thighs in a waiting position. After that, maikomi is executed every time after the completion of another movement. Here, the performer can rest their hands either on the upper thighs, or the performer can rearrange the red veil in preparation for the next trick. During the introduction and after the performers first entered the stage, the lead drummer explains the meaning of maikomi to the audience. Upon completion of the drummer's announcement, the lion dancers will then extend the left leg to the side while at the same time clapping their hands. The hands are then lifted above the head forming a triangle shape between the thumb and index finger with the palms of the hands facing towards the audience. Simultaneously, as the performers lift their hands they loudly say "Ha!" The maikomi movement concluding with the "Ha!"

is now completed. This short pause during the performance in a kneeling position provides the performers and their teachers with just enough time to make small adjustments to the costume for the upcoming trick. The drummer will use this moment to announce the next movement (新潟市南区観光協会, 0:56).

Movement Number 2: KinNo Shachihoko 金の鯱鉾 (Mythical Fish Creature)

Movement number two depicts the shachihoko, a mythical creature with the body of a fish and the head of a tiger (Figure 74). Its tail is curved and points upwards to the sky (hoko). The shachihoko was believed to have the ability to cause rain and, thus, prevent fire. The golden shachihoko is one of the decorations that was particularly popular during the Edo period and could be found on rooftops of castle towers, samurai homes, and temple gates. The most prominent shachihoko is located on the roof of the Nagoya Castle that was completed in 1615 by the Shogun Tokugawa Ieyasu.

Figure 74: Shachihoko Mythical Creature, Nagoya Castle. Copyrights: Brücke-Osteuropa, CC0. Available at: https://commons.wikimedia.org/wiki/File:Dolphin_of_Nagoya_Castle_2.JPG

For the shachihoko movement (Figure 75), six lion dancers position themselves on stage, divided into two groups and forming a triangle, facing each other. They imitate the shape of the shachihoko by going into a headstand with the elbows and lower arms placed on the ground in a triangle shape with the fingertips of both hands almost touching. The head is then placed in that triangle. The performers kick up into the headstand and flex their feet to resemble the fishtail of the shachihoko creature. The dancers will remain in this pose for about 30 to 45 seconds for the audience to appreciate the skill of the lions. Depending on the number of participating lion dancers their position on stage for this movement might change, to maintain a symmetrical image (新潟市南区観光協会, 2:44).

Figure 75: Shachihoko Movement. Copyrights: 南区産業振興課 商工観光推進室 (Commerce, Industry and Tourism Promotion Office, Industry Promotion Division, Minami-ku)

Movement Number 3: Kani no yokobai かにの横ばい (The Walk of a Crab)

The kani no yokobai movement represents the walk of a crab (Figure 76). The maritime life and Japan's cultural identity are closely linked as

Figure 76: Kani no yokobai Movement. *ibid.*

fisheries play a considerable role in its food supply, and sea creatures have inspired many Japanese folk tales. With Niigata prefecture being located directly by the sea and Tsukigata Village being in between two vast rivers, it is no surprise that sea life became a key motif of the Kakubei Jishi lion dance. Presenting the kani no yokobai movement, the dancers will stand in one line, facing the audience. Upon announcement from the drummer, they would turn around on the spot with the back to the audience and enter a handstand from which they immediately fall over into a bridge. While in the bridge position, the dancers would now walk sideways, similar to the walk of a crab, for eight counts to the right, only to repeat the same sequence of handstand, falling over into a bridge and walking to the left. The kani no yokobai is repeated four times (新潟市南区観光協会, 3:56).

Movement Number 4: Rangiku 乱菊 (Chrysanthemum Flower)

The rangiku movement resembles a chrysanthemum flower with long and irregular petals (Figure 77). This movement could be a reference to one

Figure 77: Rangiku Movement. *ibid.*

of the various origin stories of the Kakubei Jishi. The chrysanthemum flower was the insignia of the Tokugawa clan, and farmer Kakubee was known to be a distinguished carver of wooden shishi heads with the chrysanthemum insignia at the time (Groemer, 2016: 170-171). In Japan, the chrysanthemum is the imperial family emblem and was first adopted in the early Kamakura period (1185–1333). It is featured on Japanese passports, the imperial seal of Japan, and the 50-yen coin. The flower symbolizes royalty, rejuvenation, and longevity. To perform the rangiku movement, the lions execute a number of front-walkovers where the acrobats start from a standing position, bend their upper bodies forward to bring their hands to the floor and kick up into a handstand after which they immediately fall over into a bridge. From the bridge position, they turn over sideways into a frontbend by placing the hands on the floor. From here, they kick upwards and over to bring their legs back into a bridge again. This sequence of alternating forward bending and bridge positions is one dynamic motion and is repeated six times (新潟市南区観光協会, 5:28).

Movement Number 5: Sei kai ha 青海波 (Ocean Waves)

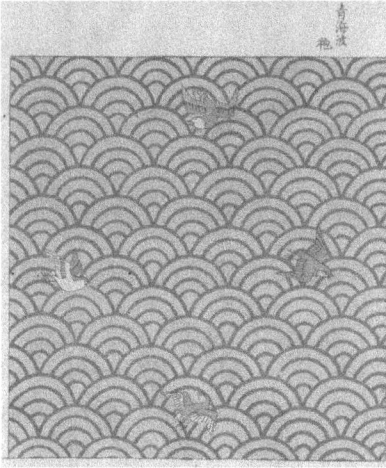

Figure 78: Sei kai ha 青海波 (Ocean Waves). Copyrights: unknown, public domain, via Wikimedia Commons. Available at: https://commons.wikimedia.org/wiki/File:%E9%9D%92%E6%B5%B7%E6%B3%A2%E3%81%AB%E5%8D%83%E9%B3%A5.jpg

The sei kai ha movement resembles the crests of the waves that emerge when the ocean crashes against a rocky shoreline (Figure 78). The sei kai ha is also a traditional pattern of waves that is used in drawings, pottery, Noh costumes, and kimono designs. To depict this movement in their acrobatic dance, four children stand in one line and move via front-walkover from a standing position to a bridge. This creates a line of rolling bridges that imitates the movement of the waves. The bridges are executed in fast succession, so the children need an advanced back limberness to make the movement appear as smooth as water (Figure 79). There are five rolling bridges executed in one movement, and the movement is repeated two times: Once to the left and once to the right (新潟市南区観光協会, 6:05).

Figure 79: Sei kai ha Movement (Ocean Waves). Copyrights: 南区産業振興課 商工観光推進室 (Commerce, Industry and Tourism Promotion Office, Industry Promotion Division, Minami-ku)

Movement Number 6: Mizu guruma 水車 (Waterwheel small)

The mizu guruma movement represents the waterwheel which is important for irrigation in the Niigata prefecture, as it was once used to grind wheat and rice. To execute the mizu guruma movement as well as the following movement tawara gorogashi (movement number 7), the lion dancers have to exchange their lion masks for a scarf or towel that is worn on their heads for protection as both movements require versions of somersaults (Figure 80).

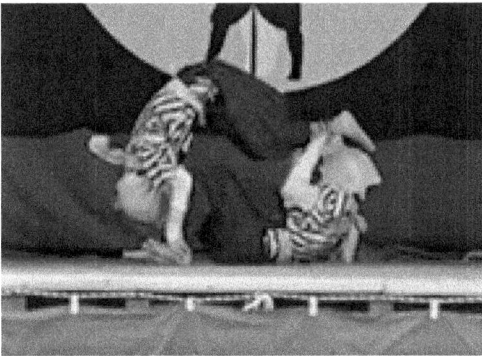

Figure 80: Mizu Guruma Movement (Waterwheel). Copyrights: Mariam Ala-Rashi, 2022.

The mizu guruma movement is a somersault movement where dancers work in pairs. There will be two duos (in total four dancers) executing the movement at the same time in opposite directions. One of the dancers kneels on the floor while the other dancer stands behind them. Upon the drummer's command, the kneeling dancer leans back and lifts their legs up so the standing dancer can grab the other's ankles. The dancer on the floor also grabs the ankles of the standing partner which now initiates the movement by leaning forward and entering into a forward somersault. In sync with the other duo of lion dancers, they roll like a wheel from one side of the stage to the other, mimicking the movement of a waterwheel (新潟市南区観光協会, 7:47).

Movement Number 7: Tawara gorogashi 俵転がし (Bale Rolling)

The tawara gorogashi movement represents the tawara which is a round bag made of woven straw for holding goods such as rice, vegetables, charcoal, and other commodities. Some agricultural cities and villages hold annual bale-rolling festivals and races that symbolize prosperity. During the bale-rolling race, large bales with a diameter of 2.5m, a length of 4m, and a weight of 1000kg are rolled down the streets of the town as fast as possible, with participants competing for time.

Figure 81: Tawara gorogashi 俵転がし (Bale Rolling) Copyrights: 南区産業振興課 商工観光推進室 (Commerce, Industry and Tourism Promotion Office, Industry Promotion Division, Minami-ku)

For the tawara gorogashi movement, two or four lion dancers wearing a towel as a head scarf enter the stage. One dancer stands on the right side of the stage, the other on the left. They face each other, entering the movement from a standing position. This movement is a somersault in which the performer bends forward, holding on to their big toes while rolling forward in a somersault from one side of the stage to the other (Figure 81). Holding the toes while somersaulting is believed to create a shape that is aesthetically very similar to that of a rolling bale. The tawara gorogashi movement is executed one time across the stage (新潟市南区観光協会, 9:20).

Movement Number 8: 淀の川瀬の水車 Yodonokawase no mizuguruma (Yodo Waterwheel large)

Similar to movement number six, this movement also represents a waterwheel. This movement, however, refers to a particular wheel in Kyoto. The Yodo water wheel was a landmark that was built in ancient times and later became a part of the Yodo water castle (淀城 Yodo-jō) in 1625, which was located at the confluence of the Katsura, Uji, and Kizu Rivers (Figure 82).

Figure 82: Yodo Water Castle 淀城 Yodo-jō. Copyrights: Anonymous/Unknown author, public domain, via Wikimedia Commons. Available at: https://commons.wikimedia.org/wiki/File:Yodo_Castle.jpg

Performed again by two dancers, the movement reflects the spinning of the waterwheel (Figure 83). However, for this movement, the dancers

Figure 83: Yodo Waterwheel Large Movement. Copyrights: 南区産業振興課 商工観光推進室 (Commerce, Industry and Tourism Promotion Office, Industry Promotion Division, Minami-ku)

wear the lion masks as they perform it from a standing position. To enter the movement, one of the dancers bends backwards to put their arms around their partner's waist. The partner now leans forward and picks up their partner to lift them over their heads while also bending backwards. Using the bodyweight and gravity for their advantage, the dancers create momentum and execute a spinning motion six times to one side then four times to the other (新潟市南区観光協会, 10:35).

Movement Number 9: Nin ba 人馬 (Horse and Rider)

The nin ba movement is executed by two lion dancers and depicts and man mounting a horse or a person climbing on top of another person's shoulders (Figure 84).

Figure 84: Nin ba (Horse and Rider). *ibid.*

For this movement, one dancer stands behind the other. The dancers in the front bend their knees and bring their hands towards their shoulders. The dancers standing behind them enter into a front-walkover and have their feet land onto the shoulders of the dancer in front of them. The dancer in the front then grabs the ankles of their partner and bends forward in order to place their partner's feet on the floor in front of them. The dancers who were standing in the back, are now standing in the front and will repeat the same movement patterns with their partners. The nin ba movement will repeated four times to the left side of the stage and four times to the right.

Upon arriving on the right side of the stage, the dancer will remain seated on the shoulders of their partner. They will now face the audience as the base (the dancer carrying their partner) will extend their arms to the side in a 90-degree angle and the flyer (the dancer sitting on their partner's shoulders) raises their arms into an O-shape with their hands over their head and their palms facing the audience. After a few seconds of giving the audience a moment to appreciate the movement, they will clap their hands once and return their arms and hands back into the previous positions (新

潟市南区観光協会, 12:04). From this position, they now move directly from movement number 9 nin ba into movement number 10 oikawa no kawa goeshi.

Movement Number 10: Oikawa no kawa goeshi 人馬(大井川の川越えし) (The Shape of the River)

The oikawa no kawa goeshi movement represents the crossing of the vast Oi River that was prone to flooding, had a large volume of water and a rapid flow. The waters of the Oi River were unpredictable and regarded during the Edo period as nearly impassable. On days when water levels were high, travelers and merchants who needed to cross the river would wait in nearby inns for safer conditions. When the water levels were finally low, they would hire people called kawagoe jinsoku which would carry the passengers on their shoulders and wooden ladders to the other side of the river (Figure 85). It is believed that during the Edo period, bridges at the Oi River could not be built due to topographical problems such as the gradient and width of the river and the volume of water. The technology

Figure 85: Crossing of the Oi River. Copyrights: Utagawa Toyokuni I, CC0, via Wikimedia Commons. Available at: https://commons.wikimedia.org/wiki/File:MET_DP143701.jpg

to build a bridge was not advanced enough during the Edo period which is why people were carried through the waters of the river by the kawagoe jinsoku.

To depict the crossing of the river, the lion dancers remain in the final position of the nin ba movement where one dancer is sitting on their partner's shoulders (see previous image 83). For the oikawa no kawa goeshi movement, they will slowly turn around over their left, walk in a narrow circle one and a half times and end up standing with their backs to the audience (新潟市南区観光協会, 13:23). From this position, they will now move directly from movement number 10 oikawa no kawa goeshi into movement number 11 shishi no ko otoshi.

Movement Number 11: Shishi no kootoshi 人馬(獅子の子落とし) (Fall of the Lion's Cub)

The shishi no ko otoshi movement represents a lion cub's fight for survival. As per the traditional tale, the lioness casts her newborn cub into a deep valley and nurtures only those cubs that are strong enough to climb back up. The movement refers to a parable of giving a child a severe ordeal to test its abilities and to raise the child to become an honest and respectable human being of society.

For the shishi no ko otoshi movement, the lion dancer who sits on the shoulders of their partner imitate the drop of the lion's cub. For this, the dancer will lower their upper body backwards (Figure 86) so that their head is close to the ground while their partner will hold on to their feet to prevent an actual drop and injury (新潟市南区観光協会, 13:44). After giving the audience a few moments to appreciate the movement, the

Figure 86: Shishi no kootoshi movement and Ninba (Tessen kazaguruma) movement. Copyrights: 南区産業振興課 商工観光推進室 (Commerce, Industry and Tourism Promotion Office, Industry Promotion Division, Minami-ku)

dancers will now move directly from movement number 11 shishi no ko otoshi into movement number 12 ninba (tessen kazaguruma).

Movement number 12: Ninba (Tessen kazaguruma) 人馬（鉄扇風車） (Iron fan windmill)

The ninba (tessen kazaguruma) movement represents the windmill. Imitating the rotating movements and blades of the windmill, the lion dancers maintain their position of the shishi no ko otoshi movement where the flyer dropped backwards, hanging from their knees and off from their partner's shoulders (see previous image 84). The base will now spin around 10 times before coming to a halt to let the flyer climb down (新潟市南区観光協会, 14:01).

Movement Number 13: Karako ningyo omumanori 唐子人形お馬乗り (Karako Doll Horse Riding)

384

The karako ningyo omumanori movement heralds the climax of the show as it is one of the final movements that are presented. The Japanese term karako (唐子) is used in terminology that describes art and refers to Chinese Tang children of the Tang dynasty. The motif of the Tang children can be found in Japanese pottery, paintings, figurines, and other forms of art, and they are symbolic for the innocence and joy of childhood (Figure 87).

Figure 87: Karako Dolls. Copyrights: Walters Art Museum, Public domain, via Wikimedia Commons. Available at: https://commons.wikimedia.org/wiki/File:Japanese_-_Brush_Rest_in_ the_Form_of_Boys_with_a_Snowball_-_Walters_49917.jpg

The karako ningyo omumanori movement represents a child riding a doll or toy horse and is presented as a duo performance with up to ten performers being on stage while working in pairs. One child performer acts as the doll horse, standing bent forward with the hands on the floor and the other child will climb on the horse's back. The drummer now commands the doll horse to turn slowly while the child sitting on top of the horse is holding its arms up in an O-shape with the palms facing the audience. The doll horse turns slowly one time.

Some shows will have an additional performer act as someone who leads the horse on a leash, to enhance the illusion of doll horse riding for the audience (Figure 88). For this, the additional performer will bring a cotton band for a leash that the horse holds in its mouth so that it can be lead in a circle (新潟市南区観光協会, 14:56). From this position, they now move directly from movement number 13 karako ningyo omumanori into movement number 14 kanazu wa jizotachi.

Figure 88: Karako Doll Horse Riding Movement. Copyrights: 南区産業振興課 商工観光推進室 (Commerce, Industry and Tourism Promotion Office, Industry Promotion Division, Minami-ku)

Movement Number 14: Kanazu wa jizotachi 唐子人形お馬乗り (かなずは地蔵立) (Standing on the Doll Horse)

For the kanazu wa jizotachi movement, the second part of the show's climax, the performers maintain their act of the child riding the doll horse but increase the level of difficulty as the flyer now brings their feet upwards to place them on the hips of the base (the horse). After finding their balance, all children that represent the horse's rider will now slowly stand up (Figure 89) and raise their arms into an O-shape (新潟市南区観光協会, 16:10). The kanazu wa jizotachi movement will shortly turn into the third part of the show's climax: The ueshitanidanno koshidame.

Figure 89: Standing on the Doll Horse Movement. *ibid.*

Movement Number 15: Ueshitanidanno koshidame 唐子人形お馬乗り(上下二段の腰だめ) (Finale Part 1)

For the ueshitanidanno koshidame, the children remain standing on top of their doll horses, however, to increase the level of difficulty even further, the children who act as the doll horses now lift their hands off the floor and extend their arms to the side while simultaneously bring their upper bodies up so that they can face the audience (see previous image 88). For this movement, the base has to maintain their leg and hip position so that the child standing on top of their hips will not fall (新潟市南区観光協会, 16:34).

Movement Number 16: Taikoni niwatirinokatachi 唐子人形お馬乗り(太鼓ににわとりの形) (Finale Part 2: The Chicken Shape)

For the taikoni niwatirinokatachi movement, the base now lowers their upper body again and place their hands on the floor. The child standing on top now slowly bends their knees as if to attempt to dismount, however, their arms now reach around the chest of the base, similar to the motion of a hug (Figure 90). With their arms wrapped around their partner's chest, the flyer now bends the back in order to lift both legs up in the air (新潟市南区観光協会, 17:07).

Figure 90: The Chicken Shape Movement. *ibid.*

Movement Number 17: Umawaganryoku kuragaeshi 唐子人形お馬乗り(馬は眼力 鞍返し) (Finale Part 3: Dismount)

For the umawaganryoku kura gaeshi, the flyer now dismounts from their partner's back by going further into the backbend, bringing the feet forward so that they land in front of their partner and return to a standing position (新潟市南区観光協会, 17:33).

Movement 18: Korenite ichidome これにてうちどめ (Bow to the Audience)

The korenite ichidome movement is a bow and "thank you" to the audience. The performers will kneel in one line, facing the audience, with their fingertips of their right hand touching the floor and the left hand on their hips. As a sign of gratitude, they will bow their heads one or two times (Figure 91), then lower the red veil in front of their faces and exit the stage. This movement is executed throughout the show in-between some of the main movements and at the end of the show to thank the audience (新潟市南区観光協会, 18:00).

Figure 91: Bow to the Audience. Copyrights: Mariam Ala-Rashi, 2022.

Excluding of Extreme Flexibility and Stylization

These 18 movements are what was recovered and selected by the Kakubei Jishi Preservation Society, and they have been performed since 1959 till today. Chuo Kondo mentions other movements which include more extreme traits of body flexibility in his book.

One of them is the turtle child (亀の子) which is a chest-stand with the feet brought under the performer's chin (Figure 92). The turtle child movement was not included in previous years nor this year, 2022. It is not listed in the repertoire of selected poses for performances either in Chuo Kondo's book nor in the brochure of the Kakubei Jishi Preservation Society.

Figure 92: Turtle Child (亀の子). Copyrights: With friendly permission from City of Edinburgh Council – Libraries www.capitalcollections.org.uk Title: A child acrobat ("Kakubeijishi") 1881, Photographer: von Stillfried-Ratenicz, Franz.

As a result of criticism during the Edo period against extreme flexibility, movements such as turtle child, were not selected for the training program and were excluded by the preservation society. As speculated earlier, the reason could be that the Kakubei Jishi Preservation Society's aim was to return to the roots of the lion dance and revive the folk performing art before it was stylized during the Edo period. Current writings by Chuo Kondo, the Kakubei Jishi Preservation Society, and the report of the Kakubei Lion Tradition Support Project refer to it as a folk performing art.

Observing the art-form the way it is presented today, it becomes clear that the focus is not on stylization as it is desired in performance art forms such as contortion. The practice of body flexibility in Kakubei Jishi performances serves as a means to depict the movements in a simplistic and authentic way. The display of stylized and extreme flexibility would likely dilute the appeal and authenticity of this folk art and shift the gaze of the onlookers on the entertainment element of the performance whereas the value of the 18 movements in their raw significance would move into the background. Today's Kakubei Jishi is about elements of cultural significance in the region, not sheer spectacle. Although at one point this was popular entertainment across Japan, today's Kakubei Jishi remains closer to home and showcases the region's sense of self. The observer might also notice that facial expressions such as smiling are not part of the performance. According to Wataru Toishi, there is no space for smiling or other facial expressions as it would not be suitable or enhance the performance in any way and that it would be rather exhausting for the children. It could be argued, that, similar to extreme flexibility, facial expressions could curtail the essence of the 18 movements. Thus, in terms of body flexibility, one could argue that the focus is not on a stylized version of an art-form but rather on the preservation of cultural heritage, by adjusting the movements to the natural abilities of the respective performer instead of forcing extreme flexibility onto them, as it was done in later parts of the Edo period.

Kakubei Jishi Costumes

Another important element of the performance and aesthetic value of the lion dance are the costumes and the make-up. As previously explored, the lion mask and the red veil give significant meaning to the movements. The overall pattern (the cut of the clothes) of the Kakubei Jishi costumes has not changed since the Kakubei Jishi tradition first began centuries ago, as it can be observed in remaining historical paintings. However, there have been decorative developments and additions in both costume and makeup over the years. The revival of the art-form by the Kakubei Jishi Preservation Society in 1933 aimed to remain as close to the original costuming as it was recorded in imagery from the Edo period. In the age of modern technology, aesthetic elements such as makeup have evolved – sparked in part by the need for an appearance suitable for both stage and television screen. When looking at historic images, it becomes clear that the main patterns for the shirts, pants, shoes, masks and veils remained unchanged over the years and the following items described in turn are part of the "standard" Kakubei Jishi uniform worn by boys and girls alike (Figure 93, 94, 95, 96, 97). Local researchers have not fully interpreted the significance of every costume element, but typically the Kakubei Jishi wear their attire during performances at temples and shrines. The costumes are symbolic and associated with the Buddhist deity Kishimojin, who embodies both

Figure 93: Kakubei Jishi performers of 2022 gather in front of the Ceremonial Building in Tsukigata after their performance. Copyrights: Mariam Ala-Rashi, 2022.

Figure 94, 95 (top): Kakubei Jishi Costume on Display in the Tsukigata Local Products Reference Room. Copyrights: Mariam Ala-Rashi, 2022.

Figure 96 (center right): Kakubei Jishi Lion Mask with Veil. *ibid.*

Figure 97 (bottom): Geta, worn by the Lion Dancers when walking to and from the stage. *ibid.*

divine and demonic aspects, and is revered for safeguarding children and ensuring a smooth childbirth and upbringing.

Tattsuke Bakama (Japanese Trousers) 裁着袴（たつつけばかま）

A hakama is a pattern used for traditional cotton trousers tattsuke bakama worn in martial arts. The trousers are wide, fitting loosely around the upper thighs and tightly from the knee down. Because they are easy to move around in, they have been used by samurai for travel and training since the middle of the Edo period (Niigata City Newsletter, 2020). The colors worn in Kakubei Jishi performances vary from historic records, due in part to Edo period troupes wearing unique color codes – and in part because money was scarce, and the dancers wore whatever colors were available and affordable. Today, the Kakubei Jishi trousers are striped in grey and black.

Tabi (Socks) 足袋

Tabi are traditional Japanese split-toed socks, usually in black, that are worn during the performance for specific movements. Other movements require the dancers to be barefoot to avoid slipping during the performance.

Geta (Traditional Japanese Plateau Sandal) 下駄

Images from the Edo period show lion dancers wearing Japanese traditional sandals during the performance that have a resemblance to flip-flops or thong beach sandals (see image 97). These are presumably made of straw or wood. The geta sandals are made of wood and have the same design but with two additional wood blocks attached to the bottom of the sole. Traditionally, geta are worn to prevent both kimono and feet from coming in contact with the ground and to keep the garments clean and dry. They are usually worn for entrance but not during a performance.

Uwagi (Traditional Blouse) 上衣 / 上着

The blouse worn by the Kakubei Jishi has a traditional pattern with wide sleeves that are wrapped and held in place with cotton ribbons, allowing an undisturbed movement range during performances. The shirts are striped in red and white, and the ribbons are light blue or turquoise.

Obi (Belt) 帯

Today's costume includes a yellow obi that is made of cotton and that is in part twisted on one end. It is worn around the waist to keep trousers, breastplate, and blouse in place.

Kote (Hand Armor) 籠手

The kote is inspired by historical hand armor that was used in Japan to protect the hands from injury during a fight. The kote was originally made of cow or deer leather, but for today's Kakubei Jishi performances it is made of light blue or turquoise cotton.

Munaate (Breastplate) 胸当（むなあて）

When analyzing images from the Edo period, it becomes evident that the munaate, a breast plate made of fabric, has been a traditional costuming element that came in various colors and designs. The manji symbol, however, was not added until later in the art-form's development. According to Tomomi Homma and Wataru Toishi, the munaate with the manji symbol has three functions:

1. It is in part fashionable and adds to the dramatic effect of the lion costume;

2. The manji symbol in particular, chosen for its positive meaning in Buddhism, is believed to protect the children from harm and guarantees good luck and safe travels;

3. The breastplate's functionality prevents the blouse from shifting and moving around during the performance.

Shishi Gashira (Lion Head) 獅子頭

The lion head at the center of the costume design is the Buddhist symbol for protection (see image 96). It is made of wood, handcrafted by local artisans and painted in red with black and gold details. It is worn on top of the performer's head during the performance. For a secure and comfortable wear, the lion dancer first wraps a white cotton cloth around their head, then places the veil on top of the white cloth. Then, the lion head is placed on top of the veil and secured in place by ribbons under the chin and the back of the head. Male and female lion heads differ, though no one is quite sure why. On top of the lion heads are chicken feathers as decorative addition. In general, the lion head worn by girls has white feathers, the lion head worn by boys has black feathers. The boy's lion head has white feathers too, but only in the back, while the girl's lion head would be decorated entirely with white feathers.

According to Wataru Toishi, it is not clear why chicken feathers were added to the lion heads. The author assumes that chicken feathers were a decorative addition that possibly reflect on the agricultural attributes of the Tsukigata Village. Furthermore, they were cheap and easy to come by (given the minimal wages of the street performers during the time of the Edo period) and added additional visual interest to the performance. However, further research is needed to confirm this hypothesis.

Maku (Veil) 幕（まく）

The red veil attached to the lion's head is used to express the lion's dynamic movement and resembles the lion's mane. Wataru Toishi states that nowadays the veil is actively used to display various landmarks of Japan. The lion dancers create various shapes by holding the veil in a certain manner. Used as a prop, it only covers the artist's face for particular tricks. During the Edo period, however, the veil stayed down and covered the dancer's faces throughout the entire performance, presumably to draw the

Figure 98: Veil covering the Lion Dancer's Face throughout the Performance. Copyrights: Utagawa Kuniyoshi, Public domain, via Wikimedia Commons. Available at: https://commons.wikimedia.org/wiki/File:Oman_ga_Ame_-Tousei_Ryuukou_Mitate.jpg

audience's attention towards the lion mask and away from the dancer's face (Figure 98).

Head Scarf

The head scarf is a simple cotton cloth or towel worn to protect the head while performing certain movements, including somersaults. This is the only time during the performance that the lion head and veil are not worn.

Make-up

To enhance the facial features and expressions while on stage, boys and girls alike wear some basic make-up simply so that their faces can be seen from a distance. The make-up consists of a light foundation, red eyeliner, and red lipstick.

Mythology, Traditions and Religion

Having examined the symbolism and costuming in Kakubei Jishi performances, the next section will explore the mythology that is found threaded through this art-form. The Kakubei Jishi acrobatic dance deeply connects with the area's religious life, social practices, community rituals, their livelihood, and their land. In addition to previous explanations of the 18 movements, this section introduces the two main religions that are practiced in Japan, Shinto and Buddhism. Before their performance, the lion dancers pray at the local shrine for safe travels, and they pray to protect the community from evil (Figure 99). The performance itself does not have a religious meaning or is considered sacred. This section further examines some of the many symbols and deities that are tied to nature, agriculture, climate, and daily life and that inspired, in part, recurring themes in the Kakubei Jishi dance. With the lion as the chosen symbol of the dance, blessings and rituals of purification and the repelling of evil are executed.

Buddhism is a widespread Asian religion or philosophy, founded by Siddartha Gautama in north-eastern India in the 5th century BC. Buddhism has no god and gives a central role to the doctrine of karma:

The 'four noble truths' of Buddhism state that all existence is suffering, that the cause of suffering is desire, that freedom from suffering is nirvana, and that this is attained through the 'eightfold path' of ethical conduct, wisdom, and mental discipline (including meditation). There are two major traditions, Theravada and Mahayana (Oxford, 2022: A).

Buddhism and Shinto are the two major religions in Japan and are not exclusively practiced (i.e., many Japanese practice both Buddhism and Shinto). It is estimated that 66.8% of the Japanese population practice Buddhism and 79.2% practice Shinto:

Figure 99: Lion Dancers enter the Shrine Grounds to Pray for the Performance and the Villagers. Additionally, they are wearing a transparent face shield to prevent the spread of the Covid-19 virus. Copyrights: Mariam Ala-Rashi, 2022.

The indigenous religion of Japan, Shintō, coexists with various sects of Buddhism, Christianity, and some ancient shamanistic practices, as well as a number of "new religions" (shinkō shukyō) that have emerged since the 19th century. Not one of the religions is dominant, and each is affected by the others. Thus, it is typical for one person or family to believe in several Shintō gods and at the same time belong to a Buddhist sect (Britannica, 2022: B).

Shinto (神道) is a Japanese religion, dating from the early 8th century and incorporating the worship of ancestors and nature spirits and a belief in sacred power (kami) in both animate and inanimate things. It was the state religion of Japan until 1945 (Oxford, 2022: B). Late professor of Shinto, Miyaji Naokazu, from the Tokyo Imperial University states in his article What is Shinto? that scholars are divided over how far back the religion can be traced back: "[...] not so recent as 3,000 or 4,000 years ago, as thought by a certain group of scholars. It appears to be very much older, probably traceable back to the Neolithic age" (Naokazu, 1966: 41). According to Miyaji Naokazu, Shinto religion was essentially the worship of nature:

> The custom of nature worship was universal. All things around men which deserved wonder, special trees, rocks, stones and even animals and vegetables were respected as deities, not to mention natural objects such as the sun, moon, and natural phenomena such as wind, rain and lightening. These were made the objects of daily worship and were believed to be closely connected with human life (Naokazu, 1966: 48).

These deities, called kami, are worshipped at public jinja shrines, household, and family shrines. Other ways of worship are rituals such as kagura dances, rites of passage and festivals. Shinto and Buddhism share similar traits and religious practices which is why many Japanese comply to both. In a study about symbols and their value, the Nazan University published the following in their article Shinto Symbols, to distinguish and identify their specific meaning:

> Shinto symbols in general are of two kinds: symbols of the kami and symbols of the faith; but a clear distinction is not always possible. The first group considered in this study includes man, animals, objects of nature, crests, sacred vessels, tablets, charms, etc.; the second includes Shinto structures and equipment, ceremonial practices, sacred music, dances, costumes, oblations and offerings, sacred vessels, and festivals; the third group consists of crests which are called secondary symbols of Shinto (Shinto Symbols, 1966: 4).

Although the lion represented in the Kakubei Jishi dance finds significance in both Shinto and Buddhism, it bears more significance in the Buddhist tradition. Hungarian musicologist János Kárpáti explains the lion's significance in his article Music of the Lion Dance in Japanese Tradition:

> The lion dance is one of the most popular [moments] of kagura ceremonies and folk feasts, the matsuris, which can be performed inside the shrines just as much as on nearby stages or in the area in front of the shrines. The word shishi itself means "lion", people do not recall the real animal but rather the image of the mythical creature. [...] The cult of the lion spread in China quite late along with Buddhism and it must have reached Korea and Japan by the transmission of Buddhist mythology. [...] The condition for the admission, or even the flourishing of

the lion figure was obviously religious tolerance and syncretism that could maintain Buddhism (with its variety of sects) and the Shinto (with its folk roots and branches). [...] Japanese life and culture is almost completely interlaced and enfolded in the various forms of the lion dance - from "exorcists" going from door to door like in Korea through the stirring scenes of folk feasts and the shishi kagura performed in the shrines to the polished no performances. This tradition is so vast and manifold that we can present and analyse only a fraction of it (Kárpáti, 2000: 109,110,112)

Religious symbols, particularly (and most noticeable) the lion mask and the manji symbol are the main elements in the costuming of the Kakubei Jishi. As previously examined, the continuation of the Kakubei Jishi

Figure 100: Hakusan Shrine Tsukigata. Copyrights: Mariam Ala-Rashi, 2022.

troupe is based on community efforts with the villagers taking part in the realization of the performance every step of the way. Most parts of the lion dancer's costumes are handcrafted. The lion dancer's parents together with local artisans craft the various elements of the costumes. As Wataru Toishi stated during his interview: "Every time something is needed for the performance, we find someone from our community to craft the necessary item."

The lion, as a mythical creature embedded in both Buddhism and Shinto, is not only represented in dances, rites of purification and "exorcism" of households. In Shinto, lions are often guardians of local shrines, as it is the case with the Hakusan shrine in Tsukigata (Figure 100) where the annual Tsukigata Festival is held and the Kakubei Jishi perform.

The Tsukigata Festival is held on the grounds of the local Hakusan shrine that worships the goddess Kukurihime no Kami (菊理媛神). The entrance of the shrine is protected by two shrine guardians that are large stone lions called Shishi 獅子 or Kara Shishi 唐獅子, also known as Koma-inu 狛犬 (lion dog) in Japan (see image 46). The lion is not native to Japan, and its significance as a protective figure in religion was imported through Buddhism as the lion was a symbolic protector of the dharma (the teachings of Buddha). Shinto priest Toya Manabu who graduated from the Department of Shintō Studies at Kokugakuin University describes in his article "Komainu": The Shrine's Guardian Figures the Buddhist iconography of the lion:

A pair of stone lion-dogs (shishi) often flank the sandō near the entrance to the shrine or the haiden (worship hall). These komainu, as the statues are known, are guardian figures believed to protect the space around the kami from evil. The ultimate origins of these lionlike figures probably extend back to ancient India or even Egypt, but the more immediate source would appear to be Chinese. Guardian lions and other divine beasts were probably imported from Tang China, along with Buddhism, via the Korean Peninsula, accounting for their alternate name, kōrai-inu, or Korean dogs. (No extant prototypes have been found in Korea.) Most komainu closely resemble the so-called Chinese lion-dog (kara-jishi). Typically, one of the creatures is depicted with its mouth open and the other with its mouth closed. This tradition has no relationship to Shintō per se but derives from Buddhist iconography, where it is used to represent the sacred utterance Aum (with a coming from the open mouth and um from closed lips). Many shrines eschew the lion-dog figure for an animal associated with the kami worshipped there (Toya, 2016).

The lion bears particular significance as the guardian of the local Hakusan Shrine of the Tsukigata Village and as the symbol of the Kakubei Jishi folk-art. Heralded as messengers of good fortune, the lion dancers receive blessings at the local Hakusan shrine from a priest, and then pray as a group to purify themselves and repel evil. This takes place on the day of the Tsukigata Festival, before they enter the stage and undertake their performance.

While the Kakubei Jishi were often viewed as entertainment, they were also often hired by private households during during the Edo period to ward off evil spirits and bless the house and its residents. For New Year's blessings, Shishi (lion) dances in general, such as the Shishimai, are still in demand during New Year celebrations and are held all around Japan. Lion dances, in various forms, are part of festivals, celebrations and community

rituals with their own unique ties to the regions where they are performed (see image 68 of Kakubei Jishi and Shishimai [middle] performing together during the Edo period).

In addition to the annual Tsukigata Festival, the Kakubei Jishi are occasionally invited to perform at the Kishimojin Temple (雑司ヶ谷 鬼子母神堂) in Zoshigaya, Tokyo. This temple was built in 1578 and enshrines Kishimojin (Japanese: 鬼子母神), the goddess of safe birth and child rearing. This deity originated in India, where she is known as Hārītī. Kishimojin, is referred to both as demon and goddess (Figure 101). Professor Reiko Ohnuma of Dartmouth University examines maternal love through Hārītī/Kishimojin's tale in her article Mother-Love and Mother-Grief: South Asian Buddhist Variations on a Theme:

Hārītī is a yaksini (female demon) who lives in the city of Rajagrha. She is married to the male demon Pancika and together they have five hundred sons, the youngest of whom is Priyankara his mother's favorite. Although Hārītī comes from a family of virtuous and benevolent demons, because of "a criminal vow formed in a previous existence," she engages in the habit of stealing and devouring all of Rajagrha's human children. As more of their children die, the people of Rajagrha finally turn to the Buddha for help. He responds by hiding Priyankara under his begging bowl when Hārītī leaves her abode. When Hārītī returns and cannot find her youngest child, she is overwhelmed with grief. Beating her breast, shedding tears of sorrow, her lips and mouth dry and burning her spirit troubled and lost, her heart torn by sufferings," she searches the entire kingdom but cannot find him. [...] She finally ends up at the abode of the god Vaisravana who takes pity on her miserable condition and tells her to go to the Buddha, for only he can restore her son. [...] The Buddha, moreover, once again brings the bereaved mother to her senses by encouraging her to universalize her grief. [...] "Hariti," he says," because you no longer see one of your five hundred sons, you experience such suffering; so what will be the suffering of those whose only child you take and devour?" [...] Once she understands the inherent connection between her own, particular grief and the suffering of other mothers, Hārītī promises to give up her child-snatching ways. Hārītī succeeds in universalizing her grief and is spiritually transformed in the process (Ohnuma, 2007: 109-110)

After her spiritual transformation, Kishimojin became the goddess of safe delivery and child rearing and was venerated as protector deity. In a 2020 interview with Tomomi Homma, advisor of the Town Development Minami-Ward of the Niigata Prefecture, the author discussed the historical meaning of the Kakubei Jishi costumes that are worn during festivals. Although the exact meanings of all costume elements have not been interpreted by local researchers, the Kakubei Jishi mostly wear their costumes when performing in front of temples and shrines as the symbolic meaning of the costumes is tied to the Buddhist deity Kishimojin. Kishimojin, a deity who inhabits godly and demonic roles, protects children and stands for a safe birthing process and happy child rearing. However, she is also quick to punish irresponsible parents and badly-behaved children (Ala-Rashi, 2020). Records and drawings from the temple's history illustrate Kakubei Jishi performances in front of the Kishimojin Temple. The lion dancer's popularity during the Edo period was significant and local vendors crafted "folk toys" made of straw that were sold in front of the temple and served as tokens for little children. This tradition was discontinued with the establishment of the Meiji era, however, and the craft was lost. In 2019, Mr. Yajima, a history researcher, noticed Kakubei Jishi straw toys in old illustrations from the Edo period and started reproducing them with the help of historic records and imagery. They are once again available at the Kishimojin temple grounds, continuing the tradition (Urban Life Metro, 2019).

The Kakubei Jishi, however, the messengers of good fortune who protect others from evil spirits and who dance for the goddess of child protection, Kishimojin, were children themselves, who were also in need of protection. Particularly during the Edo period. According to Tomomi Homma, a monk of the Tsukigata Village recommended the manji symbol (Japanese for swastika) to the traveling children as a token for a safe journey, particularly, because many of them had no relatives (Ala-Rashi, 2020). The swastika is a symbol in the form of a cross with each of its arms bent at a 90° angle halfway along, used as a religious symbol or symbol of good luck in some cultures and religions, including Hinduism, Buddhism and Jainism (Cambridge Dictionary, 2022). The word comes from Sanskrit svasti meaning 'well-being' and is an ancient symbol that can be found in various cultures and comes in various versions. Oxford Reference describes the symbol as it appears in Hinduism and its possible origins:

> A pan-Indian auspicious sign, variously explained, but probably in origin a solar symbol. Some derive it from the Sanskrit su + asti, 'well being'/'good fortune'; some also distinguish between svastikas with right-handed (clockwise-pointing) arms, which are auspicious, since they represent the sun ascending towards the summer solstice, and those with left-handed (anti-clockwise-pointing) arms, which are inauspicious since they represent the sun descending towards the winter solstice.

Manji is the Japanese word for the counterclockwise/left-facing version of the swastika symbol. The manji symbol, as it is used for the lion dance, can be found all over Japan (and many other countries that practice Buddhism) including Buddhist temples, statues, gongs, and other religious items; it is found on maps indicating the location of a Buddhist temple, it is an official kanji character, commonly used in writing, and it is found on Kamon (family) crests and family names.

Todd S. Munson, Ph.D. Professor and Chair of Asian Studies and Director of Japanese Studies at Randolph-Macon College in Ashland, Virginia examines in his article The Past, Present and Future of the Swastika in Japan the origins of the symbol and its significance in Japanese culture:

The swastika is among the oldest written symbols, dating back centuries before the development of written language. Examples have been found in South Asia, Mesopotamia, Africa, and in North, Central, and South America. In Western culture, it dates back at least to the Neolithic Period. The swastika was used by Greeks, Celts, Anglo-Saxons, Romans, and in early Byzantine and Christian art, and known by names now perhaps only familiar to Scrabble enthusiasts: fylfot, gammadion, tetraskelion. Multiple examples exist on heraldry crests, mosaics, cups, pottery, and places of Christian and Jewish worship, to name a few. Whether this diffusion is a product of human migration patterns or independent invention is a question that will likely never be answered. Moreover, in none of these early contexts is the swastika's referent clear; it may represent the sun or other astronomic phenomenon, serve as a fertility symbol, or indicate a connection to some phenomenon now lost to time. Or it may simply be a "good luck charm." The genealogy and meaning of the swastika in East Asia is somewhat clearer, as its usage in South Asian religious culture was well-established before the advent of Buddhism around 500 BCE. In earliest forms of Buddhism, there were no representations of the human form, so the first images were stylized footprints of the Buddha decorated with symbols, often featuring swastikas on each toe. As Buddhist art came to embrace the human form in the first century CE, the symbol was often used as a decorative motif on the chest, palms, and soles, and was considered one of the key identifying marks of the Buddha. [...] As both a decorative motif and written character, the swastika migrated to the Korean peninsula and thence to Japan, where Buddhism found favor with the ruling classes as early at the sixth century

CE. Over the course of a millennium, the manji 卍文 (literally "swastika symbol") established a permanent home in Japanese temple iconography, but also became an auspicious decorative motif on fabric, lacquer boxes, pottery, ceramics, and even family crests (Munson, 2016: 23-24)

As such, the significance of the manji in Japan as a protective symbol goes hand in hand with the lion's connotation as guardian figure in the Kakubei Jishi lion dance. Both symbols signify protection either for the wearer, i.e., the lion dancers wearing the manji symbol for their own protection and safe travels, or the community or household seeks purification and protection from evil spirits by summoning the lion's powers.

The remarkable efforts of the Kakubei Lion Tradition Support Project, the Executive Committee for Kakubei Jishi Traditional Activities, the Kakubei Jishi Preservation Society, artisans and the residents of Tsukigata have allowed this art-form to continue through to this day. However, this newer, gentler version of the Edo period's extreme acrobatic and contortion performance continues to find itself in distress. Due to Japan's significant population decline alongside the Covid 19 pandemic, the Kakubei Jishi art-form is facing extinction again.

The following section explores how the pandemic and the decline in population affect this folk art, in particular, and offers possible solutions for safeguarding the lion dance of Tsukigata.

CHAPTER 4: SAFEGUARDING OF THE KAKUBEI JISHI

Today, only children born in Tsukigata are allowed to volunteer for a role as a lion dancer, and unfortunately, this now makes the art-form vulnerable to two present-day issues: low birthrates and urban migration. Due to its turbulent history the Kakubei Jishi Preservation Society decided to implement restrictions upon reviving the art-form in the 1930s to avoid exploitation of the cultural heritage that belongs to the Tsukigata Village. Back then, no one could have predicted the drastic decline in Japanese population that the country is facing today. Together with urban migration, these are the two biggest threats to the continuation of Kakubei Jishi performances:

> An estimate released by Japan's Ministry of Internal Affairs and Communications shows that the total population as of October 1, 2021, was 125,502,000. This was a drop of 644,000 (0.51%) from the previous year. As the largest decline since 1950, when figures became comparable, it indicates how population decline is accelerating. [...] By age group, the working-age population, consisting of those from 15 to 64, stood at 74,504,000; a decrease of 584,000 from the previous year. This accounted for 59.4% of the total, which is the lowest ever percentage based on statistics since 1950. The senior population aged 65 and over, on the other hand, increased by 188,000 year-on-year to 36,214,000. This cohort now accounts for 28.9% of the total population, which is the highest percentage on record. Within

that range, people aged 75 years or older increased by 72,000 to 18,674,000, meaning that they account for more than half of the population of those over 65 (Nippon, 2022: A).

The population of Japan experienced a decline of 0.51% from the previous year, with the working-age population accounting for the lowest ever percentage since 1950, while the senior population aged 65 and over increased to the highest percentage on record, with people aged 75 years or older making up more than half of this population. Together with urban migration, the effect is exacerbated, threatening the continuation of Kakubei Jishi performances. Particularly smaller villages far from the bigger cities are affected by the decline as more and more young families leave the rural areas to move to the major cities for education and career prospects

To gain a comprehensive understanding of the phenomenon of urban migration in Japan, it is imperative to have a clear understanding of the country's geography which provides a deeper insight into the complex interplay of factors that shape the trends of urban migration within the country. Japan is located off the east coast of the Asian continent, between the Pacific Ocean and the Sea of Japan, and is divided into 47 prefectures. 43 of these prefectures are plain prefectures (large areas of flat land with only few trees), including Niigata. The rest are urban prefectures, in which Osaka and Kyoto are situated. Lastly, the area of the municipality that is host to the largest city on earth and Japan's capital: Tokyo. Home to 37 million people, Tokyo offers world-leading education and highly paid job opportunities. Attractive to many young families who aim to have their children accepted to one of Tokyo's major universities, many migrate from rural prefectures to the big city. Graduating from a respected university also offers the possibility to be hired by a prestigious company. This trend has led to a shrinking population in towns and villages in rural areas. In addition, the decline in Japan's population has caused an imbalance between the aging society and young adults and children. In 2022, Japan childbirths were on path to a record low, as leading Japanese news agency NHK World-Japan reported:

> Births in Japan are on a record-low pace. The health ministry says fewer than 600,000 babies were born from January through September this year. At this rate, fewer than 800,000 will be born in Japan in a calendar year for the first time since record-keeping began in 1899. The ministry says in its preliminary report there were 599,636 babies born in the first nine months of the year. That includes births to foreign nationals. That's 30,933 fewer births than during the same period last year, a drop of 4.9 percent. In all, there were 811,622 babies born in 2021. Earlier this month, the Japan Research Institute projected that about 770,000 babies would be born in 2022 (NHK World-Japan, 2022).

In comparison to other countries, Japan's population is projected to fall from a peak of 128 million in 2017 to less than 53 million by the end of the century. Italy is expected to see an equally dramatic population crash from 61 million to 28 million over the same timeframe. They are two of 23 countries - which also include Spain, Portugal, Thailand, and South Korea - expected to see their population more than halve (BBC, 2020). With falling birthrates and migration from rural areas to the bigger cities in Japan, once thriving villages and towns are turning into ghost towns. In her 2019 article What will Japan do with all of its empty Ghost Homes?, Mari Shibata reports for BBC on the trend that led to the abandoning of entire towns:

Population decline is a major issue for many countries. It's of particular concern for Japan, which after experiencing a major boom throughout the 20th Century is now seeing steep population contraction. In 2018 the lowest number of babies were born since the country began keeping records, while deaths steadily outpaced births. And, as populations decline in countries across the globe, the demand for housing will also drop as the number of households decreases. This is already happening in Japan, where the country's dramatically ageing population is fuelling a massive inventory of vacant homes. Known as 'akiya', these are homes left abandoned without heirs or new tenants. A record high of 13.6% properties across Japan were registered as akiya in 2018, and the problem is predicted to get worse; not only do relatives want to avoid inheriting homes due to Japan's second-home tax, but there are fewer citizens overall to occupy them. Akiya dot the landscape all over Japan, listed in 'akiya banks' from Tokyo prefecture to rural Okayama prefecture to mountainous Kumamoto prefecture in Kyushu, at the southern end of the Japanese archipelago. Akiya are particularly concentrated in rural areas as younger generations abandon their roots in favour of settling in cities where there are more opportunities – a phenomenon that's causing dramatic global population shift around the world (Shibata, 2019).

Japan's ministers confirmed these downward trends in 2016: "These numbers are like losing an entire prefecture," states Shigeru Ishiba, a cabinet minister in charge of efforts to revitalize Japan's especially depopulated rural areas, at a news conference" (Soble, 2016). To make matters worse, the age gap between senior citizens and the young population is increasing.

Claire Parker for the Washington Post states in her 2022 article Japan records its largest natural population decline as births fall:

> The data is bad news for those in Japan who worry about the societal effects of the country's aging and shrinking population. Nearly 30 percent of the population is over 65 years old. The decline in the working-age population has contributed to a labor shortage, which the coronavirus pandemic exacerbated, and raised concerns about a worse labor crunch to come. Experts attribute falling birthrates to a constellation of factors. "It's not about sexlessness," said Jennifer Robertson, professor emerita of anthropology and art history at the University of Michigan. "It's all of the infrastructure that goes into the healthy maintenance of a multigenerational household" (Parker, 2022).

Multiple factors were at play before the Covid-19 pandemic began, and the pandemic has only accelerated the decline. Putting a strain on the already-low birthrate, wedding ceremonies were canceled or delayed, husbands were not able to be present at the hospital during their child's birth, and grandparents couldn't assist in the care of newborns – all of which understandably dissuaded people from procreating. Furthermore, Japan has the oldest population in the world. News agency Nippon reports in its 2022 article Japan Continues to Gray: Baby Boomers Reach 75 about the threats of a growing age gap with the number of seniors aged 65 years and older reaching a record total of 36.27 million:

> Japan has by far the highest senior population ratio in the world, with 29.1% of its people over 65 years old. [...] There were 28.72 million seniors aged 70 years and over, up 390,000 (0.4 points), and 19.37 million aged 75 years and over, up 720,000 (0.6

points). As of the year 2022 the Japanese baby boomers (born between 1947 and 1949), a substantial cohort, began reaching the age of 75. With this milestone, the percentage of the total population that is aged 75 and over has exceeded 15% for the first time. Those aged 80 and over increased by 410,000 (0.4 points) to 12.35 million. According to United Nations data, Japan has the highest senior population ratio (the percentage of the population aged 65 and over) by far, at 29.1%, leading second-place Italy by 5 points (24.1%) (Nippon, 2022: B).

In other words, Japan is almost at a point where only 50% of the population is able to work. This might ultimately lead to a decline in economic strength, smaller markets, lower tax revenues and a lower GDP. Moreover, the effects of these issues are not only palpable in the larger picture of a declining economy. They have leaked into the microcosms of the Japanese society and its customs and traditions -- even affecting performing arts like the Tsukigata lion dance, Kakubei Jishi.

For smaller villages, the population decline is taking a particular toll. The estimated population of the Tsukigata Village in 2003 was 3,769. As of August 2022, the resident register of the Niigata prefecture announced that the village's population has plummeted to only 916 residents (Niigata City, 2022: D). Even the local train station had to be closed in 1999 due to low passenger numbers and the increase of motorization (Figure 102). Not only did the lion dance troupe suffer from a dwindling city population, making it more difficult to field a team of interested children, but pandemic restrictions meant that the festival simply wasn't able to be held for two consecutive years. This ultimately meant no training, no continuation and support of the traditional art-form and no possibility to attract any tourism to the remote region.

Figure 102: Closed Down Tsukigata Train Station with Kakubei Jishi Monument.
Copyrights: Masaki Ikarashi, Mayor of Minami Ward, 2022.

As of June 2022, only seven children are left to continue the tradition of Kakubei Jishi performances. As more and more young families move away from the village and into bigger cities, the future of the Kakubei Jishi looks grim. It is currently expected that only four performers will continue their training for the 2023 performance: the bare minimum needed for a performance.

In a conversation with Mayor Masaki Ikarashi, he expressed fears that the 2023 performance will be the last -- which ultimately would be the end of the Tsukigata Festival, as the decline in population is particularly palpable in Tsukigata. Many of the children will stop performing in order to focus on higher education. It is likely that they will also move to bigger cities to pursue their education and careers and never return, which only exacerbates the spiraling population decline in Tsukigata. Furthermore, it takes around three years to prepare a new dancer for performance – assuming that any volunteer to take on the tradition. Currently only children of the Tsukigata village are allowed to become lion dancers.

This provides a complicated problem without a simple solution. For possible solutions, one might have to look abroad to see how other countries are tackling the problem. Since Japan is followed closely in population decline rankings by Italy, it makes sense to start there for inspiration. The Italian government, confronted with the same dilemma, has decided on drastic measures to revive its rural areas: By selling abandoned homes for only $1. The Los Angeles Times describes the project that was initiated by Italian authorities in the article Buck the system: In Italy, old towns eager for new blood sell homes for about $1:

> More and more Italian towns and villages eager to attract new residents are putting up homes for sale for as little as one euro (it's illegal to give away property for free), a trend that was once confined to the impoverished and depopulated mountain towns in the south but that has spread since the start of the COVID-19 pandemic to wealthier northern regions like Liguria and Lombardy. Officials have latched onto the idea as a way to breathe new life into moribund rural areas. With the pandemic showing many workers that they can do their jobs remotely — and that there's life outside the urban jungle — the hope is that a good portion of prospective buyers will be younger people willing to relocate with their energy, their drive and their paychecks.[...] Prime Minister Mario Draghi's National Recovery and Resilience Plan has earmarked $2.3 billion for revitalizing Italy's historic small-town centers, rural

villages, smaller cultural heritage sites, and historic parks and gardens (Brancolini, 2021).

The project was well received, and many families from all over the world have relocated to Italy to build a new life overseas. In the past, Japan was hesitant when it came to changing immigration policies and held on to outdated immigration protocols. However, government officials can no longer ignore the problem and have announced that immigration policies will be reviewed to offer more opportunities for a foreign work force.

In the meantime, the question remains: what can Tsukigata do to prevent its intangible cultural heritage from disappearing? The author offers the following proposals as potential solutions: Lacking a local train station and with only a slow bus service available, one solution could be to initiate a shuttlebus service during the days of the Tsukigata Festival and the Kite Battle event and to make traveling to the village easier and more attractive. Other solutions could involve branching out to neighboring villages and towns, recruiting performers from outside the borders of the Tsukigata Village. This could, in turn, compel more visitors from surrounding areas to visit the village during the festival season and ultimately support the local economy and smaller businesses. Furthermore, the Kakubei Jishi could perform in other cities a few times a year to promote the art-form, assuming it could be done without disrupting the children's wellbeing, education, or family life. Another solution could be to introduce the concept of agritourism which has been successfully implemented in rural areas in South Korea, which faces similar issues as Japan. Agritourism offers visitors the opportunity to experience rural life and participate in various activities such as farming and planting crops, milking cows and taking care of farm animals. This may aid in bolstering the local economy and safeguarding the cultural legacy of the village, specifically with regards to the Kakubei Jishi.

So far, it seems that the Kakubei Jishi Preservation Society has done the remarkable – reviving what was once damaging and turning the art-form into a tradition that the villagers are proud of and that can be passed on to future generations.

All in all, the future of this folk performing art is uncertain. With a dwindling and aging population, smaller villages are fighting for survival. The effects of the larger issue trickle down to the microcosm of performing arts and endanger the intangible cultural heritage not only of Tsukigata but of many other villages in Japan. Current efforts by the government are not sufficient and the economy has taken a blow over the past years. To make matters worse, the global pandemic has accelerated the negative effects and residents of remote areas are stuck in a strenuous situation. With the migration of young families to Japan's bigger cities, villages like Tsukigata have to be innovative to maintain their cultural heritage.

CONCLUSION

In conclusion, Kakubei Jishi is a traditional performing art that originated in Tsukigata Village, Niigata Prefecture, during the Edo period. This acrobatic dance is performed by children aged 5 to 15, who display their skills in tumbling, handstands, and body flexibility poses that are commonly recognized as contortion. The term Kakubei Jishi refers to both the art form and the performers. The use of wooden lion masks and traditional Japanese costumes with wide-sleeved shirts and pants is characteristic of the performance. The Kakubei Jishi are accompanied by live music, played by a group of three musicians, consisting of two drummers and a flute player. The performers are referred to as artists and actors by the locals, who perceive this form of entertainment as an acrobatic dance, rather than a circus act. Notably, body flexibility is a crucial element of the Kakubei Jishi performance, which holds significance in the history and development of acrobatics, contortion, and body flexibility in East Asia, particularly Japan. The performances are held twice a year during the Tsukigata Festival, in June and September, either at the Tsukigata Rural Environment Improvement Center or on the grounds of the Hakusan Shrine. The festival was canceled in 2020 and 2021 due to the COVID-19 pandemic. However, with the introduction of new vaccines and the implementation of appropriate safety measures, such as social distancing and PCR testing, the festival was able to be held again in 2022 after a two-year hiatus.

The consensus among scholars is that the lion dance was likely created during the mid-Edo period (1603-1867). Evidence supporting this assertion can be found in the writings of the Kakubei Jishi Preservation Society, which are featured in the chapter entitled "Origin of Kakubei Lion" in the Niigata City Designated Intangible Folk Cultural Property brochure. According to these texts, the earliest known mention of the Kakubei Jishi dates back to approximately 1756, when it was first referenced in a book called Echigo Nayose by Maruyama Genjun (1682-1758). Another source, Echigo Yashi, was published in 1815 and provides further support for the development of the lion dance during this period.

Two theories regarding the origin of the Kakubei Jishi have been examined. According to the first theory, the art-form was invented by Kakubei's sons to trick the audience into doing handstands and expose their feet in order to identify their father's murderer. The second theory suggests that a farmer from Tsukigata invented the art-form during the Edo period to generate additional income through street performances, given the annual floods and harsh winters that destroyed the harvest. Despite the geographical situation pointing towards the latter theory, interviews with the local community suggest that a large group of residents of Tsukigata and Mito believe in the first theory. However, there is no concrete evidence to support this theory. It is possible to argue that the final form of Kakubei Jishi, as we know it today, was rooted in Edo period folk dance and folk acrobatics, incorporating elements of body flexibility. However, born out of necessity and opportunity, this folk performing art quickly developed into a popular spectacle and street performance that would entertain the masses.

With Edo becoming the capital of Japan, the city attracted many artists seeking to earn a living. Among these artists, street performers were highly sought after, and the Kakubei Jishi of Tsukigata quickly gained popularity. The dance form that displayed an array of spiritual, cultural and mythical elements became so beloved that it led to a significant increase in the number of Kakubei Jishi troupes in a short period of time. The average troupe would consist of four lion dancers and three musicians as oyakata of the group. Children began training at the age of three and started performing at the age of seven, becoming professionals by the age of eight. These troupes offered "exorcism" services to households for a nominal fee, which were believed to purify homes and drive away bad spirits, evil, famine, and disease. As the demand for these performances grew, so did the need for further development of techniques and tricks used by performers. However, the lives of the child performers who joined these troupes were far from easy. During the Edo period, education was not compulsory, and children often helped their parents with farm work. Many questions arise regarding the lives of these child performers, including where they came from, how they were provided with education, food, shelter, and safety, and what their working hours and "payment" looked like. These children were often exploited, beaten, kidnapped, and abused, and received no school education. Based on historical records, it is apparent that there was a significant degree of competition among the numerous Kakubei Jishi troupes that traversed the streets.

Photographic and other material evidence from performances of Kakubei Jishi during the Edo period illustrates the exceptional level of flexibility exhibited by child performers, which is comparable to that of contemporary contortionists. Accounts from inhabitants of Tsukigata village indicate that children were actively sought after as lion dancers, owing to their inherent flexibility. To sustain their popularity and remain competitive with other street performers, the Kakubei Jishi continually innovated their acrobatic-dance routines, incorporating new tricks and stylized movements into their repertoire.

The Meiji Restoration in 1868 marked a significant shift in Japan's political landscape, marking the end of the military rule of the Tokugawa shogunate and ushering in a period of modernization and Westernization. This era of change had a profound impact on various aspects of Japanese society, including education and the treatment of minors. In particular, the government introduced compulsory education between 1900 and 1911, as well as implementing measures to protect children from exploitation, which contributed to the decline of Kakubei Jishi street performances. The perception of the public towards these performances also shifted during this period, as people became more aware of the dire circumstances of the child performers. Many of these children were orphans and had been given away or sold to troupe elders or were even kidnapped and trafficked. The children were denied an education and were forced to work for their basic needs, which often included accommodation and daily bread. The exploitation of child performers was so severe that troupe leaders instructed the burning of documentation and records upon their death to destroy evidence of their mistreatment. The modernization of Japan during the Meiji period (1868-1912) led to a gradual change in the collective perception of the child as someone who needed protection and care, which became more prevalent in the following years. As a result, the decline of Kakubei Jishi street performances was welcomed, as the exploitation of child performers had been exposed and measures were put in place to protect minors.

During the Meiji period, Japan underwent a major transformation from a feudal society to a modern, industrialized nation. As part of this transformation, new labor laws were implemented to protect employees from exploitation and prohibit child labor. In addition, mass media began to criticize society for tolerating child abuse, including the exploitation of child performers in street shows like the Kakubei Jishi. By the end of the

Meiji period, most Kakubei Jishi troupes had disappeared due to changing societal values and the implementation of mandatory education. During World War I, newspaper coverage of street performers also ceased, leading to a gap in literature about the Tsukigata lion dance. In 1947, the Child Welfare Act was finalized to further regulate and prohibit child exploitation in the entertainment industry. However, leaders of the Tsukigata Village recognized the cultural significance of the Kakubei Jishi and established a research society in 1936 to reclaim the tradition as a cultural heritage. Through years of research and community efforts, the lion dance was eventually recognized as an "Intangible Folk Cultural Property" of Niigata City. The revival of the Kakubei Jishi became a community project in which local families, musicians, and craftsmen took pride. Children were allowed to join the troupe with parental permission, and new training structures were established to ensure a positive experience for child performers.

The Executive Committee for Kakubei Jishi Traditional Activities, together with the Kakubei Jishi Preservation Society, have collected and restored historical information on training techniques, acrobatic tricks, poses, costume designs, and music that were performed by the Kakubei Jishi in the past. These recovered acrobatic tricks are now performed by schoolchildren in the 20th and 21st centuries. Children can now volunteer to become Kakubei Jishi performers with their parent' permission, and showcase their skills and flexibility at the annual Tsukigata Festival held in June. The children practice once a week on Saturdays and spend a full day preparing for performances. Many of their parents, who were former Kakubei Jishi performers themselves, assist with performance preparations, including applying make-up and sewing costumes. The students wear costumes which not only serve as decorative items but also provide significance and context to the various movements and tricks.

Today, there are no specific criteria or physical requirements, such as extraordinary flexibility, for children who wish to participate in the Kakubei Jishi lion dance. Both girls and boys are equally encouraged to perform, and there are no gender-specific movements or tricks. The lion dance repertoire comprises acrobatic tricks, including tumbling, handstands, and body flexibility, which sometimes resemble contortion poses. Although children during the Edo period were forced into extreme flexibility poses, such practices are no longer common. Modern Kakubei Jishi training does not include any specific flexibility training. Instead, children showcase their natural abilities and flexibility during performances. If a child is unable to perform a particular pose or trick, it is modified to suit the child's natural level of flexibility. For example, if a child cannot perform a backbend, they can execute a front bend instead. There is no expectation for children to practice flexibility at home.

The Kakubei Jishi Preservation Society aimed to revive the folk performing art of lion dance and return it to its roots before its stylization during the Edo period. There were various factors that contributed to the society's objection, including the dark history of the lion dance during the peak of the Edo period, criticism from society during the Meiji Restoration, and the Tsukigata Village's desire to distance itself from the criminal perception associated with Kakubei Jishi leaders. Records from the Edo period indicate that the lion dance underwent a transformation and became stylized to attract a broader audience and compete with other street performers. Extreme body flexibility, such as chest-stands, were commonly performed by Kakubei Jishi during the Edo period, but they are not present in today's performances.

The Kakubei Jishi lion dance is not the only performance art that has undergone changes over time. Chinese and Mongolian contortion, which we know from circus performances today, evolved from folk acrobatics and dances and were adapted by the entertainment industry into a circus discipline for popular, secular consumption. Similarly, Kakubei Jishi, a form of folk acrobatics and street performance, underwent significant stylization during the Edo period to compete in a crowded entertainment market. However, the establishment of the Kakubei Jishi Preservation Society signaled a return to the perceived authentic form of the lion dance. This effort aimed to distance the art-form from its dark past, promote healthy training practices for child performers, revive the folk performing art, and promote tourism in the region by showcasing a traditional art-form as accurately as possible. Unfortunately, due to the scarcity of historic records, it is difficult to determine the accuracy of this recreation. Future research that compares archival imagery from the Edo period with contemporary lion dance performances could shed light on this matter, but it is beyond the scope of this study.

The incorporation of national customs, such as the shape of the golden shachihoko of the Nagoya Castle and the Oi River crossing, along with elements from religious practices found in Buddhism and Shintoism, were key factors in the appeal of Kakubei Jishi. This connection between folk acrobatics, traditions, and spiritual practices illuminates the aesthetic evolution of the performance from the Edo period to the present day. The Kakubei Jishi is centered around symbolic movements, which aim to convey specific meanings through the use of folk acrobatics and body flexibility, rather than simply presenting extreme body flexibility for spectacle. Although many more movements and acrobatic tricks were reportedly developed and performed during this time, these have not been preserved. The exact process of movement development during the Edo period is unclear, but it is speculated that performers drew inspiration from the landmarks, natural phenomena, and sights they encountered while on tour. Today, there are 18 distinct dance moves listed in Chuzo Kondo's book "Local Performing Arts-Kakubei Lion," which have been adapted by the preservation society for the continuation of the art form.

Each movement in the Kakubei Jishi dance represents natural phenomena, spiritual and mythical connotations, or depictions of agricultural elements. Although the dance incorporates symbols and deities tied to nature, agriculture, climate, and daily life, it is not considered a religious or sacred performance. Even as a secular performance, the lion dancers pray for safe travels and to protect the community from evil at the local shrine prior to performing. The chosen symbol for the dance, the lion, is used for blessings, purification rituals, and repelling evil. Lions are considered mythical creatures embedded in both Buddhism and Shinto and are often represented in dances, purification rites, and exorcism of households. In addition, lions are often guardians of local shrines, such as the Hakusan shrine in Tsukigata where the annual Tsukigata Festival is held and where the Kakubei Jishi perform. Historically, the Kakubei Jishi were hired to perform at private households during the Edo period to ward off evil spirits and bless the house and its owners. Today, Shishi (lion) dances in general, such as the Shishimai, are still in demand during New Year celebrations and are held throughout Japan. Lion dances in various forms are also part of festivals, celebrations, and community rituals with unique ties to the regions where they are performed.

The Kakubei Lion Tradition Support Project, the Executive Committee for Kakubei Jishi Traditional Activities, the Kakubei Jishi Preservation Society, local artisans, and residents of Tsukigata have made significant efforts to preserve the Kakubei Jishi art-form. However, this contemporary version of the Edo period's highly acrobatic performances is facing new challenges. With Japan's declining population and the COVID-19 pandemic, the future of the art-form is in peril once again. In the 1930s, the Kakubei Jishi Preservation Society imposed restrictions on reviving the art-form to prevent the exploitation of children and of the cultural heritage of Tsukigata Village. Only children born in Tsukigata were allowed to volunteer as lion dancers. However, the current decline in the Japanese population and urban migration have emerged as the two biggest threats to the survival of Kakubei Jishi performances. In particular, smaller villages located far from larger cities are struggling as young families leave rural areas to pursue education and career opportunities in urban centers.

Tokyo, with a population of 37 million, is a hub of world-class education and lucrative job opportunities. This draws many young families seeking to secure spots for their children at top universities in Tokyo, resulting in a migration from rural areas to the city. Obtaining a degree from a prestigious university also opens up opportunities to work for renowned companies. This phenomenon has contributed to a population decline in rural towns and villages, exacerbating the already imbalanced demographics between the aging population and younger generations in Japan. Prior to the onset of the Covid-19 pandemic, multiple factors had contributed to this trend, but the pandemic has only accelerated the problem. These issues have also impacted Japanese communities and their customs and traditions, including performing arts such as the Tsukigata's lion dance, Kakubei Jishi. Smaller villages such as Tsukigata have been particularly affected, with the village's population plummeting to only 916 residents as of August 2022.

As of June 2022, the number of children who are continuing the Kakubei Jishi performances has dwindled to only seven. The outflow of young families from the village to bigger cities has further threatened the future of the Kakubei Jishi tradition, with only four performers expected to continue their training for the 2023 performance, the minimum requirement for a performance. Mayor Masaki Ikarashi has expressed his concerns that the 2023 performance may be the last, which would bring an end to the Tsukigata Festival, as the population decline in Tsukigata has been particularly pronounced. In addition, many children are likely to give up performing in order to focus on higher education, and are expected to move to bigger cities to pursue their education and careers, thus exacerbating the population decline in Tsukigata. The complex issue is further compounded by the fact that it takes around three years to train a new dancer for the performance, assuming that there are volunteers to take on the tradition. Currently, only children of the village are allowed to become lion dancers. The village's efforts to address the issue have not kept up with the fast-declining numbers of village residents. Tsukigata Village's population drastically declined from an estimated 3,769 residents in 2003 to only 916 residents as of August 2022.

In order to prevent the intangible cultural heritage of Tsukigata from disappearing, several strategies were put forward by the author. One potential solution involves improving transportation options to the village during the Tsukigata Festival by implementing a shuttle bus service or making travel to the area more attractive. Another possible approach involves extending recruitment efforts to include performers from neighboring villages and towns, which may increase interest in the festival and support the local economy. Additionally, promoting the Kakubei Jishi through performances in other cities a few times a year could raise awareness of the art form, provided that it does not have a negative impact on the wellbeing, education, or family life of the children involved. Agritourism may present another viable solution as it supports the local economy and helps preserving the cultural heritage of the village.

The Kakubei Jishi Preservation Society has achieved a remarkable feat by transforming a once harmful art-form into a cherished tradition that can be passed down to future generations. However, the future of this folk performing art remains uncertain as rural villages, including Tsukigata, struggle to survive due to declining and aging populations. This issue extends beyond Tsukigata and endangers the intangible cultural heritage of many other villages in Japan, with current government efforts deemed insufficient and the economy suffering. Moreover, the global pandemic has worsened the situation, particularly for residents of remote areas. To preserve their cultural heritage, villages such as Tsukigata must be innovative in the face of the migration of young families to larger cities.

The story of the Kakubei Jishi holds a poetic quality, as it began as a means to save a struggling village and now ends as a way to revive the village's economic woes by promoting tourism. The fierce lion dance is believed to ward off malevolent spirits, making it a symbol of protection and hope for the villagers. It remains to be seen whether the lion will continue to guard the village and preserve its prosperity, but for now, one can only wait in hopeful anticipation.

十足番

丸光兵衛獅子

Figure 103: Kakubei Jishi. Copyrights: 江戸職人歌合 （石原正明著）, Public domain, via Wikimedia Commons. Available at: https://commons.wikimedia.org/wiki/File:Kakubei.jpg

BIBLIOGRAPHY

2012-2014 Report Kakubei Lion Tradition Support Project (2014). Niigata: Executive Committee for Kakubei Jishi Traditional Activities.

Ala-Rashi, M. 2020. Mapping Contortion ins Japan. Part Three: Cultural Heritage. [online] Available at:
https://circustalk.com/news/mapping-contortion-in-japan-part-three-cultural-heritage-the-lion-dance [Accessed: 30. November 2022]

Azuma, M. (1951). LABOR LEGISLATION IN JAPAN. The Annals of the Hitotsubashi Academy, 1(2), 181–195. http://www.jstor.org/stable/43750609

BBC, 2020. Fertility rate: "Jaw-dropping" global crash in children being born. [online] Available at: https://www.bbc.com/news/health-53409521 [Accessed: 19.03.2023]

Brancolini, J. 2021. Buck the system: In Italy, old towns eager for new blood sell homes for about $1. [online] Available at: https://www.latimes.com/world-nation/story/2021-10-27/italy-super-cheap-homes-one-euro [Accessed: 02, December 2022]

Britannica, T. Editors of Encyclopaedia. 2022. (A). Meiji Restoration. [online] Available at: https://www.britannica.com/event/Meiji-Restoration [Accessed: 13. October 2022]

Britannica, T. Editors of Encyclopaedia. 2022. (B). Religion of Japan. [online] Available at: https://www.britannica.com/place/Japan/Resources-and-power [Accessed: 29. November 2022]

Cambridge Dictionary, 2022. Swastika. [online] Available at: https://dictionary.cambridge.org/dictionary/english/swastika [Accessed: 29. November 2022]

Circus Talk, 2020. Mapping Contortion in Japan– Part Three: Cultural Heritage & The Lion Dance [online] Available at: https://circustalk.com/news/mapping-contortion-in-japan-part-three-cultural-heritage-the-lion-dance [Accessed: 10. June 2022]

Enjoy Niigata, 2022. Shirone Giant Kite Battle. [online] Available at: https://enjoyniigata.com/en/event/1885?fbclid=IwAR2phkn-rwroTf9vhLOtZqPZhTmVW03G4F9LkV5ZrmMTns5mxM-v54HXiGaYA [Accessed: 10. June 2022]

Groemer, G. (2001). The Creation of the Edo Outcaste Order. Journal of Japanese Studies, 27(2), 263–293. https://doi.org/10.2307/3591967

Groemer, G. 2016. Street Performers and Society in Urban Japan, 1600-1900. The Beggar's Gift. Abingdon: Routledge (Taylor & Francis). Kindle Edition.

Invitation to Nohgaku. 2018. A Thriving and Classical Theatre Form. [online] Available at: https://www2.ntj.jac.go.jp/unesco/noh/en/history/history3.html [Accessed November 12, 2022]

Japanese Law Translation. 2007. Child Welfare Act. [online] Available at: https://www.japaneselawtranslation.go.jp/en/laws/view/11/en [Accessed October 10, 2022]

Kárpáti, J. (2000). Music of the Lion Dance in Japanese Tradition. Studia Musicologica Academiae Scientiarum Hungaricae, 41(1/3), 107–117. http://www.jstor.org/stable/902570

Kondo, C. 1997. Local Performing Arts-Kakubei Lion. Niigata City: Kyoritsu Printing Co., Ltd.

Merriam-Webster.com Dictionary, s.v. handstand. [online] Available at: https://www.merriam-webster.com/dictionary/handstand. [Accessed October 5, 2022]

Motomori, E. 2019. The Disappearance of the Kakubei-Jishi Child Performers: Rethinking the Construction of Modern Childhood. [online] Available at: https://meigaku.repo.nii. ac.jp/?action=pages_view_main&active_action=repository_ view_main_item_detail&item_id=2935&item_no=1&page_ id=13&block_id=21 [Accessed: 13. October 2022]

Munson, T. (2016). The Past, Present and Future of the Swastika in Japan, Traditional and Contemporary Asia: Numbers, Symbols, and Colors, Volume 21:3, 23-26.

Naokazu, M. (1966). What Is Shinto? Contemporary Religions in Japan, 7(1), 40–50. http://www.jstor.org/stable/30232984

NHK World-Japan, 2022. Number of Births in Japan on Pace for Record Low. [online] Available at: https://www3.nhk.or.jp/nhkworld/en/news/20221125_39/ [Accessed: 02, December 2022]

Niigata City, 2022. (A) Outline of Minami-ku. [online] Available at: https://www.city.niigata.lg.jp/minami/kohoshi/map.files/p1-2.pdf [Accessed: 10. June 2022]

Niigata City, 2022. (B) Niigata City 2022 Statistical Data. [online] Available at: http://www.city.niigata.lg.jp/multilingual/e_index/e_data.files/all_graph_eng22.pdf [Accessed: 10. June 2022]

Niigata City, 2022. (C) Important Cultural Property Former Sasagawa Residence (Sasagawa House) [online] Available at: https://www.city.niigata.lg.jp/minami/shisetsu/yoka/bunka/kyusasagawake.html [Accessed: 10. June 2022]

Niigata City, 2022. (D) Basic Resident Register population by town name. [online] Available at: https://www.city.niigata.lg.jp/shisei/gaiyo/profile/00_01jinkou/kihon_kujinko/jyuukimachir04.html [Accessed: 28. November 2022]

Niigata City Designated Intangible Folk Cultural Property. (n.d.). History of Kakubei Jishi. [Brochure]. Kakubei Jishi Preservation Society.

Niigata City Newsletter, 2020. Minami Ward Office Newsletter No. 321. [online] Available at: https://www.city.niigata.lg.jp/minami/kohoshi/minamikaze/r02/minami_0816/minami_321_1.html [Accessed: 23, November 2022]

Nippon, 2022: A. Shrinking Japan: Even Tokyo sees first Population Decline in 26 Years. [online] Available at: https://www.nippon.com/en/japan-data/h01310/ % [Accessed: 19.03.2023]

Nippon, 2022: B. Japan Continues to Gray: Baby Boomers Reach 75. [online] Available at:
https://www.nippon.com/en/japan-data/h01446/#:~:text=Japan%20has%20by%20far%20the,820%2C000%20over%20the%20previous%20year. [Accessed: 02, December 2022]

Norma, C. (2008). A Past re-imagined for the Geisha: Saviour of the 1950's Japanese sex industry. Traffic, 10, 37-56.

Nogawa, M. 2014. Reconstruction of the History of the Kakubei Jishi. In: 2012-2014 Report Kakubei Lion Tradition Support Project. Niigata: Executive Committee for Kakubei Jishi Traditional Activities. Pages 4-6.

Ohnuma, R. (2007). Mother-Love and Mother-Grief: South Asian Buddhist Variations on a Theme. Journal of Feminist Studies in Religion, 23(1), 95–116. http://www.jstor.org/stable/20487889

Oxford English Dictionary, 2022. (A) Buddhism. [online] Available at: https://www.oxfordlearnersdictionaries.com/definition/english/buddhism [Accessed: 28. November 2022]

Oxford English Dictionary, 2022. (B) Shinto. [online] Available at: https://www.oxfordlearnersdictionaries.com/definition/english/shinto?q=shinto [Accessed: 28. November 2022]

Parker, C. 2022. Japan records its largest natural population decline as births fall. [online] Available at: https://www.washingtonpost.com/world/2022/06/03/japan-low-births-population-decline-2021/ [Accessed: 02. December 2022]

Plaza Homes, 2022. School Grade and Age Structures in Japan. [online] Available at: https://www.realestate-tokyo.com/living-in-tokyo/education/school-grades-ages/ [Accessed: 25. October 2022]

Romano & Goswami, 2022. Meiji Development: Modernization of Education-Educational Reform. [online] Available at: https://sites.rutgers.edu/rutgers-meets-japan/our-exhibition/meiji-development-modernization-of-education/ [Accessed: 13. October 2022]

Shibata, M. 2019. What will Japan do with all of its empty 'ghost' homes? [online] Available at: https://www.bbc.com/worklife/article/20191023-what-will-japan-do-with-all-of-its-empty-ghost-homes [Accessed: 02. December 2022]

Shinto Symbols. (1966). Contemporary Religions in Japan, 7(1), 3–39. http://www.jstor.org/stable/30232983

Soble, J. 2016. Japan Lost Nearly a Million People in 5 Years, Census Says. [online] Available at: https://www.nytimes.com/2016/02/27/world/asia/japan-confirms-a-decline-in-population.html [Accessed: 02. December 2022]

Toya, M. 2016. "Komainu": The Shrine's Guardian Figures. [online] Available at: https://www.nippon.com/en/views/b05206/ [Accessed: 28. November 2022]

Urban Life Metro, 2019. 御年90歳、幻の江戸郷土玩具「麦わら細工の角兵衛獅子」を復元した人に会いに行った [online] Available at:
https://urbanlife.tokyo/post/14980/ [Accessed: 28. November 2022]

Videos

新潟市南区観光協会, 2018. 角兵衛獅子. [online] Available at: https://www.youtube.com/watch?v=zSOf_fRey3M&ab_channel=%E6%96%B0%E6%BD%9F%E5%B8%82%E5%8D%97%E5%8C%BA%E8%A6%B3%E5%85%89%E5%8D%94%E4%BC%9A [Accessed: 10. November 2022]

List of Figures

My sincere gratitude goes to all the individuals who gave their permission to use their illustrations/photographs.

Figure 1: Shishimai-Lion Dance Hong Kong. Copyrights: Jakub Hałun, CC BY-SA 4.0 <https://creativecommons.org/licenses/by-sa/4.0>, via Wikimedia Commons. Available at: https://commons.wikimedia.org/wiki/File:20091004_lion_dance_Hong_Kong_Kowloon_6823.jpg

Figure 2: Kakubei Jishi. Copyrights: 南区産業振興課　商工観光推進室 (Commerce, Industry and Tourism Promotion Office, Industry Promotion Division, Minami-ku)

Figure 3: Butsudan Shrine. Copyrights: No machine-readable author provided. Gakuro assumed (based on copyright claims)., CC BY-SA 3.0 <http://creativecommons.org/licenses/by-sa/3.0/>, via Wikimedia Commons
Available at: https://upload.wikimedia.org/wikipedia/commons/a/aa/Butsudan_at_ShinDo_Buddhist_Temple.jpg

Figure 4: Sickles manufactured in Tsukigata. Copyrights: Mariam Ala-Rashi, 2022.

Figure 5: Nakanokuchi River entering Shinano River. Copyrights: 新潟市, CC BY 2.1 JP <https://creativecommons.org/licenses/by/2.1/jp/deed.en>, via Wikimedia Commons. Available at: https://upload.wikimedia.org/wikipedia/commons/c/ca/NiigataCityOpenData_kuusatsu001.jpg

Figure 6: Tsukigata Bridge. Copyrights: Mariam Ala-Rashi, 2022.

Figure 7: Rice Fields Tsukigata. Copyrights: Mariam Ala-Rashi, 2022.

Figure 8: Greenhouse Tsukigata. Copyrights: Mariam Ala-Rashi, 2022.

Figure 9: Fruit Plantation Tsukigata. Copyrights: Mariam Ala-Rashi, 2022.

Figure 10: Local Manufacture Tsukigata. Copyrights: Mariam Ala-Rashi, 2022.

Figure 11: Bonsai Tree Nursery Tsukigata. Copyrights: Mariam Ala-Rashi, 2022.

Figure 12: Niigata Map. Copyrights: Niigata City, 2022. (A) Outline of Minami-ku. Available at: https://www.city.niigata.lg.jp/minami/

Figure 13: Fruit Plantation (Grapes) Tsukigata. Copyrights: Masaki Ikarashi, Mayor of Minami Ward, 2022.

Figure 14: Fruit Plantation (Peaches) Tsukigata. Copyrights: Masaki Ikarashi, Mayor of Minami Ward, 2022.

Figure 15: Fruit Plantation and Flower Fields Tsukigata. Copyrights: Masaki Ikarashi, Mayor of Minami Ward, 2022.

Figure 16: Local Fruit Market Tsukigata (A). Copyrights: Masaki Ikarashi, Mayor of Minami Ward, 2022.

Figure 17: Local Fruit Market Tsukigata (B). Copyrights: Masaki Ikarashi, Mayor of Minami Ward, 2022.

Figure 18: Drainage and Water Control Systems Tsukigata (A). Copyrights: Mariam Ala-Rashi, 2022.

Figure 19: Drainage and Water Control Systems Tsukigata (B). Copyrights: Mariam Ala-Rashi, 2022.

Figure 20: Drainage and Water Control Systems Tsukigata (C). Copyrights: Mariam Ala-Rashi, 2022.

Figure 21: Mountain Range Niigata. Copyrights: Mariam Ala-Rashi, 2022.

Figure 22: Manhole Cover with Kakubei Jishi and Local Fruit Trees, Tsukigata. Copyrights: Mariam Ala-Rashi, 2022.

Figure 23: Food Packaging with Kakubei Jishi, Tsukigata (A). Copyrights: Mariam Ala-Rashi, 2022.

Figure 24: Food Packaging with Kakubei Jishi, Tsukigata (B). Copyrights: Mariam Ala-Rashi, 2022.

Figure 25: Grain Elevator with Kakubei Jishi, Tsukigata. Copyrights: Mariam Ala-Rashi, 2022.

Figure 26: Multipurpose Hall, Tsukigata. Copyrights: Mariam Ala-Rashi, 2022.

Figure 27: Tsukigata Local Products Reference Room 郷土物産資料室 [角兵衛獅子]. Copyrights: Mariam Ala-Rashi, 2022.

Figure 28-36: Kakubei Jishi Bronze Statues. Copyrights: Mariam Ala-Rashi, 2022.

Figure 37: Guest House Goo Goo, Tsukigata. Copyrights: Mariam Ala-Rashi, 2022.

Figure 38: Main Road, Tsukigata. Copyrights: Mariam Ala-Rashi, 2022.

Figure 39: Traditional Buildings, Tsukigata. Copyrights: Mariam Ala-Rashi, 2022.

Figure 40: Sasagawa Residence, Tsukigata. Copyrights: 新潟市, CC BY 2.1 JP <https://creativecommons.org/licenses/by/2.1/jp/deed.en>, via Wikimedia Commons Available at: https://commons.wikimedia.org/wiki/File:NiigataCityOpenData_kyusasaga-wake02.jpg

Figure 41: Main Gate - Sasagawa Residence, Tsukigata. Copyrights: 新潟市, CC BY 2.1 JP <https://creativecommons.org/licenses/by/2.1/jp/deed.en>, via Wikimedia Commons Available at: https://commons.wikimedia.org/wiki/File:NiigataCityOpenData_kyu-sasagawake01.jpg

Figure 42: Garden - Sasagawa Residence, Tsukigata. Copyrights: yamakidoms, CC BY-SA 2.0 <https://creativecommons.org/licenses/by-sa/2.0>,File:%E6%97%A7%E7%AC%B9%E5%B7%9D%E5%AE%B6%E4%BD%8F%E5%AE%85_(2728026495).jpg

Figure 43: Shirone Giant Kite Battle Tsukigata (A). Copyrights: Masaki Ikarashi, Mayor of Minami Ward, 2022.

Figure 44: Shirone Giant Kite Battle Tsukigata (B). Copyrights: Masaki Ikarashi, Mayor of Minami Ward, 2022.

Figure 45: Lion Mask for Kakubei Jishi Performance しし頭. Copyrights: Mariam Ala-Rashi, 2022.

Figure 46: Hakusan Shrine with two Lion Statues as Guardians, Tsukigata. Copyrights: Mariam Ala-Rashi, 2022.

Figure 47: Lion Statue, Hakusan Shrine, Tsukigata. Copyrights: Mariam Ala-Rashi, 2022.

Figure 48: Lion Statue in Front of the Stage for the annual Kakubei Jishi Performance, Hakusan Shrine, Tsukigata Festival. Copyrights: Mariam Ala-Rashi, 2022.

Figure 49: Torii (Gate) of the Hakusan Shrine with handcrafted straw decorations for the Tsukigata Festival. Copyrights: Mariam Ala-Rashi, 2022.

Figure 50: Map of Edo around 1840's. Copyrights: Scanned University of Texas Libraries, Public domain, via Wikimedia Commons. Available at: https://commons.wikimedia.org/wiki/File:Edo_1844-1848_Map.jpg

Figure 51: Kakubei Jishi in Edo. 江戸勝景 (Picturesque Scenery of Edo). Copyrights: Utagawa Hiroshige, Public domain, via Wikimedia Commons. Available at: https://commons.wikimedia.org/wiki/File:NDL-DC_1301981-Utagawa_Hiroshige-%E6%B1%9F%E6%88%B8%E5%8B%9D%E6%99%AF-crd.jpg

Figure 52: Popularity of the Kakubei Jishi in Edo. Copyrights: Kobayashi Kiyochika; Kobayashi Kiyochika died 1915; Kobayashi Tetsujiro, Public domain, via Wikimedia Commons. Available at: https://

commons.wikimedia.org/wiki/File:Straatartiest_uit_Edo-Rijksmuseum_RP-P-1989-220.jpeg

Figure 53: 逆立ちする子供たち - コピー Children Standing on Their Heads. Copyrights: 図.阿久根巖、「おもちゃ絵　四種」『逆立ちする子供たち―角兵衛獅子の軽業を見る、聞く、読む』(小学館(2001年4月1日)p.5～8. Provided and permission to use granted by Masaki Ikarashi, Mayor of Minami Ward.

Figure 54: Ceremonial Building used on the day of the Tsukigata Festival for performance preparation (A). Copyrights: Mariam Ala-Rashi, 2022.

Figure 55: Second Floor of the Ceremonial Building that used on the day of the Tsukigata Festival for performance preparation (B). Copyrights: Mariam Ala-Rashi, 2022.

Figure 56: Kakubei Jishi masks and veils in the Ceremonial Building. Copyrights: Mariam Ala-Rashi, 2022.

Figure 57: Kakubei Jishi Training. Copyrights: Provided and permission to use granted by Masaki Ikarashi, Mayor of Minami Ward.

Figure 58: Extreme Flexibility of Kakubei Jishi Performers during the Edo Period. Copyrights: Provided and permission to use granted by Masaki Ikarashi, Mayor of Minami Ward.

Figure 59: Kakubei Jishi Child Performers during the early Meiji Period. Copyrights: Provided and permission to use granted by Masaki Ikarashi, Mayor of Minami Ward.

Figure 60: Kakubei Jishi with Drummer and Flute Player. Copyrights: Provided and permission to use granted by Masaki Ikarashi, Mayor of Minami Ward.

Figure 61: Drums and Flutes used to accompany Kakubei Jishi Performances (A). Copyrights: Provided and permission to use granted by Masaki Ikarashi, Mayor of Minami Ward.

Figure 62: Drums and Flutes used to accompany Kakubei Jishi Performances (B). Copyrights: Provided and permission to use granted by Masaki Ikarashi, Mayor of Minami Ward.

Figure 63: Drawings of Edo Period Kakubei Jishi Performances (A). Copyrights: Permission to use granted by Masaki Ikarashi, Mayor of Minami Ward.

Figure 64: Drawings of Edo Period Kakubei Jishi Performances (B). Copyrights: Permission to use granted by Masaki Ikarashi, Mayor of Minami Ward.

Figure 65: Drawing of a chest-stand pose performed by Kakubei Jishi artist during the Edo Period. Copyrights: Permission to use granted by Masaki Ikarashi, Mayor of Minami Ward.

Figure 66, 67, 68: Drawings of Edo Period Kakubei Jishi Performances exhibited in the Local Produce Reference Room, Tsukigata.

Figure 78: Sei kai ha 青海波 (Ocean Waves). Copyrights: unknown, public domain, via Wikimedia Commons. Available at: https://commons.wikimedia.org/wiki/File:%E9%9D%92%E6%B5%B7%E6%B3%A2%E3%81%AB%E5%8D%83%E9%B3%A5.jpg

Figure 79: Sei kai ha Movement (Ocean Waves). Copyrights: 南区産業振興課 商工観光推進室 (Commerce, Industry and Tourism Promotion Office, Industry Promotion Division, Minami-ku)

Figure 80: Mizu Guruma Movement (Waterwheel). Copyrights: Mariam Ala-Rashi, 2022.

Figure 81: Figure 81: Tawara gorogashi 俵転がし (Bale Rolling) Copyrights: 南区産業振 興課 商工観光推進室 (Commerce, Industry and Tourism Promotion Office, Industry Promotion Division, Minami-ku)

Figure 82: Yodo Water Castle 淀城 Yodo-jō. Copyrights: Anonymous/Unknown author, public domain, via Wikimedia Commons. Available at: https://commons.wikimedia.org/wiki/File:Yodo_Castle.jpg

Figure 83: Yodo Waterwheel Large Movement. Copyrights: 南区産業振興課 商工観光推進室 (Commerce, Industry and Tourism Promotion Office, Industry Promotion Division, Minami-ku)

Figure 84: Nin ba (Horse and Rider). Copyrights: 南区産業振興課 商工観光推進室 (Commerce, Industry and Tourism Promotion Office, Industry Promotion Division, Minami-ku)

Figure 85: Crossing of the Oi River. Copyrights: Utagawa Toyokuni I, CC0, via Wikimedia Commons. Available at: https://commons.wikimedia.org/wiki/File:MET_DP143701.jpg

Figure 86: Shishi no kootoshi movement and Ninba (Tessen kazaguruma) movement. Copyrights: 南区産業振興課 商工観光推進室 (Commerce, Industry and Tourism Promotion Office, Industry Promotion Division, Minami-ku)

Figure 87: Karako Dolls. Copyrights: Walters Art Museum, Public domain, via Wikimedia Commons. Available at: https://commons.wikimedia.org/wiki/File:Japanese_-_Brush_Rest_in_the_Form_of_Boys_with_a_Snowball_-_Walters_49917.jpg

Figure 88: Karako Doll Horse Riding Movement. Copyrights: 南区産業振興課 商工観光推進室 (Commerce, Industry and Tourism Promotion Office, Industry Promotion Division, Minami-ku)

Figure 89: Standing on the Doll Horse Movement. Copyrights: 南区産業振興課 商工観光推進室 (Commerce, Industry and Tourism Promotion Office, Industry Promotion Division, Minami-ku)

Figure 90: The Chicken Shape Movement. Copyrights: 南区産業振興課 商工観光推進室 (Commerce, Industry and Tourism Promotion Office, Industry Promotion Division, Minami-ku)

Figure 91: Bow to the Audience. Copyrights: Mariam Ala-Rashi, 2022.

Figure 92: Turtle Child (亀の子). Copyrights: With friendly permission from City of Edinburgh Council – Libraries www.

capitalcollections.org.uk Title: A child acrobat ("Kakubeijishi") 1881, Photographer: von Stillfried-Ratenicz, Franz.

Figure 93: Kakubei Jishi performers of 2022 gather in front of the Ceremonial Building in Tsukigata after their performance. Copyrights: Mariam Ala-Rashi, 2022.

Figure 94, 95: Kakubei Jishi Costume in Display in the Tsukigata Local Products Reference Room. Copyrights: Mariam Ala-Rashi, 2022.

Figure 96: Kakubei Jishi Lion Mask with Veil. Copyrights: Mariam Ala-Rashi, 2022.

Figure 96: Geta, worn by the Lion Dancers when walking to and from the stage. Copyrights: Mariam Ala-Rashi, 2022.

Figure 98: Veil covering the Lion Dancer's Face throughout the Performance. Copyrights: Utagawa Kuniyoshi, Public domain, via Wikimedia Commons. Available at: https://commons.wikimedia.org/wiki/File:Oman_ga_Ame_-Tousei_Ryuukou_Mitate.jpg

Figure 99: Lion Dancers enter the Shrine Grounds to Pray for the Performance and the Villagers. Additionally, they are wearing a transparent face shield to prevent the spread of the Covid-19 virus. Copyrights: Mariam Ala-Rashi, 2022.

Figure 100: Hakusan Shrine Tsukigata. Copyrights: Mariam Ala-Rashi, 2022.

Figure 101: Goddess and Demon Hariti, known as Kishimojin in Japan. Copyrights: UNESCO / Dominique Roger, CC BY-SA 3.0 IGO <https://creativecommons.org/licenses/by-sa/3.0/igo/deed.en>, via Wikimedia Commons. Available at: https://commons.wikimedia.org/wiki/File:Culture,_Campaign,_Mandut_-_UNESCO_-_PHOTO0000002130_0001.tiff

Figure 102: Closed Down Tsukigata Train Station with Kakubei Jishi Monument. Copyrights: Masaki Ikarashi, Mayor of Minami Ward, 2022.

Figure 103: Kakubei Jishi. Copyrights: 江戸職人歌合 （石原正明著）, Public domain, via Wikimedia Commons. Available at: https://commons.wikimedia.org/wiki/File:Kakubei.jpg

ABOUT THE AUTHOR

Mariam Ala-Rashi is a cultural anthropologist specializing in the field of dance and performance studies. She holds a Master of Arts degree from the University of Roehampton in London, UK. Mariam Ala-Rashi has amassed extensive professional experience as a dancer and dance instructor, having worked in various locations across Europe and Asia, where she has received numerous accolades for her work.

Her passion for dance led her to pursue further studies in contortion, which she undertook as a full-time student at the Beijing International Art School for a period exceeding four years. Following her time at the school, she continued her contortion studies at the Mongolian National Circus for another two years. During her time in East Asia, Mariam Ala-Rashi also undertook extensive fieldwork as an author and researcher, focusing on dance and circus arts.

Currently residing in Japan, she holds positions as a lecturer at four universities, where she imparts her expertise in higher education. Mariam Ala-Rashi continues to engage in anthropological research in dance and performance studies, maintaining close contact with her contortion coaches and classmates from China and Mongolia.

OTHER BOOKS BY MODERN VAUDEVILLE PRESS

Juggling: Or How to Become a Juggler (annotated edition)

Rupert Ingalese, annotated by Thom Wall
ISBN – 978-1733971201
99 pages
MSRP: $15 USD

The fully annotated edition of Rupert Ingalese's 1921 "how to juggle" manual. This book covers basic juggling technique, tricks with hats and canes, practice methodology, and more. Ingalese's manuscript provides an interesting look at the state of juggling pedagogy in Britain's music hall era. Annotations by juggler and circus researcher Thom Wall bring insight and context to Ingalese's descriptions and instructions.

Pottery in Motion

Sam Veale
ISBN – 978-1733971232
71 pages
MSRP: $15 USD

British juggler Sam Veale's *Pottery in Motion* is the first of its kind - a straightforward book that provides aspiring plate spinners both the specifics of the props (such as plates, sticks, and rack) and comprehensive instruction on the skill of plate spinning itself. This small but detail-packed guide appeals to individuals looking to learn plate spinning and provides the knowledge to take it to a performance-ready level, just add practice.

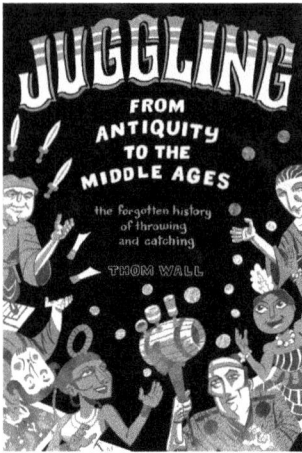

Juggling: From Antiquity to the Middle Ages

Thom Wall
ISBN – 978-0578410845
129 pages
MSRP: $25 USD

As with dance, so with juggling—the moment that the performer finishes the routine, their act ceases to exist beyond the memory of the audience. There is no permanent record of what transpired, so studying the ancient roots of juggling is fraught with difficulty. Using the records that do exist, juggling appears to have emerged around the world in cultures independent of one another in the ancient past. Paintings in Egypt from 2000 BCE show jugglers engaged in performance. Stories from the island nation of Tonga place juggling's creation with their goddess of the underworld—a figure who has guarded a cave since time immemorial. Juggling games and rituals are pervasive in isolated Inuit cultures in northern Canada and Greenland. Though the earliest representation of juggling is 4,000 years old, the practice is surely much older—in the same way that humans were doubtlessly singing and dancing long before the first bone flute was created.

This book is an attempt to catalogue this tangible history of juggling in human culture. It is the story of juggling, represented in art and writing from around the world, across time. Although much has been written about modern jugglers–specific performers, their props, and their routines–little has been said about those who first developed the craft. As juggling enters a golden age in the internet era, *Juggling: From Antiquity to the Middle Ages* offers a look into the past—to the origins of our art form.

Spanish Edition:
Malabares - desde la Antigüedad hasta la Edad Media: la historia olvidada de lanzar y cachar

Thom Wall, et. al.
ISBN – 978-1733971263
179 pages
MSRP: $25 USD

Malabares - desde Antigüedad hasta la Edad Media, es un divertido viaje por países, por épocas. Desde el Antiguo Egipto y sus ya famosas malabaristas profesionales de la tumba nº 15 de Beni Hasan, a los juegos para niñas de la isla de Tonga y otras zonas del Pacífico Sur; pasando por los edictos del rey Alfonso X de Castilla sobre la regulación de los juglares o los antipodistas aztecas actuando ante el Papa Clemente VII en el siglo XVI. También reserva un espacio al final del libro para, aprovechando su faceta de lingüista, realizar unas reflexiones acerca de la propia definición de la palabra "juggling"[malabarismo] a lo largo del tiempo y sus orígenes. Es, por tanto, un libro ideal no solo para malabaristas o cirqueros, sino para cualquiera con curiosidad sobre la historia, en especial de aquellos hechos que en ocasiones pasan más desapercibidos en los textos cotidianos.

A través de este libro aprendemos sobre leyendas y juegos antiguos, fantaseamos con grandes artistas y actuaciones que nunca podremos ver y que nos hacen dudar sobre esa tan manida sentencia que a veces afirma "esto nunca se ha hecho antes". *-Malabares en su Tinta*

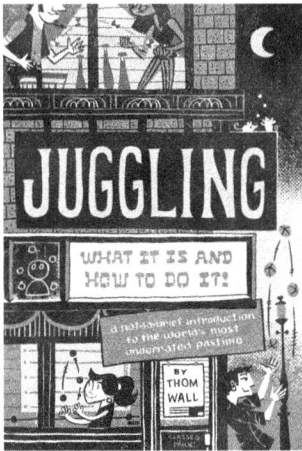

Juggling: What It Is and How to Do It

Thom Wall, et. al.
ISBN – 978-1-7339712-5-6
224 pages
MSRP: $25 USD

Juggling: What It Is and How to Do It teaches learners of all ages how to juggle – one of the world's oldest artforms. With a kind demeanor, humor, and enthusiasm, this authoritative manual explains the process of juggling through four different modalities, bolstered by the latest physical education research.

Juggling is an accessible primer that a middle-schooler can hit the ground running with, or that families can enjoy together. The result of six years of work by 2021 International Jugglers' Association *Excellence in Education* award winner and former Cirque du Soleil juggler Thom Wall and featuring guest chapters by some of today's juggling masters, *Juggling* provides great content for even the most serious adult learner.

Book plus Juggling Kit!
Includes juggling balls by Alchemy Juggling

| **MSRP: $60 USD**

This exclusive kit makes the perfect gift for any aspiring juggler. Includes one copy of *Juggling: What It Is and How to Do It* and three professional-grade beanbags.

Beanbag specs: 90g ea., approx. 2.75" diameter. Machine washable / dryable. Made in USA.

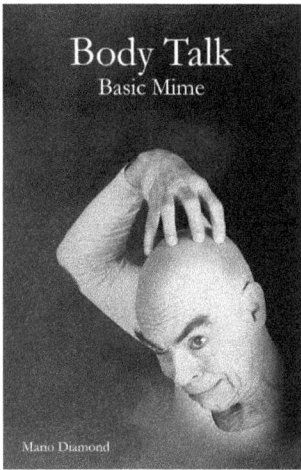

Body Talk: Basic Mime

Mario Diamond
ISBN – 978-1733971218
73 pages
MSRP: $15 USD

Body Talk: Basic Mime covers the fundamental skills of mime in an easily accessible workbook format. Diamond brings over 40 years of teaching and performance experience to *Body Talk*, which includes rich photography illustrating various mime techniques.

"[*Body Talk: Basic Mime*] should be required reading for any theater participant looking to incorporate elements of mime into their routines." - *Midwest Book Review*

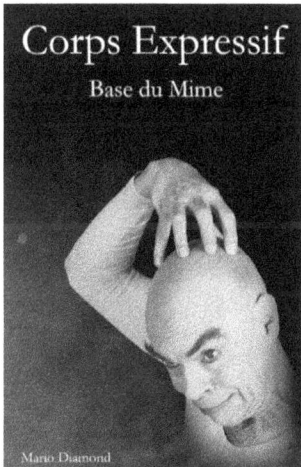

French Edition: Corps Expressif: Base du Mime

Mario Diamond
ISBN – 978-1958604984
68 pages
MSRP: $15 USD

Mario a écrit un tour de force sur l'art du mime. Ce livre est éloquent et concis... riche en outils pour les élèves comme pour les professeurs, facile à comprendre et rempli d'exercices pratiques. Ce livre est brodé de segments historiques et anecdotiques qui en font un manuscrit amusant, plein d'observations charmantes et bouffonnes qui font de Mario un artiste phénoménal, prodigue de la caractéristique définitive du mime, la personnalité.

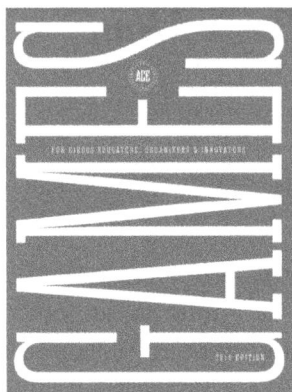

Circus Games (v1.1)

Compiled by Lucy Little & the American Youth Circus Organization (AYCO)
ISBN – 9781733971225
124 pages
MSRP: $15 USD

With over 100 games organized for optimal use in cooperative movement based settings, this is a must have for every circus school, teaching artist, and arts education program! Games are organized by age, number of participants, energy level, and social/emotional learning outcome, and also includes special notes for working with a variety of populations that may require adaptation or modifications to each game. Find more info about the project here: https://www.americancircuseducators.org/gamesproject/

The ABC Tour

Jon Udry
ISBN - 978-0578410852
MSRP: $25 USD

Ever felt like a challenge? For juggler and comedian, Jon Udry, the ABC Tour — 26 letters, 26 shows — seems the perfect way to shake things up.

What started as a silly idea he believed would take two to three months to complete, ended up being a mammoth three year project that included some of the toughest, most brutal and most enjoyable performances of his life.

From attempting to juggle while wearing roller skates and the unexpected discoveries of performing at a Naturist's Resort, to the challenges that came with working in rainforest conditions covered in ants or in snowy conditions at -10°C, Jon tells the full story from A to Z.

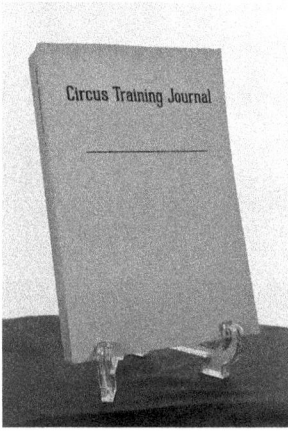

Circus Training Journal

Thom Wall & Rebecca Starr,
Consultant editor: Sarah Baker
ISBN – 978-1-7339712-9-4
9×6" paperback
380 pages
MSRP: $20 USD

What's measured is managed! The *Circus Training Journal* is the result of a year of collaboration between Thom Wall and Rebecca Starr, head aerial coach at Circadium: School of Contemporary Circus. This undated journal, spanning three months of daily training, tracks workouts, nutrition, goal-setting, and more. Heavyweight groundwood paper optimized for ballpoint and pencil.

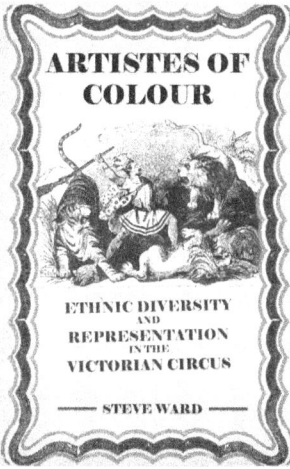

Artistes of Colour

Steve Ward, PhD
ISBN – 978-1-7339712-7-0
317 pages
MSRP: $25 USD

In a society that places an increasing value in ethnic diversity and cultural identity, the contribution that performers from a variety of ethnic backgrounds made to the development of the circus in the nineteenth century is often dismissed and largely forgotten. Using contemporary records and images, *Artistes of Colour* explores the wealth and depth of talented black and other performers of colour, and the contribution they made to the success of the nineteenth century circus. Ward draws iconic figures from the margins of history and gives them the recognition they deserve, illustrating what the BBC calls "a field of study that has been overlooked far too long."

Long-listed for the American Society for Theatre Research 2022 Book Award.

Coming Soon:

Captain George

Amelia Osterud, Edited by Fritz Grobe
MSRP: $25 USD
Coming in 2024!

The life and times of the world's most celebrated illustrated man.

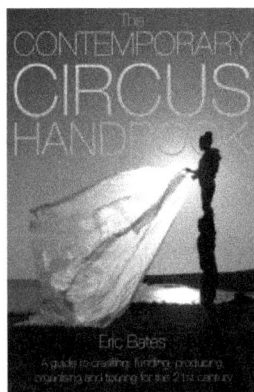

The Contemporary Circus Handbook: A guide to creating, funding, producing, organizing and touring shows for the 21st century

Eric Bates
ISBN – 978-1-958604-03-8
MSRP: $25 USD
Coming July 2023!

The Contemporary Circus Handbook contains interviews with more than 25 professionals, from Gypsy Snider of the celebrated contemporary circus company "The Seven Fingers" to Lydia Bouchard of La Resistance about their work in the performing arts world. Combining Eric Bates' (Cie Barcode, Cirque du Soleil, et. al.) hard won wisdom as well as tips and insights from his contemporaries, what emerges is an invaluable blueprint of how to progress from the seed of an idea for a show to the full touring timeline. The scope of the book is wide but deeply hands-on, diving into practical details on how to find an agent, start your own company, secure funding and build your niche brand. *The Contemporary Circus Handbook* truly is a unique offering to the circus world, full of insider tips and years of accumulated knowledge from industry insiders.

www.ingramcontent.com/pod-product-compliance
Lightning Source LLC
Chambersburg PA
CBHW070048030426
42335CB00016B/1836